THE REPUBLIC OF KOREA

THE REPUBLIC OF KOREA

Economic Transformation and Social Change

David I. Steinberg

Westview Press / Boulder and London

Westview Profiles/Nations of Contemporary Asia

Photo credits: pages 7, 12, 14, 17, 70, 72, and 86 courtesy of the Korean Cultural Service, Korean Overseas Information Service, Ministry of Culture and Information, Embassy of the Republic of Korea, Washington, D.C. Pages 16 and 184 courtesy of the Seoul Olympic Organizing Committee and the Seoul Asian Games Organizing Committee. All other photos are by the author.

Jacket photos (clockwise from upper left): automobile factory assembly line; Hyangwon Pavilion in Kyongbok Palace; transplanting rice by hand; Korean children. Second and fourth photos courtesy of the Korean Cultural Service, others by the author.

Published in 1989 in the United States of America by Westview Press, Inc., 5500 Central Avenue, Boulder, Colorado 80301, and in the United Kingdom by Westview Press, Inc., 13 Brunswick Centre, London WC1N 1AF, England

Library of Congress Cataloging-in-Publication Data
Steinberg, David I.
  The Republic of Korea : economic transformation and social change
  /David I. Steinberg.
    p. cm.—(Westview profiles/Nations of contemporary Asia)
  Bibliography: p.
  Includes index.
  ISBN 0-86531-720-8
  1. Korea—History. 2. Korea (South)—History. I. Title.
II. Series: Westview profiles. Nations of contemporary Asia.
DS907.18.S73 1989
951.9—dc19   88-5750
                                                                                        CIP

Printed and bound in the United States of America

The paper used in this publication meets the requirements of the American National Standard for Permanence of Paper for Printed Library Materials Z39.48-1984.

10   9   8   7   6   5   4   3   2   1

Dedicated to the people of the Republic of Korea
and to Koreans everywhere

Contents

Tables and Illustrations

Photographs

Preface

Writing a single, general volume of prescribed length on a culture as intricate as Korea's is a task to be attempted only with great trepidation. Analyzing the complexities of this unique culture, one so rapidly changing and increasingly assuming a major, pivotal role in the world economic order, is daunting. Tracing comprehensively its historical and evolving relations with its neighbors, its social, economic, and political peregrinations over some two thousand years, if not the five thousand years that is sometimes claimed, is mesmerizing.

Such study for the contemporary period is particularly difficult. Korea is not only constantly evolving physically, socially, and intellectually; it is also the subject of a twentieth-century minefield of disputation. Analysis of the Japanese colonial period and present Korean-Japanese relations heightens nationalistic sentiments and excites tensions on both sides of the Straits of Tsushima; it is significant that the adjacent area is called the Japan Sea in Tokyo and the Eastern Sea in Seoul. The mere mention of North Korea in any but a clearly pejorative sense often produces consternation in the South. The acerbic politics of the various republics of South Korea reflect factionalism and engender vigorous debate. Relationships with the United States are continuously subject to revised analysis as Korean nationalism and anti-U.S. feeling grow, as trade tensions become more acute, and as U.S. documents of the postliberation period are declassified. Korean participation in the Vietnam War has been largely ignored in the academic literature. Because of Korea's rapid growth, it is frequently propounded as a model for economic development, and its rapid expansion has been the source of much folklore and myth for ideological, administrative, and political reasons.

There have been simplistic Western interpretations of Korean history and contemporary politics and economics, and in some sense they may be excused. Until the Korean War, there were few works on Korea in Western languages. Whereas China since Voltaire and Japan since Perry have had pivotal intellectual, artistic, and economic impacts on Western thought and society, Korea was ignored on its own volition until the latter days of the nineteenth century. Overshadowed by the cultural font of East Asia—China—and by the modernization, military power, and economic pervasiveness of Japan, Korea even when in the limelight seemed a pale imitation of its neighbors.

In the early 1960s, in spite of a military occupation and a prolonged war resulting in the largest U.S. commitment of troops to the Asian mainland until that time, fewer than half a dozen U.S. academicians could be considered "experts" on Korea. Fortunately, that situation has changed. A new, younger generation of Americans and of Koreans writing in English has lifted the mist through which Korea was only dimly perceived by foreigners. These scholars have given depth and breadth to such analyses; as the Korean economy has expanded, so has the study of that society. We are all in their debt.

This book, as one of a series on various countries of Asia, is by its nature limited. It is by intent an overview, an idiosyncratic précis of continuously evolving trends in the Republic of Korea. (North Korea will be the subject of a separate book.) This book cannot satisfy the specialist; the perceptive generalist will want more detail than the nature of this publication and its length allow. I share this frustration. Yet, if this short work yields a balanced portrait of a valiant and remarkable people, and if my inherent sympathy for the Korean culture and its people, its history and problems, its dynamism and difficulties becomes evident, then the effort will be worthwhile. A quarter-century involvement in Korea, including five years' residence, extensive trips, field research, and a family that is half Korean lead me to hope that these positive emotions are clearly present; but equally, I would also hope that this empathy does not cloud the objectivity of analysis.

Some technical remarks are in order. Various romanization systems have been propounded, some officially authorized. Except in cases in which other romanizations have become accepted or adopted by individuals (for example, Syngman Rhee, Park Chung Hee), I have followed in this book a modified McCune-Reischauer system most commonly used in general publications. Diacritical marks, representing a short vowel sound, are included for Korean words and historical eras or figures (e.g., Kokuryŏ), as is the long vowel (e.g., wakō). Such marks are eliminated in commonly accepted place names and contemporary names, although the diacritical marks are included in the Dramatis Personae section for reference. Normally, family names—which are single syllables with a few exceptions—come first (*Park* Chung Hee), except when Western usage has become established, as in Syngman *Rhee*. The reader new to Korea should note that surnames are limited in that country, and individuals with similar names are unlikely to be related, as 55 percent of Koreans have four surnames: 22 percent named Kim; 18 percent named Lee, Rhee, Yi, etc.—all romanizations of the same Chinese character; and so on. Clan location is more important than name.

In references to the Republic of Korea, South Korea and Korea (in the contemporary period) are used interchangeably. The Democratic People's Republic of Korea is generally termed North Korea. For the premodern period, Korea refers to the whole peninsula, whereas the term "peninsula" is used to designate the area and people of both North and South today. In contrast to usage in South Korea, which does not diplomatically recognize the Democratic People's Republic of Korea, North Korea is spelled with a capital N. Use of any of these terms is not intended to be either pejorative or judgmental.

World recognition of Korea, and a resurgence of Korean self-confidence, has come from economic development, and thus I have concentrated on this theme, although others might have been chosen. A book of this type is intended as an overview, a sophisticated introduction to a society through such a theme. Trends in Korean history or culture have been stressed to illuminate the present; concepts have been emphasized to demonstrate historical continuity. My intention is to excite the reader to turn to more specialized studies for detailed data, which often have inherent fascination. The bulk of the statistics for this study come from the Economic Planning Board of the Republic of Korea, as well as from other works cited in the Suggested Readings section. Although Korean statistics are considered excellent overall, the careful reader will note some discrepancies both in the text and with other material.

It is, then, to the Korean people that this work is dedicated. My residence in Korea, my vocational and avocational research, and the many trips since my first visit in 1962 provide perspective and continuity for this study, which by its nature is an attempt to make contemporary Korea more accessible through its historical and cultural setting.

David I. Steinberg
Bethesda, Maryland

Acknowledgments

It is with great appreciation and a sense of gratitude that I acknowledge a variety of individuals and institutions that have made this work possible, although none of them should be held responsible for the results.

A special debt is due my wife, Ann Myongsook Lee, and her family as well, who exemplify much of the best of the Korean tradition. She has read and commented on the manuscript, as have my children.

Peter H. Lee, the University of California, Los Angeles, scholar as well as relative, did the same and gave permission to quote from the poems he has translated. John Girling of Australia National University gave valuable suggestions from a cross-cultural perspective. John Bennett, president, Korea Economic Institute, commented extensively and helpfully on the draft, as did Yang Key-beck of the Library of Congress; Cho Soon, Faculty of Economics, Seoul National University; and Vincent Brandt of Tufts University. Josh Turner of Helena, Montana, provided detailed and constructive suggestions on both substance and style. The editors at Westview Press, especially Sally Furgeson, provided assistance in their usual careful, probing manner, improving the quality and continuity of the text.

Some of the photographs were provided by the Office of Information and Culture of the Korean Embassy in Washington, D.C., and these are reproduced with that office's permission and with my thanks to Chan Yong Lee, director.

I also thank The Asia Foundation for giving me five years' residence in Korea; the Agency for International Development's Center for Development Information and Evaluation for providing numerous opportunities to engage my penchant for work on Korea; and the World Bank and its Task Force on Concessional Flows, which enabled me to look at the effectiveness of foreign economic aid to Korea.

xv

The Suggested Readings section lists some of the authors to whom I am indebted. The lack of extensive footnoting, a requirement of this series, should not obscure the wealth of existing data on aspects of Korea; these data may be found in the works included in this section. Many more individuals have contributed substantially to this book. A comprehensive list of the hundreds of people—public and private, academicians and villagers—who have become unwitting coconspirators would be inappropriate, for they might be charged with the errors that are mine alone, and for which, in sins of commission or omission, fact or interpretation, I bear sole responsibility.

D.I.S.

1

Introduction:
Geography as Destiny

Every peninsula fancies itself an island. Conversely, there is no island that does not envy a peninsula.
— Vassily Aksyonov, *The Island of Crimea*[1]

Korea's geographic position has tragically affected its people and history. Perhaps only Poland, also located astride and flanking major avenues of political turmoil, has been as constantly buffeted as Korea. Both have profited from as well as contributed to their culturally, economically, and militarily dominant neighbors. Korea, because of its peninsularity and the relative homogeneity of its culture, is unique. Korea has been a political as well as a military battlefield for more than two thousand years; control over the peninsula has been an essential, if not a dominant, motif of the Northeast Asian scene.

Continuously threatened by pressures from the north—whether early transhumant tribes, Mongols, Manchus, or later both the tsarist and communist Russians—Korea was also invaded by China from the south and Japan from the east. Changes of foreign governments or dynasties never freed Korea from the threat of alien occupation or control. Culturally, Korea has wavered between attempted insularity from and identification with the Chinese culture on the mainland.

In sweeping geopolitical perspective, the contemporary Korean scene almost seems a reincarnation of the past. Technological change in communications or weaponry has speeded information and proliferated the possibility of death, but it has not materially affected national interests in the Korean area. The region's intense rivalries still focus on the Korean peninsula. There, the United States and Japan face the Soviet Union and China together with North Korea much as China faced Japan over Korea in the Sino-Japanese War of 1894–1895 and Japan fought Russia in the Russo-Japanese War of 1904–1905.

1

The Republic of Korea (South Korea)

From Korea's vantage point, how different from those struggles of the nineteenth century were major power interests in the Korean War? How basically different, indeed, were all these interests from those motivating the Japanese invasion of Korea in 1592 in an attempt to conquer China, or from the Mongol invasions of Korea in the thirteenth century in an effort to control Japan, or from other numerous and repeated attempts by various powers since the sixth century to use or neutralize Korea? From as early as the end of the nineteenth century (not only from World War II), proposals to prevent the control of all or part of the Korean peninsula from falling within various unfriendly spheres of influence have involved cutting the Gordian knot and dividing Korea in half. Geopolitically, Eastern-Western bloc relationships may appear salient today, but continental-insular tensions along a geographical east-west axis have had remarkable historical continuity.

A north-south axis remains relevant as well. Sino-Soviet rivalry forced each nation to woo North Korea and to neutralize or use South Korea much as the imperial Chinese tried to subjugate and include the peninsula in the Sino-centric world order. The non-Chinese nomadic "barbarians" of the north did the same in their campaigns against the southern sedentary Chinese. The Sino-Soviet split seems singularly persistent in perspective.

Geopolitics may remain vital today, but economic rivalries and policy issues, previously on the periphery, are rapidly assuming an importance never before relevant. South Korea is now a large and varied market; as its wealth increases, its population of over 40 million will consume an even greater magnitude of more-sophisticated products. More important, South Korea has become the twelfth largest trading nation in the world. Its exports are ubiquitous.

At the edge of this peripheral geopolitical abyss but at the center of a new economic order in East Asia, one for which few if any Koreans were prepared a generation ago, the Korean people have and do exhibit remarkable cultural tenacity. Yet, they have recognized their position as underdog in these struggles, acknowledging that role in their oft-quoted proverb, "When whales fight, the shrimp suffers." Over the past two decades, since the 1960s, perhaps for the first time in several hundred years, Korea's confidence in its own capacity is again pronounced, a result of impressive economic performance and resolution that can best be described as both extraordinary and unanticipated following the Korean War. How the Korean economy grew is a major emphasis of this book.

The cultural continuity, distinctiveness, and resolution of the Korean people are pronounced, as are their eclectic interests. Koreans have selectively grafted heterogeneous foreign elements onto a distinctively

4

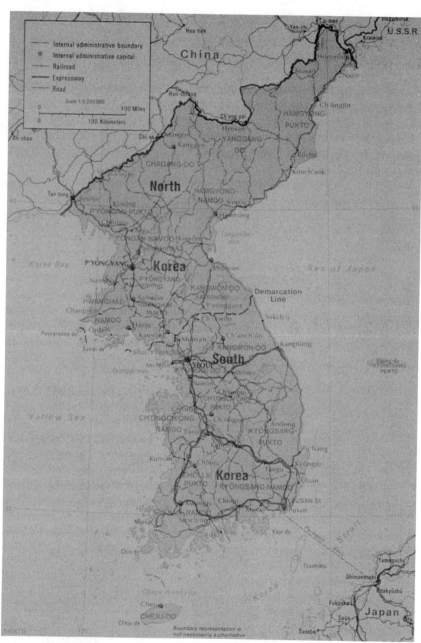

The Korean peninsula

Korean base, both transforming the foreign concepts and modifying the root culture but still retaining Korean individuality. In spite of many influences—Buddhism from India via China, Chinese Confucianism, Western Christianity, Japanese life and economic policies, Marxism in the north, the U.S. presence in the south, and diverse trends in the contemporary international scene—Korea remains a distinctive, unique culture. A certain "Korean-ness" is present in such diametrically antagonistic regimes as the Republic of Korea in the south and the Democratic People's Republic of Korea in the north and in the industrialization and economic growth of both.

In this century alone, Korea has withstood what may aptly be called the cultural genocide of the later years of Japanese colonial rule, national division, a foreign military occupation, a civil war, and the onslaught of Western internationalism in the South and Marxism in the North. Yet the Korean people have retained their cultural identity. Those who approach Korea as a simple appendage of the Chinese cultural world order, a peripheral dependent nation in the Japanese or U.S. industrial complex, or solely as a pawn in international world trade or power politics misperceive the vibrancy of a people, their special contribution to world culture, their importance in contemporary international affairs, and their unwillingness to be considered—South or North—as anything but Korean.

This identity exists and extends beyond mere linguistic affinities, but it is not easily articulated, any more than such definitions come facilely to mind for the Japanese or the English. Giving language to their identity has become of increasing concern to some Koreans as their society has evolved, as more Koreans (perhaps 6 to 7 million, or about 10 percent of the combined population of North and South) are resident outside the peninsula, and as the insularity of the Koreans, through foreign exposure and training, diminishes. The search to define the Korean identity in the face of constant, indeed increasing, flux is the subject of much research and even the focus of a Korean government institute. This search is sometimes confused with the perceived governmental need for a South Korean ideology, one that competes with Marxism or the *chuch'e* (autonomy, or self-reliance) concept of Kim Il Sung in the North. Simple negativism toward communism and North Korea, so stridently invoked, has increasingly proven inadequate as an identity, an ideology, or as a basis of analysis; yet, constant use of terms such as "democracy" or the "free world" to describe the South are similarly inexact and only marginally helpful.

Until this century was half over, Korea rarely impinged on Western public consciousness except as the backdrop to the wars of the latter part of the nineteenth century. Because of its self-invoked international isolation as the "hermit kingdom," the overwhelming attractions of China from the Age of the Enlightenment, and later the Western romance with things Japanese, Korea was ignored or mistaken. Korean art seemed but a pale imitation of Chinese art; Korean painting was regarded as derivative, its pottery almost unknown except as a branch of the Japanese ware, its literature (often written in classical Chinese) considered obscure. Korean society was controlled by a minor, although long-lived, dynasty whose legitimacy was dependent on China, one that increasingly become enfeebled over 518 years of factional strife exacerbated by foreign incursions. In the early twentieth century, with world inattention but with U.S. connivance, Korea was left to the whims of the Japanese military. Except for a few foreign missionaries and a small number of exiled Korean patriots whose voices went largely unheeded, there was little concern in the West with the fate of the Koreans in their homeland.

Finally liberated from Japanese rule and occupied by foreign troops, South Korea was forced into a civil war that brought vast destruction to the peninsula. The devastated economy and fragile political system, together with what seemed like the obliteration of the culture and society, made South Korea a likely candidate for oblivion in the eyes of Westerners, for whom it persisted only as a bad memory among foreign combatants.

It is almost inconceivable that, under what seem to have been insuperable odds, Korea has become a candidate for economic "model-hood," a developmental state of grace approaching economic saintliness to be emulated internationally. From what had been called a "basket case" or a "rat hole" down which economic assistance was endlessly poured without apparent effect, Korean accomplishments, especially in comparative perspective, are now justly extolled worldwide. The dynamics of its achievements, however, are less well understood, folklore often replacing fact on Korean growth.

A nation industrializing, Korea attracts international attention as its products and people spread widely throughout the world. Writing on the Korean economy is as much a growth industry as the economy itself. The Korean economic experience, inter alia, is used to bolster academic theories or political ideologies, to demonstrate the efficacy of foreign assistance or, in contrast, the importance of stopping foreign aid, and to promote political legitimacy. But too little is known, even in influential foreign circles, of the nature of Korean society—how that society has affected what Korea has accomplished as well as the problems that Korea continues to face. Many of these issues stem from the country's geographic position, astride various lanes of continuous national aggrandizement.

This book will concentrate on the process of economic growth, for which Korea today is renowned. We will examine some of the salient

Republic of Korea national flag (*Taegukki*)

forces that helped to produce this remarkable change as well as draw lessons from that experience. Equally important are themes in Korean history and society that help explain such vast changes and their implications for the future. We will also consider the continuous cultural tenacity of the Korean people and their flexibility in adapting and adopting selective elements from abroad—two seemingly discordant traits that in fact harmonize within the Korean context. We will explore the evolution of the class structure in Korea and the changes it is now experiencing. Predicting the Korean future is an undeveloped art, but trends in a new Korea are discernable, even if in miasmal form.

Korean culture historically has been eclectic. It has adopted and adapted a variety of influences, some important, others trivial. It has identified itself with some of the dominant forces in the region, although at other times warding off cultural absorption. It could amalgamate a Confucian morality and court system, producing a somewhat genetically modified stock because of its own base. It could reject important Japanese influences while adopting others and could embrace U.S. concepts and methods but significantly alter many of their salient features.

Korea has survived as a separate and distinct culture because emotionally it has been an island, self-sufficient in its own cultural pride. It has been a metaphorical as well as a literal peninsula, relying on and influenced by other ties—cultural, economic, or security-related. Caught between the two concepts of insularity and peninsularity, the Korean people happily have managed to avoid the excesses of each. In its new internationally active incarnation, which this book explores, Korea has managed almost unconsciously to incorporate productively the two opposing forces, if not without some strain then with a minimum of cultural dislocation and trauma. It is a consummation to which many nations devoutly could aspire.

2

Land and People

It may be said of Korea that there is no country of comparable significance concerning which so many people are ignorant.
Cornelius Osgood, *The Koreans and Their Culture*[1]

Korea breeds cartographic images. In Korean folklore, it is pictured as a rabbit, its ears nestling along the Russian border. Metaphorically, it was the shrimp among the whales. The early Buddhist monk Toson likened Korea to a ship or to a tree with its roots in Mount Paektu on the Manchurian border. Mountainous Korea was to early European sailors like "a sea in a heavy gale." Korea in hostile hands was in the contemporary period a potential dagger pointed at the heart of Japan or, as an alternative, a bridge from Japan to the mainland. Koreans have been harassed by the major powers of the region, the passive voice reflecting accurately a previous national perception. Even the weather seems to reflect these crosscurrents: The winters bring severe Siberian winds, snow, and cold from the north; the summers are a monsoon season of humid heat, rain, and typhoons from the south.

KOREA AS NORTHEAST ASIAN NEXUS

In prehistoric times, Korea was part of a physical link, a literal bridge, with Japan. In historic times, it has been both a cultural and military metaphorical bridge in Northeast Asia, the transmission site or center of competing interests. It was the avenue through which much Chinese cultural influence and Buddhism entered Japan, affected materially by its Korean passage. It was also repeatedly the military nexus for control over the region. Korea served as the staging area for the Mongols' attempted invasions of Japan in the thirteenth century. Japan invaded Korea in 1592 and 1597 as the first steps in its proposed conquest of China. The Manchus did the same in the early seventeenth century to protect their flank as they invaded China. Japan fought China over

9

Korea in 1884–1885 and Russia in 1904–1905 for the same reasons. Japan colonized Korea to secure its interests on the Asian mainland in 1910, and today both Japan and the United States view the defense of South Korea as essential to the maintenance of the regional balance of power.

Viewed from the mainland, the peninsula (approximately the size of Rumania or New Zealand) is a mountainous appendage potentially outflanking the competing forces of the north and south over the East Asian heartland, close to the borders of societies traditionally differentiated between those essentially agricultural and those practicing herding. The peninsula's location engendered continous conflict between the stable, sedentary rice culture of the south and the nomadic tribes of the north. As early as the third century B.C., the Chinese Han Dynasty colonized the northern portion of Korea to ensure its control against the nomadic tribes of what is now Manchuria. In the late sixth century, the Chinese Sui Dynasty was overthrown after its exhaustion in ineffectual attempts to subdue Korea as part of its struggles against the northern barbarians. Later, the Khitan, the Jurchens, Mongols, and Manchus all attempted to control or neutralize Korea in their wars with the Chinese to the south. Similarly, the People's Republic of China felt that it could not let the borders of northern Korea fall into hostile hands in 1950. Both tsarist and Soviet Russia have attempted to exert influence on Korea, and both China and the Soviet Union, after the Sino-Soviet split, have carefully attempted to cultivate North Korea in their own rivalry.

GEOGRAPHY AS OBSTACLE

Internally, South Korea, with 38,022 square miles (98,477 square kilometers), has no major geographic divisions, no distinctive or extensive plains or major mountains that naturally divide many nations. Although it contains 3,579 islands, its major insular feature is Cheju, called in early European maps "Quelpaert," a separate subtropical province that is dominated by the extinct volcano Mount Halla. Korea is so generally mountainous, however (only 20 percent of the land is arable), that there may be no place where one can stand and not view hills and mountains. The few rivers are not navigable by oceangoing vessels for any distance, although the Naktongkang in the south winds for 323 miles (521 kilometers), the Hankang in the west for 319 miles (514 kilometers), and the Kumkang (south of the Han) for 249 miles (401 kilometers), the latter two flowing into the Yellow Sea. In the days before road traffic became efficient, small vessel coastal commerce was important. A few country boats also sailed down the Naktong toward the sea. In the nineteenth century, small foreign ships on the Han River could reach

Mt. Sorak, a popular resort area for citizens throughout Korea

Village in which the houses have been rebuilt under the *Saemaul* (New Community) rural development program

Mapo, then a village some miles from the walls of Seoul but now virtually a part of its downtown area. Until recent times, no major Korean city was built on the coast because of fear of the ravages of foreign, mainly Japanese, pirates.

The combination of restricted valleys and lack of major river systems meant Korea, unlike China, did not need extensive mobilization of labor and development of administrative mechanisms for central flood control and management of massive, rather than localized, irrigation. Its particular geography was the reason Korea never developed the highly effective means of centralized management for such purposes, as did a hydraulic society like China, even though Korea emulated the Chinese court and administrative organizational structure. Korean bureaucracy may have been weaker because of the lack of such a challenge. Neither did Korea develop a feudal society with localized centers of power, as did medieval Europe or Japan.

Korea is essentially a country of relatively small fertile valleys and larger coastal plains interspersed among waves of mountains oriented along a north-south axis. The mountainous nature of the terrain fostered the development and continuation of separate tribal systems in an early period but was not severe enough to prevent the formation of three kingdoms. By the seventh century, the country had evolved into a unified state that persisted until the end of World War II. Thus, because of this history and ethnic unity, the division of Korea along the 38th parallel in 1945 represents a separation far more traumatic than, for example, the similar division of Germany.

The borders of the eight provinces that make up mainland South Korea (Cheju Island being the ninth) are in some sense historic or arbitrary. They are rarely based on pronounced geographic features—a river or the top of a mountain—in contrast to the *kun* (counties, of which there are 139), into which provinces are divided, and the *myŏn* (townships, numbering 1,274) that make up countries. Cities with over a million population—Seoul, Pusan, Taegu, Inchon—are special cities and are administered directly from the capital, not through the provinces. Provinces more often codified distinct economic and social units of Korean society in spite of a centralized Korean political administration. In the modern period, economic divisions have disappeared and social distinctions have broken down, although regional loyalties are still politically significant.

ETHNICITY AND LANGUAGE

The Koreans today are, in international terms, a homogeneous people of Mongoloid race, even though their origins may be traced to a series of tribes on the peninsula and in what is now Manchuria, with strong prehistoric Siberian cultural influences. Throughout the peninsula Koreans speak the same language, one that is part of the Altaic group that stretches from Turkey and Finland across central Asia to the Pacific. This linguistic group also includes Mongolian, Uzbek, and Manchu (and perhaps Japanese). Although many Chinese concepts and loan words (perhaps 50 percent) are now an integral part of the language and have been so for some fifteen hundred years, they have been incorporated into a very different linguistic and grammatical structure, more different, for example, than German is from English. Chinese is tonal; Korean and all Altaic languages are not. Chinese sentence structure (subject, verb, object) more closely resembles that of English; Korean sentence structure (subject, object, verb) is more like that of German. In many cases, Koreans will have both an indigenous and a Chinese-origin term for the same object or concept, as English speakers may have both an Anglo-Saxon and a Latin or Greek term.

Korean is intelligible throughout the peninsula, but inhabitants of Cheju Island, because of its isolation, have maintained a dialect that is unique. Regional accents remain and are a cause for humor by those from Seoul, the primate city that is, and has been since 1392, the cultural and intellectual hub of Korean life. In spite of the overall homogeneity,

Although birth rates have fallen in the Republic of Korea, children and primary schools seem ubiquitous.

provincial stereotypes—first recorded in the tenth century—persist. They derive partly from differences among the rival kingdoms dating from the period before Korea was unified under one administration, and they have retained a certain mild piquancy. Some, such as those regarding the Cholla provinces of the southwest, were reinforced by political rivalries in the postindependence period; the combination of regional historic differences and individuality exacerbated contemporary problems that had disastrous consequences, culminating in the Kwangju Rebellion or Incident of 1980 (see Chapter 6). In the light of this event, some Koreans have questioned whether the notion of cultural homogeneity may be a myth. Although Koreans may feel these differences acutely as a type of regional factionalism, in any comparative perspective they remain marginal in a remarkably unified people.

The linguistic and cultural unity of Korea has been and remains an important, although unquantifiable, element in Korea's phenomenal economic growth. Both North and South Korea are the only countries in Asia that have no statistically significant minority groups, no culturally distinct peoples, immigrants or indigenous, who have or do control the economic hierarchy or remain at the bottom of the social ladder. This ethnic and linguistic homogeneity has enabled the mobilization of the society for developmental or political goals and has enhanced economic

TABLE 2.1
Population and Urbanization, 1960-1986

Population of South Korea		Population by Province (Nov. 1985)		
				percent
1949	20,189,000	Kyonggi	4,794,000	11.8
1958	23,331,000	South Chungchong	3,002,000	7.4
1961	25,402,000	North Chungchong	1,391,000	3.4
1967	30,131,000	South Cholla	3,748,000	9.3
1970	32,241,000	North Cholla	2,202,000	5.4
1975	34,707,000	South Kyongsang	3,519,000	8.7
1980	37,436,000	North Kyongsang	3,013,000	7.4
1983	39,929,000	Kangwon	1,726,000	4.3
1987	42,082,000 (midyear est.)	Cheju	489,000	1.2

	1960	1982
Urbanization as a percent of total population	28	61
percent of urban population in Seoul	35	41
percent of urban population in cities over 500,000	61	77

1985

	number (millions)	percent
Total population	40.4	
Seoul	9.6	23.8
Pusan	3.5	8.7
Taegu	2.0	5.0
Inchon	1.4	3.4

Urbanization is defined as cities (si) over 50,000, of which there
are 57. There are also 191 market towns (up). The Seoul population
density is 11,458 per square kilometer. The North Korean population
(1985) was estimated at 20,380,000.)

Source: Derived from Economic Planning Board yearbooks and
statistics.

equity. If Korea had significant internal cleavages, these were along
hereditary class lines that have become increasingly blurred, rather than
along ethnic ones.

In contrast to many countries today, where tribalism or ethnicity
looms larger than civic consciousness, North and South Korea are both
nations and states; that is, they are identified by their peoples conceptually,
if not diplomatically, as one. Perhaps one could posit that the Korean
peninsula is a single (temporarily) divided nation that now is two states
that at some future time and under conditions still obscure will regain
its geographic integrity and reaffirm its ethnic nationhood.

The population of the two Koreas in 1986 totaled some 62 million,
of whom about two-thirds reside in the South (Table 2.1). South Korea's
population has more than doubled since independence in spite of its
family planning program, which is one of the most successful in the

A view of Seoul, facing south toward the "southern mountain," a public park in the center of the city

world. Its present population growth rate is 1.21 percent per year. More than 10 million people—one-quarter of the nation—live in Seoul, and by 1990, Seoul and Korea's second largest city, Pusan, will have about 40 percent of the total population in South Korea; in 1988, these two cities and their metropolitan regions contained half the nation's population. Urbanization is arguably the single most important change in modern Korea, a theme to which we will return.

In spite of the numbers of Koreans who do not live on the peninsula, South Korea has a population density of 1,060 people per square mile (408 people per square kilometer), the highest in the world after Bangladesh and Taiwan; Japan has 876 people per square mile (303 people per square kilometer). South Korea has a population ratio to arable land of 4,919 persons per square mile (1,702.2 persons per square kilometer).

THE KOREAN DIASPORA

In addition, significant Korean minorities live outside the peninsula. About 2 million Koreans are located in China, mostly in the Yanbian Korean Autonomous Prefecture of Jilin Province in Manchuria. There may be 1 million ethnic Koreans in the Soviet Union. Some 389,000 migrated to the Russian Maritime Provinces when Japan colonized Korea, and others were resettled in Soviet central Asia. Perhaps over 600,000 Koreans are now resident in Japan, a small fraction of the millions who

Swimming pool in an apartment complex

were imported into Japan when Korea was a Japanese colony to perform lower-class industrial and economic chores associated with Japan's war efforts. There may be 1 million Koreans in the United States, although the census of 1980 indicated that the official figure was 432,000. Los Angeles has the largest Korean population of any city outside Korea. As the Korean economy has expanded, some highly educated Koreans have migrated back to Korea, but others have left to work overseas, especially as the construction industry dilated in the late 1970s. In 1982, officially some 168,000 Koreans were working in the Middle East, but at the height of the boom a few years earlier there may have been half a million.

Although the movement of Koreans and Korean economic influence overseas may seem to set a precedent in Korean history, in fact in the seventh and eighth centuries the Yellow Sea was Korean and the Koreans controlled the trade in the region. The unification of Korea, and the internal attention this required, together with the rise of the Japanese *wakō* (pirates), ended that period of Korean economic expansion, one that was not to reappear for twelve hundred years.

*   *   *

There has, then, been a remarkable persistence in the continuity of the Korean tradition and its people as a distinct cultural entity in spite of the diverse pressures to which Korea has been subject. The reemergence of Korea as an important factor in its own right, rather than solely as a pawn in regional struggles, is a result of a complex series of forces, some of which are to be found in this cultural continuity and in the origins and history of the Korean people.

3

Origins and Early History of the Korean People

The origins of the people today known as Korean are obscure. Research on later periods is easier because all Confucian societies, including Korea, has kept voluminous records; the prehistoric beginnings, however, are still murky, and archeological evidence is limited. One need not accept the claim of five thousand years of Korean art to recognize that there are at least two thousand years of a continuous situational, historical, and artistic tradition traceable and clearly labeled Korean, as well as earlier remains indicating that peoples have inhabited the Korean peninsula for three millennia.

PREHISTORY

Strong evidence exists of the Siberian ancestry of the peoples who have come to be known as Korean, but the backgrounds of the earlier paleolithic and neolithic peoples are unknown. Scattered paleolithic remains, mainly stone tools and implements, have been discovered in both the northern and southern portions of the peninsula, indicating that these peoples lived in caves and huts and were hunters and gatherers.

Neolithic evidence is widespread throughout the region. Early neolithic remains from about 4000 B.C. indicate the use of polished stone tools and pottery—a round-bottomed, plain ware similar to some found in Siberia, pointing perhaps to a common ethnicity or origin. By 3000 B.C., there were well-established communities. The people used stone spears and flint axes but likely were still nonagricultural. Houses were partly dug into the ground and perhaps covered with thatch. A distinctive combware decoration on pottery is evident from this era and indicates that perhaps both the technology of and aesthetic or magical interest in such designs were widespread. Identical designs have been found in eastern Siberia, Manchuria, and parts of Mongolia.

By the late neolithic, perhaps 1800 B.C., stone plows and sickles were introduced, demonstrating that the population was largely sedentary and that agriculture was in its rudimentary stages. Millet has been found, acorns were used for food as well, and millstones were employed. Pit dwellings were common. Shell mounds have also been discovered, indicating that some of the peoples subsisted by gathering shellfish and fishing. Weights for nets and fishhooks show that this was an important economic source for sustenance. A new form of pottery with a thunderbolt design appeared, which seems to have had its origins in Manchuria.

Evidence from the later period and neighboring peoples points to the clan as the basic element of social organization. Leaders were probably elected from among the elders, there was communal labor, and shamanism seems to have been practiced. These three neolithic periods probably indicate three separate waves of immigration into the peninsula, but it is likely some fusion occurred, for continuity exists between those neolithic groups and the people today known as Koreans.

By the eighth century B.C., bronze was evident; bronze daggers have been widely found and predominate until the introduction of iron in the fourth century B.C. It seems likely that this technology was introduced from north China, which already had a flourishing bronze culture of very high artistic attainments. Many dwellings were built on slopes, agriculture predominated, and rice cultivation was introduced, presumably from China as well. A distinctive burial pattern for the powerful was the dolmen—large, often massive, flat stones mounted on stone underpinnings. Of different types, these monuments are prevalent in Korea and in parts of Manchuria but are absent from China, indicating their North Asian origins. They are found in parts of Europe and may have spread both east and west from wherever they originated. Iron was introduced into Korea by the Chinese, whose coins from this period have been found there, and by the Hsiung-nu, a migrant pastoral people from the north. Iron and other cultural elements were transmitted through Korea to Japan and absorbed into what became the Yayoi culture. Some of the material attributes of prehistoric Korea are recognizable in Korean life today. Distinctive pottery was prevalent; for the burial of important personages, two large urns were placed mouth to mouth. The *ondŏl*, under-floor flue heating of contemporary Korea, dates from this period.

The most ancient state known on the peninsula was that of Old Chosŏn, the name that has sporadically been used for Korea since that period. It incorporated a portion of what is now southeastern Manchuria and was located in the Taedong River valley in northern Korea. Its legendary founder (and thus the mythic progenitor of the Korean people) was Tan'gun (traditionally placed about 2333 B.C.), the son of heaven who married a girl who had been transformed from a bear. The Tan'gun myth is still celebrated in Korea, for however archaic it may now sound, it is distinctly Korean (that is, non-Chinese) in origin and appeals to a sense of Korean distinctiveness and nationalism.

CHINESE DOMINANCE

Direct Chinese influence began to be felt in the region to the north of Korea—the Liaotung peninsula, site of the present city of Dalian (formerly Darien, under the Japanese)—with the establishment of a commandery in that area in the fourth century B.C. by the Chinese state of Yen (Yenching was the old name for Beijing). By 194 B.C., however, Chinese influence became apparent on the peninsula when Wiman, whom legend has it may have come from China with a group of retainers, became the ruler of Chosŏn. Although ties between the city-states that federally were known as Chosŏn were relatively weak, Chosŏn was in contact with the Hsiung-nu, which worried the Chinese.

To outflank the Hsiung-nu, who were persistently attacking northern China and against whom the Chinese constructed the Great Wall, the early Han Dynasty in China conquered Korea in 108 B.C. and eventually established a set of four commanderies in the north. This period, known as the Lolang (Nangnang in Korean), lasted several hundred years. The superior technology and bureaucratic mechanisms of the foreign regime were a strong cultural and administrative attraction for the various tribes and city-states on the peninsula. During this period, there developed a set of tribally organized states or groupings that eventually fused into what has become Korea. These were Puyo in the north and Mahan, Chinhan, and Pyonhan in the south.

THE THREE KINGDOMS AND UNITED SILLA

For more than half a millennium, three states evolved with vague, changing boundaries and overlapping and shifting alliances—with one another and with China and the "barbarian" (in Chinese terms) tribes in the north—and vied for power on the peninsula. These were Koguryŏ in the north, the legendary founding date of which is 37 B.C.; Paekche in the southwest, founded in 18 B.C.; and Silla in the southeast, which was founded in 57 B.C. and which was the kingdom that eventually, in A.D. 668, unified Korea for the first time. These dates begin an era sometimes known as the Proto–Three Kingdoms period. The real emergence of these small city-states into kingdoms, however, came significantly later following the collapse of the Chinese Lolang commandery; Koguryŏ ousted the Chinese in 313, and the first historically recognized ruler of Silla was Naemul (356–402).

These kingdoms spread their control over parts of the peninsula (and eastern Manchuria in the north). Silla remained continuously centered at Kyongju in the southeast, but Paekche, which began in the region of present-day Seoul, occasionally moved its capitals, ending in Puyo in the southwest. Other, smaller states rose and fell during this period, the most important of which was Kaya, located strategically between Silla and Paekche in the south-central region in the Naktong River valley. The territory of Kaya was not extensive but later came to be regarded as a vital precedent for Japan's territorial ambitions on the peninsula.

During the period of the Three Kingdoms and the United Silla kingdom that followed, Korea was a transmission belt, receiving and exporting culture and technology in the region. It seems to have done this both passively and actively, sometimes modifying culture in the process of its transmission. In discussions of this period, it is accurate to avoid considering the region by the modern national designations, such as "Korea" or "Japan," which at that time had no meaning. Such designations only tend to blur reality and overly engage nationalistic pride. The peoples who inhabited the Japanese island of Kyushu and the southern coast of Korea at this time were probably similar in culture and without political boundaries as understood today. There was considerable interchange between the islands and the peninsula and, indeed, between both and the mainland of China. About one-third of the registered noble families in the Japan of 815, for example, were of Korean descent. In this early period, the people on what is now the southwest coast of Korea unofficially controlled much of the trade in the Yellow Sea and between China and Japan. Korean expatriate colonies were scattered along the north China coast, and when the Japanese sent tribute or Buddhist missions to China, they often went in ships controlled and manned by these people.

It was through the peninsula, and especially Paekche, which was strategically situated along the west coast closest to Japan and China, that much of early Japanese culture was transmitted. Buddhism came into Japan from China through Korea, and much of the art of the classical Japanese Nara period can be traced to artisans from Paekche.

As partial historical justification for their expansion on the mainland of Asia in the nineteenth and twentieth centuries, the Japanese claimed that a Japanese empress had conquered the kingdom of Kaya (now known as the site of origin of the popular zitherlike instrument, the *kayagŭm*), justifying the modern Japanese colonial takeover of Korea as recovery of part of its earlier lost territories. There is no historical evidence for this claim, for the Japanese sources cannot be documented and are ambiguous, whereas Korean records do not refer to it. It is

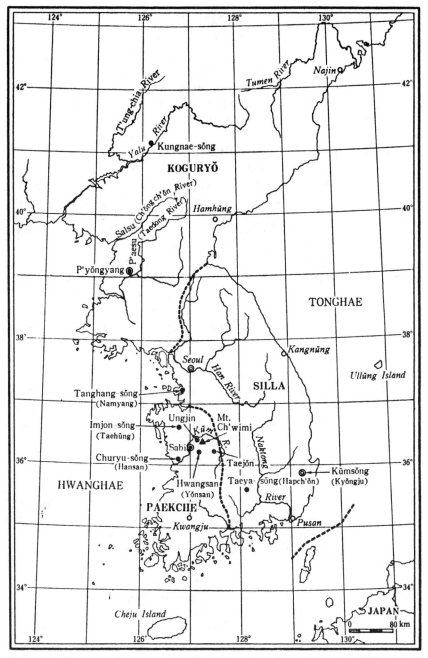

The unification struggle among the Three Kingdoms (seventh century). Reprinted, by permission of Harvard University Press and Ilchokak, from Ki-baik Lee, *A New History of Korea* (Cambridge, Mass.: Harvard University Press, 1984), p. 68.

clear, however, that Kaya and the Wa (the Japanese of that period) were allied sporadically, and Wa troops did assist the Kaya against the other two kingdoms. The early culture of the whole region, however, was so intertwined that modern nationalistic distinctions simply obfuscate reality while raising ethnocentric ire, and modern claims of domination by the peoples on either side of the straits, based on a millennium-old incident, are dubious at best.

These three kingdoms had considerable power. Koguryŏ, a "warrier aristocracy" in the north, was strong enough—under the leadership of one of Korea's most famous military leaders, Ulchimundŏk—to defeat several major invasion attempts by the Chinese Sui Dynasty (589–618), and so disastrous were those defeats that the dynasty was weakened and soon was overthrown by the T'ang Dynasty (618–907), whose forces, led by Emperor T'ai-tsung, were also repulsed.

Eventually, however, with the assistance of the T'ang, which had designs on the whole peninsula, Silla was able to overcome its traditional enemies, conquering Kaya in 562, Paekche in 660, and Koguryŏ in 668, thereby unifying Korea for the first time in its history. The concept of the unity of the Korean peoples dates from this period and represents a strong historical force of great emotional significance to Koreans everywhere. Unity continued uninterrupted in spite of foreign invasions until the foreign-initiated division of the country into North and South Korea in 1945, a division Koreans today, both in South and North, cannot accept as permanent. China recognized Silla's domination south of the Taedong River (near present Pyongyang), north of which was Parhae, a post-Koguryŏ kingdom that included part of Manchuria and that lasted until the advent of the Koryŏ Dynasty in 936.

The great remains of this period are to be seen in Kyongju (known at that time as the "City of Gold"), a site that testifies to the power, wealth, and artistic achievements of the Korean people of the Silla period. A census (held every three years) of Kyongju, which contained about a quarter of the Silla population, in the ninth century enumerated 178,936 households (certainly over half a million people, possibly many more), meticulously listed by status and individuals by age and sex, as well as by material possessions. Its purpose evidently was to fix taxation rates and corvée labor requirements. The great burial mounds, together with the wealth of Buddhist monuments, the remains of which are still extant, indicate that the kings of Silla were able to mobilize extensive labor (and thus the agricultural resources to feed this force) for this monumental construction.

With the ascendancy of Silla, technology was also cultivated; the remains of the earliest extant observatory in the world, built between 632 and 647, as well as an icehouse of the same period, still exist. One can still see the sculptured stone channels, surrounded by gardens, through which water flowed carrying cups of wine for the courtiers who sat along its sides composing poetry for the occasion. Korea has the world's oldest existing wood-block printing (of Buddhist texts), dating from 751. Bronze construction was exceptional; the bell in the Kyongju museum, for example, dated 771, is 11 feet (3.4 meters) high and 7.5 feet (2.3 meters) in diameter. Buddhist monuments, such as the man-made grotto on top of a mountain at Sökkuram (outside Kyongju), were engineered with a fine sense of proportion and knowledge of mathematics. The first rays of the sun rising from the Eastern Sea strike the Buddha's forehead, creating a halo effect.

All three kingdoms showed a strong tendency toward patrilinial and hierarchical power. All were centralized, aristocratic states, with a very strong tradition, perhaps best known in Silla but apparently common to the area, of rank based on hereditary principles. In Silla, this was called "bone rank," and it influenced all forms of social and political behavior. The Silla aristocracy was organized into gradations of seventeen ranks, with only the top rankings allowed to have effective power. Chinese records of the period indicate that high officials might have as many as three thousand slaves and other property. Beneath the aristocrats were an extensive but unknown percentage of the population who were servants or slaves, many perhaps better termed serfs, who farmed the land for their overlords and were bound into hereditary service.

Confucianism became the court-adopted bureaucratic ideology; Buddhism was the state religion. A National Confucian College was established in 682 and a civil service examination system in 788. The system differed from its Chinese model, as it was open only to the higher aristocracy. There was an inherent attitudinal conflict between the Confucian concept of an intellectual and moral egalitarianism (which produced or reinforced hierarchical structures based on parables of family relations) and the bone-rank system based on lineage. The lower aristocracy over time attempted to change the system by liberalizing access to power, but with little result, as the higher aristocracy resisted such changes. At the same time, there was constant tension between the king and the aristocracy over effective power, with centralization of authority in the hands of the court. To ensure control, military reforms were instituted by the king, changing a tribally based system of six military garrisons into a system of nine divisions and ten garrisons to protect the borders and ensure domestic peace—that is, by breaking down tribal loyalties to keep the aristocracy from threatening the throne.

Buddhism had been introduced earlier in the Three Kingdoms period and remained a major cultural force. It was a result of introduction from the apex rather than conversion from below; after the royal family adopted Buddhism, it then spread to the commoners. Major temples were built, such as Pulguksa ("Temple of the Buddha Land") in Kyongju in 751, and monks traveled to China and India to bring back scriptures and new scholarly exegeses.

Although the Chinese were expelled from the peninsula by Silla in 676, their strong cultural impact remained. The Chinese written language was required for court use, and Chinese stylistic and artistic influences beyond Buddhism were profound. The earliest extant landscape depiction in world art is a temple floor tile from Paekche from the seventh century; it is markedly Korean but probably based on earlier Chinese landscape concepts. Confucian learning was cultivated, and literature was composed in a Koreanized Chinese script called *hyangch'al*, which used some Chinese characters to represent Korean sounds.

Silla was an absolute monarchy, with society mobilized for state purposes. The aristocratic youth were organized into the *hwarang* ("flower of youth"), an elitist youth mobilization to protect the court and the state (the name and concept were revived in the republican period a thousand years later). Much of what is today regarded as distinctively Korean may be dated from the Three Kingdoms and United Silla periods.

As the court expanded and became more luxurious, more funds were needed by the center, thus putting severe strains on the social periphery. Peasant rebellions became common, and new dynasties sprang up. A short revival of the division of Korea, into what became known as the Later Three Kingdoms, proved ephemeral. A member of the gentry from Kaesong, named Wang Kon, founded a new dynasty called Koryŏ, from which comes the name Korea.

THE KORYŎ DYNASTY, 936–1392

The founder of the Koryŏ Dynasty set up his capital in Kaesong (just north of today's Demilitarized Zone) and by 936 had extended his boundaries to cover the whole of the peninsula. Like Silla, Koryŏ was a state in which lineage played a critical role in social organization, but of a somewhat different nature. Koryŏ also had internal military problems, as well as trouble securing its northern frontier.

The Koryŏ rule was essentially a civilian administration, continuing the Confucian bureaucratic tradition and with an effective presence through the nation. The highest administrative body was the *Samsŏng*, or Three Chancelleries, which balanced power with the *Chungch'uwŏn*, or Royal Secretariat to the king. Koryŏ administration was an aristocratic political centralism. Officials were paid (for their lifetimes) from the proceeds of land temporarily granted by the king; and only families of those of higher ranks were able to retain these holdings beyond the officials' tenures.

Koryŏ diversified power among a variety of clans from different regions, restructuring the aristocracy. Social status was hereditary, but there was considerable upward mobility, as poorer relatives of the aristocracy were able to sit for the examinations, of which there were three classes, each open to different levels. The highest examination, available only to the most elite, was in classics, and during the entire dynasty only 450 men passed it; six thousand passed an examination on composition (in Chinese); the last category was available to those from the lower aristocratic ranks and was more technical in nature. The Koryŏ period also saw the rise in clan and regional private academies to teach the classics to the sons of the aristocracy. The higher aristocracy was able to perpetuate itself, through the examinations and because an official who ranked Grade 5 or above could automatically have one son enter the bureaucracy. In 992, a national university was established with six colleges, including classics, law, and accounting; a different rank was required for entry to each. Below the aristocracy were free peasants and below them were special artisans or service workers—potters, miners, transport workers, and others. In addition, there were numerous slaves.

The civilians at the core of the ruling group discriminated against the military, which in 1170 staged a military coup led by Ch'oe Ch'ung-hŏn. He was able to establish military supremacy for some sixty years, in much the same way that, four hundred years later, the shoguns were able to control the emperor in Japan until the Meiji Restoration of 1868.

The military problems were not only internal. The state was threatened by the Khitan and the Jurchen to the north at various times and built a 300-mile (480-kilometer) long wall, completed in 1044, to protect the northern frontiers. The Koryŏ king was asked by the Chinese Sung Dynasty to attack these tribes, which also threatened China proper, but Koryŏ refused. Meanwhile, the Japanese *wakō* attacked settlements on both coasts, forcing the population inland.

The Mongols, however, proved the greatest threat to Koryŏ and eventually conquered China, setting up the Yüan Dynasty. In 1231 the Mongols invaded Korea on their march to conquer Japan and, during the next thirty years, launched six invasions of Koryŏ. Forced into corvée labor to build ships and to provision them for the invasion, the Korean population suffered badly in the unsuccessful efforts by the Mongols to extend their domain. Japan claimed that it was saved by the *kamikaze*, the "divine wind" that destroyed the Mongol fleets in 1274 and 1281.

The strength of the Mongols clearly did not lie in their seafaring ability. The water barrier seemed to be a significant element in enabling the truncated Korean regime to continue. The Korean court, to escape

Mongol rule, fled in 1232 to the west coast island of Kanghwa, a few hundred yards from the mainland near the mouth of the Han River. There the court was able to continue; it surrendered in 1259 but did not return to Kaesong until 1270. Accommodations with the Mongols were reached; Koreans presented daughters to Mongol royalty, and a modus vivendi was established. In spite of the Kanghwa exile, culture flourished. It was during this period that the court had constructed the vast corpus of Buddhist Tripitaka (scriptures) on wooden type, a collection that today is still extant. Although clay type was invented in Sung China in the eleventh century, in 1234 the Koreans invented the world's first movable metal type and in the last year of the dynasty, in 1392, established a National Office for Book Publication.

In retrospect, as the following Yi Dynasty is considered quintessentially Confucian, so the Koryŏ Dynasty is known for the flowering of Buddhism. Buddhism thrived under royal patronage, along with Confucianism, and seventy temples were built in Kaesong alone. Some of the finest Korean temples belong to this period, and Buddhist sculpture and painting were exceptionally developed. Buddhist temples expanded along with the clergy, for whom the state established a separate examination system. Large temples with great wealth and land began to establish their own private armies to protect their property. Pottery reached its peak of subtlety with the flowering of celadon wares for the court. Trade was extensive with the northern tribes and with the Chinese Sung Dynasty. There is even a record of an Arab ship reaching the port that serviced Kaesong; Arabs had centuries earlier established continuous trading relationships with the Chinese at Canton, where they had built a mosque.

The dynasty decayed, however, and the agricultural base could not support ever-increasing court and national needs. Farms became larger and were run for their absentee landlords in the capital. Corvée labor increased. As taxes were raised, peasant rebellions mushroomed, and commoners found it advantageous to become indentured serfs as a means for survival. The end of the dynastic cycle was in sight. The Koryŏ Dynasty was overthrown in a military coup by General Yi Sŏng-gye, who had made his initial reputation in supressing the pirates. Ordered to march north to attack the Chinese Ming Dynasty (1368–1644), he instead turned his army homeward and took over the peninsula.

In spite of foreign incursions, even domination for a period, the Koryŏ Dynasty set many of the social patterns and institutions on which the following Yi Dynasty was built and achieved as well standards of art and culture that today are still admired.

4

The Flowering and Decline of Traditional Korea

The 518 years of the Yi Dynasty constitute one of the longest recorded histories of dynastic succession on the East Asia mainland. Korea had brilliant periods of artistic splendor and innovation. During those turbulent years, however, it underwent foreign invasions that damaged the economy beyond recovery, attrition in leadership, intensified factionalism that seriously impaired the capacity of the state to use available talent to cope with its many problems, and a diminished tax base that resulted in greater demands on a smaller group of peasants and thus in peasant rebellions. How was this dynasty able to continue in the face of these problems?

The answer may lie in three major historical developments. Chronologically, the first development was the generally effective administration of the first two hundred years of Yi rule, during which the early dynastic administration prospered on a broad and expanding economic base (for which land reform was critical). Then, following national devastation by Japan, self-imposed isolation (together with that of Japan during approximately the same period) gave the dynasty time during which it might have dealt with its internal administration—time it did not, however, use effectively. Third, the international rivalries in the nineteenth century required a weak buffer state in the region, allowing the Korean regime to continue until Japan, with Western acquiescence, annexed Korea in 1910.

THE YI DYNASTY, 1392–1910:
THE FLOWERING OF A CULTURE

The consolidation of Yi Dynasty rule, requiring certification from the suzerain power—China—ushered in a period of an intense, court-centered administration scrupulously modeled on the Chinese pattern.

The new dynasty early carried out a sweeping land reform that transformed the old economic order, giving the new dynasty great fiscal power by increasing the state lands and revenues while destroying the basis of the Koryŏ aristocratic wealth. A more intense Confucianism became the dominant ideology of the court. It was during the Yi Dynasty that the *yangban* (literally, "two classes"—civilian and military—but mainly referring to the civilian gentry, or upper class) became the decisive force in administration. Official Korea in this dynasty was essentially a *yangban* enclave, and this group, or whatever faction of it was in power at the time, severely curtailed the theoretically absolute power of the monarch. Relatively small at first, this group began to expand rapidly some centuries later, until it constituted more than 20 percent of the population. It perpetuated itself by limiting access to competitive examinations for official positions to its own social strata.

It became more difficult to attain upper class status under the Yi Dynasty than during the Koryŏ period; illegitimate sons of *yangban* and their descendants no longer sat for the examinations, nor could those from the two most northern provinces. "Protected" (noncompetitive) appointments were severely constrained. Commoners could not take the examinations that were the prerequisites to official positions. If a family did not manage to have members pass within four generations, it gradually lost status. This general pattern was a direct descendant of the Silla hierarchical system, modified to meet Yi needs. The expansion of the *yangban* group placed severe strains on the economy, because *yangban* wealth was based on income from rural land and was not subject to normal taxation, thus generating no court income. At other times, it also fostered virulent factionalism, sometimes over minute issues of Confucian protocol, or on substantive national issues. Factionalism became a dominant theme of Korean court, and even contemporary, politics.

Losers in these struggles were sometimes executed, but more often they were exiled to remote districts such as Cheju Island or the wild east or southern coasts, where they would have no power over central decisions. They did not mobilize the periphery against the center but rather attempted to regain influence and return to the court. In spite of this factor, certain families were able throughout the dynasty to retain leadership through personal and economic influence and the examination system, for to compete effectively in the latter required economic means and the leisure it produced. The Kim family from Andong, North Kyongsang Province, was one such family that supplied ministers to the court for hundreds of years. Clans built and maintained private schools, called *sŏwŏn*, to educate their sons for the examinations and thus to perpetuate their status. These schools were often important centers for scholarship and intellectual debate as well. They were also an economic problem, for like the Buddhist monasteries of the Koryŏ period, they took off the tax registers land that had supported the central administration.

State administration was a Chinese court in miniature, and institutions were established to foster scholarship and the arts. The modern Sŏnggyungwan University in Seoul is the direct descendant of the Confucian Academy, where students studied for the higher examinations. They regarded themselves even then, as now, as the guardians of political morality; as early as the fifteenth century, students demonstrated against court actions that undercut the Confucian tradition, such as undue royal interest in Buddhist activities.

As the dynasty progressed, there developed in rural areas a large group of "decayed" or "fallen" *yangban*, the *hyangban*, or rural gentry, whose economic status (as distinct from social standing) was probably little different from that of many commoners. Below the *yangban*, who controlled most of the wealth, were the *chung'in*, the hereditary technocrats who ran the working levels of the administration. They were the professional (as opposed to the literati) artists, clerks, scribes, doctors, and artisans. Below them were the *ajŏn*, the hereditary petty clerks. These latter two groups were exceedingly important, for they provided administrative continuity, as more senior *yangban* officials were constantly transferred to prevent them from developing local loyalties. The bulk of the population were the *sangmin*, or commoners. There were, in addition, government artisans, who were essentially lower-level skilled workers who produced goods for the state; in the mid-period of the dynasty there were two thousand of these artisans in Seoul and thirty-five hundred in the provinces.

Slavery was important in Korean history—although little has been written about it—and it was extensive. In the fifteenth century, there were three hundred fifty thousand slaves on the government register alone, but the number had declined to two hundred thousand by the seventeenth century. Through various means, slaves were able to move up out of their status, and by 1801 the roster of government slaves was ordered burned, but such registers were continued. Private slavery went on, and the revolts of the nineteenth century often included the burning of slave registers. Slaves may have totaled about 40 percent of the population at various times and may have been ten times more common in Korea than in China or Japan. Slavery included many who in Europe were called serfs.

Changing social status is illustrated (perhaps not typically) by social class identification in official registers in Taegu from 1690 to 1857. At the earlier date, *yangban* were 9.2 percent of the population, *sangmin*

53.7 percent, and slaves 37.1 percent (of which one-fifth were household, or private, slaves). By the later date, the figures had changed to 70.2, 28.2, and 1.5 percent, respectively. Thus, there was official social mobility, although the economic changes may have been minimal.

As the dynasty consolidated its power, Buddhism was downgraded, and temple construction was prohibited in the capital, Seoul. By 1507, the state effectively cut off all support to Buddhism. Buddhist orders had in many cases become wealthy from the donation and acquisition of land, which the central government confiscated in an effort to decrease the power of the monkhood and to return land to the tax registers.

The greatest king of the Yi Dynasty was Sejong (r. 1418–1450), under whose direction culture flourished. In 1420 he founded the Royal Academy, the *Chiphyonjŏn,* to encourage scholarship. Most important, he sponsored the development in 1443–1444 of *han'gŭl,* the unique scientific Korean alphabet. Writing and publishing flourished with the invention of movable type.

Other important developments mark this early period of the dynasty. The first rain gauge was invented in Korea in 1441 and introduced throughout the country the following year, two hundred years before such gauges were developed in Europe. Astronomical clocks and clepsydras were constructed. In 1401 mulberry bark was used as money, with copper coinage introduced in 1423 and iron currency in 1464. The era was one of intellectual excitement and innovation. This splendid period was truncated first by the incessant factional disputes among the *yangban* close to the court, feuds that often lasted for generations and impeded effective state management. More immediately decisive were the Japanese invasions.

THE IMJIN WARS (1592–1598) AND THEIR AFTERMATH

On the Garrison Tower
In the moonlit Hansan Isle
A great sword beside me.
I sit alone, sunk in sorrow.
Listen, a reed leaf whistle in the dark—
It pierces my entrails, eye, they shake.

Admiral Yi Sun Sin (1545–1598)[1]

The military leader of Japan, Hideyoshi, intent on conquering China, invaded Korea in 1592 in his first efforts to strike at the mainland. His well-organized army quickly devastated the country, destroying cultural objects and undermining the economic capacity of the state. The Korean court at this time called on Admiral Yi Sun Sin, who is credited with inventing the world's first ironclad ships, averaging about a hundred feet (30.5 meters) in length. Both the technology and Admiral Yi's knowledge of the southern coast, its islands and inlets, gave the Koreans their only victories in this war, forcing the Japanese to retreat as their lines of supply were cut. In eight major engagements in 1592, some two hundred fifty Japanese ships were sunk and, later, half the Japanese fleet was destroyed in Pusan harbor. (Admiral Yi is still regarded as Korea's premier military hero, and a shrine was built to him under the Park Chung Hee regime.) In the meantime, the Chinese Ming Dynasty sent troops to support the Korean effort.

In 1597, Hideyoshi once again invaded Korea. Admiral Yi, who had been exiled because of the rabid factional disputes that were to characterize the dynasty, was called back to lead the Korean naval forces. Only Hideyoshi's death a year later forced the Japanese to withdraw, although in this second invasion the Koreans put up much stiffer resistance with Chinese support. The effect of these wars, however, was profound for Korea. Never again until modern times did independent Korea develop a tax base sufficient to cover an expanding central administration and the needs of a modernizing state. From that period on, the nation was in economic decline.

The effects of these wars are still apparent. The Japanese brought to Kyushu thousands of Koreans, many of whom were potters, and the rise of the Japanese pottery industry may be traced to this period. The intense unease of many Koreans about Japanese intentions toward the peninsula thus predate the colonial period and have their origins in the Imjin Wars. Historical markers attesting to this devastation and its perpetrators abound in contemporary Korea.

Unfortunately for Korea, the Imjin Wars were followed closely by the rise of Manchu power in Manchuria. Intent on taking over China, which they did in 1644, founding the Ch'ing Dynasty (1644–1911), the Manchus invaded Korea to protect their flank. The Manchu invasions of 1627 and 1637, when they occupied Seoul, completed the economic disruptions that the Japanese had initiated. Economic turmoil, together with the rise of the new Manchu Dynasty in China, prompted Korea to enter a period of intense isolation, accessible only through very selective routes. Trade with Japan was regulated through Pusan in the southwestern corner of the peninsula and carried out by the lord of the Japanese island of Tsushima, astride the straits between the two countries. Modest trade along the northern frontier with Manchuria was severely limited by the Manchu authorities as to volume and season.

More important were the tribute missions to China, which were often large and in effect functioned as trading and diplomatic missions. Chinese records indicate that Korean envoys were extremely interested in new technology that either the Chinese had developed or the Jesuits and others from Europe were introducing. By this route Christianity first entered Korea, as Koreans in the tribute mission to China became interested in Catholicism in the period 1608–1623 (there had been several Christians in the Japanese invading forces during the Imjin Wars, but they had no material impact on Korean society). Increasing Korean isolationism and fears that Catholicism could upset the ancestrally oriented social order led in the later part of the eighteenth century and during the first half of the nineteenth century to persecutions of both Korean Catholics and Chinese and French priests (who had entered from China). Many Catholics were martyred for their faith, in 1801, 1839, and 1866; in 1866 about five thousand Koreans were executed along with nine French priests. The first Westerners to be recorded in Korea were seventeenth-century sailors on a Dutch ship wrecked off Cheju. They were captured, brought to the court at Seoul, kept for years, finally escaping to return to their homes. One produced the first Western account of Korea.

Korea's insulation from the outside world thus did not prevent important progressive changes from taking place in the society—changes that, however, did not retard the dynasty's gradual decline. These innovations included the practice of transplanting rice and knowledge of the use of fertilizer, which led to higher yields that could support an increase in population; the introduction of extensive coinage; and the development of commerce.

Most important, however, was a new, critical look at the Confucian tradition. Confucianism, contrary to popular Western stereotypes, had never remained stagnant either in China or Korea. Neo-Confucianism, based on the philosophy of Chu Hsi (1130–1200), brought to Confucianism a supernatural dimension from Buddhism and was an important influence on intellectual life in Korea. There developed, in addition, a new Confucian school, called *Sirhak*, or the "School of Practical Learning." Scholars had become dissatisfied with sterile debate and the arcane aloofness of traditional Confucianism from the reality of a nation in obvious economic decline. The *Sirhak* group wanted to rationalize the civil service examination system, the foundation of the bureaucracy; its members wanted to build up industry, technology, and commerce; and they advocated a critical examination of the Confucian classics and more study of Korean history. Had they been given the scope to implement some of their ideas, the history of Korea might have been changed, for they might have produced an administration concerned with Korean realities. Instead, they were suppressed by groups who were inimical to progress and innovation. Koreans reexamining their history have recently revived interest in this scholarship.

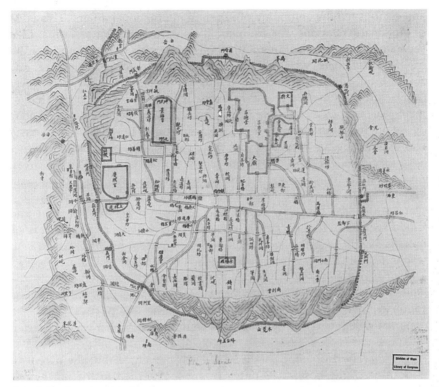

Seoul in the nineteenth century

FOREIGN OPENINGS AND NATIONAL COLLAPSE

The Western expansion into East Asia in the latter half of the nineteenth century could not leave Korea unaffected. The opening of Japan by Admiral Perry in 1854, followed by the intensity with which Japan began to modernize following the Meiji Restoration in 1868, forced Korea into modern exposure. Korean forces had defeated U.S. attempts to sail up the Taedong River to Pyongyang in 1866 and had burned the U.S. ship *General Sherman* and killed its crew. The same year, after the martyrdom of some of their monks, the French attempted to exert influence but were repulsed. In 1871, the Americans returned and bombarded the coast of Kanghwa off the mouth of the Han River near Seoul but also were forced to withdraw. The Japanese finally compelled the opening of Korea, as the Americans had forced such an opening on Japan.

The Treaty of Kanghwa with Japan was signed in 1876. It opened three ports of trade, allowed a Japanese diplomatic mission in Seoul, and established the autonomy of Korea in international affairs. This issue of diplomatic relations was complex. If Korea was subject to China, then separate diplomatic relations with foreign states were inappropriate. But exclusive relations with China imposed obligations for defense and support on China that China could not meet; the issue was never satisfactorily resolved even when Korea became independent in 1896 (a memorial arch in Seoul celebrates that event, which followed China's defeat in the Sino-Japanese War). By that time, however, the dynasty was doomed by the economic and power rivalries of the period. Neither a Korea dependent on an impotent China nor an independent but weak Korea could autonomously function. The peninsula was a power vacuum into which all interested foreign powers would attempt to move.

In the last two decades of the nineteenth century, Korea—and China even more so—became a hotbed of international rivalry as various nations sought to establish claims on its resources. In 1882, China sent troops to Korea to protect it against Japan, but that year Korea signed a number of treaties with various European nations as well as with the United States in an attempt to block sole Japanese penetration of the country. England took over an island off the south coast with the apparent intention of forestalling Russian influence, which was increasing in Korea.

This forced opening might have been prevented, but the ascent to the throne of the boy king Kojong (r. 1864–1907) led to the regency of his father, the Taewŏn-gun (the "Great Prince of the Court"). The Taewŏn-gun was isolationist and turned Korea inward at a time when a forward-looking policy might have been in Korea's best interests. Fearful of all its neighbors and cognizant of colonial expansion in the region, the Koreans sought and succeeded in signing a diplomatic treaty with the United States in 1882, for to Koreans the United States was the major power with the least interest in colonizing the peninsula.

In 1884, Korean reformers attempted to restructure the government to meet the modern requirements of a nation-state. After a short flurry of reform, reaction set in, and the conservatives, supported by the Chinese, gained the upper hand, suppressing such changes. During the same period, foreign concessions and investments began to flow into Korea, including telegraph links with Japan in 1883, the Seoul-Inchon railroad in 1896, and various mining concessions. A postal service was initiated, a customs facility developed, and a major Western missionary effort launched that involved the development of modern education for youth, with a special contribution made to the education of women, and modern medical services. These were to have profound effects on Korean society.

Korea in 1750 (courtesy of the Library of Congress)

Change and ferment were occurring internally in Korea, however. In reaction to economic decline, and spurred by the introduction of Western thought, there developed a syncretic religion called the *Tonghak* (or "Eastern Learning"; later called *Ch'ŏndogyo*, the "Religion of the Heavenly Way"), which combined Western (Catholic) and Korean elements. This group formed the vanguard of a series of peasant revolts that were destructive to the economy of the southwestern part of the state.

To stem growing anti-Japanese feeling in Korea, the Japanese engineered the assassination of Queen Min, who was thought to be against Japanese influence. The king fled to the Russian legation in Seoul and ran the country from there for about a year, thereby increasing Japanese anxiety about Russian intentions in the area.

In the meantime, on the pretext of maintaining order because of the Tonghak Rebellion—a peasant revolt based on syncretic religious beliefs, including Christian elements, that began in the southwest, spread, and was threatening the regime—the Japanese (and then the Chinese) introduced troops into Korea, resulting in the Sino-Japanese War of 1894–1895, in which China was severely defeated. Korea thus became "independent," but under Japanese hegemony, and China ceded Taiwan to Japan under the provisions of the Treaty of Shimonoseki.

Japanese expansion exacerbated Russian fears and interests in the region. This led to the Russo-Japanese War of 1904–1905, which was fought in large part in Manchuria, where the Japanese were attempting to gain a foothold, as were the Russians in their search for an eastern warm-water port. The Russian defeats on land, and the sinking of the European Russian fleet by the Japanese in the battle of the Tsushima Straits, prompted President Theodore Roosevelt's intervention and led to the Treaty of Portsmouth in 1905, which established Japanese supremacy in Korea. That same year, a secret U.S.-Japanese protocol was signed. The Taft-Katsura Agreement gave Japan a free hand in Korea in return for Japanese acquiescence in the U.S. assertion of its supremacy in the Philippines.

The Japanese victory in the Russo-Japanese War led to Tokyo's imposition of a protectorate over Korea. Foreign affairs and economic matters were placed in Japanese hands; it was just a matter of time before Japan would formally annex the Kingdom of Korea, which had existed as a unified, independent nation since 668.

5

The Japanese Colonial Period

The land is no longer our own.
Does spring come just the same
To the stolen fields?

—Yi Sang-hwa (1900–1943)
"Does Spring Come to Stolen Fields?"[1]

No period of Korean history is fraught with more controversy than that of the Japanese colonial era, and no topic is more likely to excite passion. These sensitivities are easily understandable, even to foreign observers, but the depth and extent of Korean feeling on this subject are more profound than outsiders might imagine, more intense than the reactions of many other peoples to their Western colonizers.

The reasons may partly be found in residual negative attitudes toward the Japanese and their aggression in the Yi Dynasty, their brutality in the first two decades of their colonial administration, their attempted cultural genocide during the later years of that period, and the world's expedient abandonment of Korea in 1905 and again in 1919 despite treaties and altruistic general statements about self-determination of nations.

These negative attitudes merge uneasily with ambivalence about Japanese economic power and capacity. Many Koreans respect the ability of the Japanese to unify socially for national goals and the attractions of some elements of Japanese culture and life. This was at one time coupled with an almost inchoate pessimism about Korea's economic future as compared to that of Japan and, even today, with continuing distress over Korean internal politics. All these disparate factors color Korean analysis of the Japanese period and influence in Korean history.

39

JAPANESE RULE: THE COSTS AND THE BENEFITS

Viewed chronologically, the Japanese record in Korea is continuously tragic. Abandoned by the United States under the Taft-Katsura Agreement, the Korean pawn was taken by Japan as a result of the Russo-Japanese War of 1904–1905, and a Japanese protectorate was established in 1905. Under a series of military governments following Japanese annexation in 1910, massive amounts of the best Korean arable land were alienated to the Japanese, who were encouraged to emigrate to Korea. The Japanese brutally suppressed the March 1, 1919, independence movement, based poetically and naively on Woodrow Wilson's Fourteen Points following World War I.

Later, Japan attempted to obliterate Korean history, language, and even personal names in an effort to integrate Korea culturally into the Japanese empire. This effort followed Japan's previous attempts to amalgamate Korea as an agricultural and industrial component of its expansionism in the region. The Japanese encouraged Koreans to emigrate to Japan to work at menial jobs in war-related industries. The Korean independence movement—fragmented abroad in China, the United States, and Russia—was ineffective in altering the course of events in Korea. Thus, history reveals an unmitigated series of degradations of the collective and individual Korean persona.

The results of Japanese rule from a developmental perspective were different. The Korean peninsula in 1945, at the close of the Japanese period, had advantages that many other colonies did not share. The North, with considerable heavy industry and hydroelectric power, could exploit its natural resources; the South had light industry and modern irrigation, agriculture, and research facilities. A rail and road transportation network blanketed the peninsula, and modern port facilities had been constructed. A considerable portion of the population was educated in Japanese (although only 5 percent went beyond primary school). Numbers of Koreans had attended Keijo Imperial University (now Seoul National University), and more had received higher education in Japan (less than 1 percent attended any college, however). Koreans received training in lower-level industrial, managerial, and administrative skills. The basis had been established for economic growth. Even the disastrous Korean War could not obliterate this foundation, but a different set of political and economic objectives and a different leadership was required for it to become effective.

For whom, however, was this infrastructure built and the Koreans trained? Clearly and correctly, the Koreans argue that it was for the Japanese, to serve their expansionist and military interests. The welfare of the Korean people was not a primary, or even a secondary, concern.

I do not wish to denigrate the real suffering and humiliation of the Korean people or justify colonialism. At the close of the Japanese period, however, and with the repatriation of the Japanese colonists, a unified Korea would have been in a position to make important economic strides in its own development. Unfortunately, the division of the nation and the Korean War retarded that process for about a generation.

THE EARLY PERIOD OF JAPANESE RULE

Japanese rule formally began with the establishment of the Office of the Government-General and the incorporation of Korea into the empire in 1910. Yet, the Protectorate, begun in 1905, under which Japan was to control Korean foreign relations, had effectively initiated Japanese rule and penetration.

Japan had stationed troops in Korea in 1904. In September of that year, the Japanese inaugurated military control over the whole country, beginning the process of railroad construction and telecommunications expansion. On September 17, 1905, Korea was forced to agree that control of foreign relations would be passed to the Japanese Foreign Office. On February 1, 1906, the function of Resident-General was established; the Resident-General controlled not only foreign relations but also the whole of the Korean internal administrative structure.

King Kojong, however, remained on the throne. After he surreptitiously sent an emissary to the Hague Peace Conference in June 1907 to protest Japanese policy, he was forced to abdicate in favor of his son the following month, and a third Japanese-Korean agreement legally terminated Korea's modest internal autonomy.

Control over the Korean currency and the introduction of Japanese banking into Korea gave the more-affluent colonists the economic means to manipulate Korea beyond the legal implements already at their disposal. The Oriental Development Company, a Japanese government-sponsored conglomerate formed in 1908, the purpose of which was to spur Japanese investment, was a pivotal means of Japanese expansion.

By obtaining title to untitled, crown, and military land, the company within the first year gained access to some 74,100 acres (30,000 hectares). This acquisition was to grow to 380,926 acres (154,221 hectares), and the number of tenant farmers working for the company reached 300,000. At its height, the company owned about 20 percent of the arable land in the country. This was made possible through an extensive eight-year land survey that began in 1910. The survey forced registration of all land, enabling the Japanese effectively to expropriate the land of masses of unsophisticated Korean owners or operators. There were more than 34,000 legal protests, mostly by Koreans, over the seizure or registration of land in that period. The Japanese nationalized more than 4 million hectares (9.9 million acres) of village and grave forests, turning over exploitation rights to their own lumber companies. Korean investment was effectively discouraged with the passage of a company ordinance in 1910, forcing the registration of all Korean firms, with the Government-General retaining the legal right to dissolve them. In 1912, Korean fisheries were brought under the control of the Japanese as well. Japanese emigration was also encouraged, and by 1908 there were 126,000 Japanese in Korea; by 1911, the figure had risen to 210,000. In the 1940s, Japanese civilians in Korea numbered 704,000 and Japanese military numbered 179,000.

This type of colonial experience differed greatly from that of any other colony in East or South Asia. Westerners ruled there with relatively small numbers, whereas the extent and intensity of Japanese penetration and settlement in Korea were unique in Asia. The Japanese role in Korea was more akin to France's role in Algeria: the propinquity of the colony to the colonial power, the extent of immigration to and emigration from it, and the attempts at administrative absorption. This may also help account for the depth of Korean resentment against the Japanese.

THE KOREAN INDEPENDENCE MOVEMENT

We do hereby declare and proclaim that Korea is an independent country and that the Koreans are a free people. To all countries in the world we announce this is so that the great cause of the equality of mankind shall be made clear; and we make this known to our posterity, generation after generation to come, to enable them to enjoy forever their just right to national self existence.

We declare this with an authority supported by a five thousand year-old history, and proclaim this with the united loyalty of 20 million countrymen; we uphold this for the uninterrupted and free development of the nation.
. . .

Now we are standing up for the great cause. All conscience is on our side and truth is marching with us! Let us all men and women, young and old, cheerfully set forth out of the ancient dreariness and take part in a fulfillment of a joyful resurrection with tens of thousands of living. The spirit of our forefathers, a thousand generations in the past, are helping us from within and the favoring climate of the whole earth protects us from without. To begin is to succeed. Let us press forward courageously toward the light ahead.

—*Declaration of Independence*, March 1, 1919

The Koreans did not take the loss of their sovereignty lightly. Although the official army had been placed under Japanese control, the volunteer Korean Righteous Army and local resistance fighters, incorporating both *yangban* and commoners, fought some pitched battles (but more often guerrilla actions) against the Japanese. Between 1907 and 1910, some one hundred and fifty thousand Koreans demonstrated and fought against the colonizers. Although the Japanese claimed that resistance ended by 1912, it may have continued sporadically until 1915. Elements of the Korean resistance fled to Manchuria, where they continued periodically to harass the Japanese until 1919, and others went to Shanghai.

In 1907, the *Sinminhoe*, a secret organization devoted to regaining Korean independence, was formed, and by 1910 it had some three hundred members throughout the country. That same year it was destroyed by the Japanese, and some of its members were tortured and imprisoned. This was one of a number of small, militant, anti-Japanese groups that began to form by 1904 and were active in the pre-1919 period; such groups indicated the extent of Korean intellectual resistance to the Japanese.

The flowering of the spirit of Korean independence is without question the March 1, 1919, Independence Movement, known in Korean as *Samil Undong* ("3-1," first day of the third month, movement). This date is still celebrated as a national holiday. Excited by the statements of Woodrow Wilson at the Paris peace conference, in which Wilson called for the self-determination of nations, Korean students' demonstrated in Tokyo on February 8, 1919. The acme of the movement, however, came when a diverse and influential group of thirty-three Koreans, including Christian, *Ch'ŏndogyo,* and Buddhist leaders, peacefully met on March 1 in Pagoda Park in Seoul and publicly read a proclamation of independence. The signers of the declaration, who made no effort to escape, were arrested, tried, and convicted. This moving, poetic statement excited Koreans throughout the country, causing demonstrations that were brutally put down by the Japanese police and military. Two million Koreans participated in the movement. In the course of its nationwide suppression by the Japanese, 47,000 people were arrested, women and children were intentionally killed, 7,509 Koreans died, and 15,961 were wounded.

Korea became a police state under Japanese rule. Ubiquitous police suppressed all overt efforts at Korean dissent. Foreign missionaries, however, who often ran schools and hospitals, were a focal point for Korean nationalism, for they were less subject to Japanese harassment until World War II. Because the Japanese controlled the press and all external communications, this group was the single source from within Korea to spread the story of Japanese atrocities to the outside.

The focus of the struggle for independence thus shifted outside Korea. A Korean provisional government-in-exile was formed in 1919 in Shanghai, where the international settlement harbored many diverse causes. The movement was led by Kim Ku, who after World War II was a rival to Syngman Rhee and was assassinated in 1949. Already in the United States in 1919, Syngman Rhee was only prevented from presenting Korea's cause to the Paris peace conference because U.S. authorities refused him permission to leave the country. The United States was unwilling to jeopardize more important relations with Japan.

THE JAPANESE OCCUPATION: THE LATER PERIOD

Following the suppression of the domestic independence movement in 1919, the Japanese modified their policies to eliminate some of the harshness of their rule. A civilian leader replaced the military one. As Japan moved closer to its 1931 occupation of Manchuria, the buildup of the economy was stressed. The movement toward war both on the mainland and in the Pacific changed the content of much of the Japanese occupation. The Japanese military, in control within Japan, formulated policies designed to integrate the Korean state culturally as well as economically into the Japanese empire.

The physical battle for Korean independence shifted to Manchuria and, to a much lesser degree, to the Russian Maritime Province. In Manchuria, after the pitched battles that were fought in the early 1920s inside Korea, the most famous was in 1920 at Ch'ŏngsanni, where Koreans defeated Japanese troops of much greater strength. After the start of the Sino-Japanese War in 1937, the provisional government-in-exile, which had been established by Korean nationalists in Shanghai, moved to Chungking when the Japanese occupied Shanghai and the Chinese capital retreated into the interior. Other Koreans joined Mao Tse-tung in Yenan and later became known as the Yenan faction in North Korea under Kim Il Sung's leadership. Manchuria reemerged as a center of guerrilla activity during World War II; Chinese communist efforts to harass the Japanese reinforced Korean independence aspirations. It was from these movements, supplemented by Soviet interests in opposing Japanese control, that Kim Song Ju, who later became Kim Il Sung—taking the name of a famous earlier partisan—got his start; he eventually became the leader of North Korea.

There were protests in Korea as well and assassination attempts against Japanese leaders. On June 10, 1926, mass demonstrations for independence occurred at the funeral of Korea's last monarch. In 1929, students in Kwangju began demonstrations against the Japanese because one of the Japanese had insulted a Korean female student; the protests spread to 194 schools and involved some 54,000 students. In 1925, the Korean Communist party was founded, in part as a reaction to the colonial occupation. A previous party had been organized in Shanghai in 1920.

Japan sought to eliminate the cultural identity of the Korean people. History was rewritten. Although early records of the cultures on the Korean peninsula and in Japan (too early in history to call them either Korean or Japanese) and their relations were always sparse and unclear, the Japanese propounded historical precedents for their occupation of Korea based on dubious historical materials. They discouraged the traditional Korean schools, which dropped in number from about 2,000 to 600. It became illegal to use Korean names on official documents; all instruction in the schools and discussions in public were mandated to be in Japanese beginning in 1938. A Japanese curriculum was enforced from 1941. Books on Korean history and culture were suppressed, and scholarship on Korean subjects was discouraged. This situation was different from that of any other colony in the region. In other colonies, advancement may have required knowledge of the language and culture of the colonizers, but in Korea the indigenous language was prohibited by law. In effect, this was a policy of cultural genocide.

Although the wealth of many landlords was adversely affected, the Japanese did not destroy the *yangban* class but rather used this educated and powerful group for its own ends. In the early years of the occupation, the Japanese even created seventy-six Korean peers to reward cooperation. A segment of the Korean *yangban* elite could take advantage of Japanese opportunities: One-third to one-quarter of the student body of Keijo Imperial University was open to Koreans; other Koreans who had money were educated in Japan, and ambitious but destitute commoners went into the Japanese army.

The Japanese occupation, however, wrought extreme economic hardships on most Koreans. Korea was developed and exploited for the Japanese realm. The development of impressive hydroelectric facilities together with the industry that relied on that power were important to the incipient, and then actual, Japanese war effort. In fact, Korean annual economic growth between 1911 and 1938 averaged 3.5 percent, compared to 3.4 percent in Japan. In that same period, manufacturing rose by 10 percent per year (from an infinitesimal base). In contrast to many colonial powers, Japan did not import primary products for processing from Korea but instead established processing facilities in the colony.

Korea was also exploited as a rice-exporting region to make up part of the deficits that the main islands suffered. About half of rice production was exported to Japan. Thus, per capita consumption of rice in Korea declined and was only partly replaced by coarser grains, such as barley and millet. Nutritional standards dropped and poverty increased. This traditional agrarian export pattern, together with a wealth of farmers and a dearth of natural resources, convinced foreign planners in the early 1950s that Korea should be an agricultural exporting country, a concept that was never implemented.

By 1930, 75 percent of farmers were in debt, and three-quarters of that debt was to Japanese financial institutions. Tenancy and partial tenancy became the norm; some 12 million people (2.3 million families) were tenants, paying exorbitant rents. There was migration out of rural areas; in 1925, 2.8 percent of such migrants went to Manchuria and Siberia, 16.9 percent to Japan, and 46.4 percent to Korean urban areas, where living standards were also low. As the war effort intensified, Korean labor was drafted into Japanese industry. By the close of the war, 2.4 million Koreans had worked in Japan, many in the mines, some in other menial positions, thus freeing Japanese for military or other civilian jobs with better pay. Within Korea, 4.1 million workers were forced to serve the Japanese in various positions. Finally, beginning in 1943, Koreans were conscripted into the armed forces (Korean college students were drafted in 1944).

The legacy of the Japanese colonial period remains vibrant today. Korean laws and administrative regulations are largely holdovers from the Japanese (who in many cases adapted them from the Germans). Japanese modern farming, irrigation, and agricultural research services formed the basis on which Korea was able to expand and modernize its rural sector. Japanese industry, taken over at the end of the war by Korean entrepreneurs who had held relatively junior positions in those firms, sometimes became major Korean corporations. In 1945, the Japanese left behind in Korea substantial corporate assets. The leading 2,000 firms were worth some $4.6 billion. Sixty-eight percent of these firms were owned by Japanese; 27 percent were under joint Japanese-Korean control, but with the Japanese predominant; and only 5 percent were completely Korean-owned. Educated Koreans over fifty speak Japanese, having been schooled at least through primary level in that language. In contrast, the North Korean leadership claims legitimacy partly on the basis of its anti-Japanese activities.

In some sense, the Japanese administrative centralization and state control, guidance of the economy, and suppression of unions, all reinforced by traditional values, became an inchoate model for the two Koreas in startlingly different political systems. In contrast to Taiwan, another Japanese colony, increases in agricultural production in Korea required coercion. In Taiwan, which had no large landlord class, farmers directly benefited. In Korea, increased agricultural production was seen as enriching the landlords, not the farmers themselves.

The intentional and harsh Japanese suppression of Korean language and culture gave birth on liberation to a vast demand for and expansion of Korean education and interest in all things Korean. The experience of the colonial period resulted in the closure of Japanese relations for the generation between 1945 and 1965. Japanese could not be taught in Korean universities as a foreign language. Although anti-Japanese sentiment restricted Korean growth for that period, it was a natural reaction to the colonial era.

But Japan had an unacknowledged and, later, positive economic influence as well. It became both a developmental model and a rival to be surpassed. Various Korean economic policies may be traced to Japanese influences—individuals trained, institutions formed—but Japan remains an example to Koreans of what Korea may accomplish. Many Koreans are determined to overcome the humiliation of the colonial era, and the present stigma of being a Korean resident in Japan, by demonstrating that Korea is capable of surpassing the accomplishments of its former colonial masters.

6

The Republics of Korea

The tasks of the State vary in accordance with the time. They are basically three: founding, consolidation, and reform. . . . If one were to cling to consolidation when reform is needed, it can be likened to a sick child who refuses medicine and waits for death.
—Yi Yulgok, in a report to King Sunjo (c. 1590)[1]

The Japanese surrender on August 15, 1945, ending World War II and the colonial era in Korea, caught the United States unprepared to deal effectively with Korea and with the exuberance of the Korean people after their liberation. None of the twenty-five thousand U.S. troops that were to constitute the occupation force could immediately be released from Okinawa. The vanguard, led by General John Hodge, did not arrive in Seoul until September 8, and no trained Korean specialists were available. Policy consisted of only a vague concept, a result first of the Cairo Declaration of December 1, 1943, calling for independence for Korea "in due course"; of the Yalta Agreement of February 1945, which specified a four-power trusteeship; and then the Potsdam Conference of July 1945 on the Soviet entry into the Pacific war (and, thus, Soviet occupation of the North). None of these ideas relating to the future of Korea were ever discussed with Koreans; insofar as these concepts delayed independence, they were plans that all Koreans would violently oppose.

PRELUDE: LIBERATION AND MILITARY OCCUPATION

The decision to divide the acceptance of the surrender between Soviet and U.S. forces at the 38th parallel, about 30 miles (some 48 kilometers) to the north of the capital, Seoul, was an arbitrary one made by two young U.S. officers, Dean Rusk (later secretary of state) and Colonel Charles Bonesteel (later commander of UN forces in Korea); their aim was simply to keep Seoul in U.S. hands. Although this was a seemingly "equitable" geographic division, they did not realize that a division of Korea (between Russian and Japanese spheres of influence) had been suggested along a similar line in the later part of the nineteenth century. There was no thought that this was to be a permanent division; it was a demarcation of convenience, for no troops were available to back it up should the Soviets have decided to push south, and no troops were available to go north.

While General Hodge in Okinawa prepared to come to Korea, the Soviets, who had trained a large cadre of Koreans, including Kim Il Sung, in the Soviet Far East, moved immediately to assist in the formation of people's committees and other local bodies, placing their cadre in command. These committees were also formed in the South. Liberation produced in both North and South embryo "people's republics" in reaction to all the forces that had been aligned with the Japanese, including wealthy landowners. Fearful that chaos might prevail and intent on fostering a relatively conservative regime, General Hodge (who was unprepared and without reliable colleagues in the Korean community) kept the Japanese in positions of authority. This policy caused outraged, and understandable, protests from the Koreans. Many of the hated Japanese police forces, composed of Koreans, were retained and used to suppress demonstrations against rice collections and rising urban rice prices. Hodge refused to deal with locally elected or appointed bodies, opting for more conservative representation.

The three-year U.S. military government of Korea was conservative, generally well intentioned, but not particularly efficient. Although the United States had trained specialists for the occupation of Japan and had major programs for the military in the Japanese language, Korea— on the periphery of U.S. attention—was ignored. Relief was provided, schools built, and Japanese-owned land was distributed in what was to be the first phase of land reform in the South. Politically, however, southern Korea was in ferment. Peasant agitation was widespread, and unrest permeated the society as leading figures jockeyed to obtain power. Syngman Rhee returned to Korea from the United States, already an old man of seventy who had spent more than a generation in exile.

As the cold war and containment policy against the Soviets, mainly focused on Europe, began to be articulated in the United States, Korea was initially considered eligible for massive economic assistance, along with Turkey and Greece. This project was dropped, however, because of the magnitude of the funds involved. In fact, the cold war and containment had begun in Korea with the arrival of U.S. troops and in the preliberation demarcation.

The UN called for free, supervised elections throughout the peninsula, but these were held only in the South, on May 10, 1948; there, a Constituent Assembly was voted into being that was to be the basis for forming a constitution and the new government of the Republic of Korea. Syngman Rhee was elected speaker and then president. On August 15, 1948, the anniversary of liberation day, the Republic of Korea was born. The Democratic People's Republic of Korea was instituted on September 9, 1948, but on December 1 the UN General Assembly declared that the Republic of Korea was the sole legitimate government on the peninsula.

THE FIRST REPUBLIC: SYNGMAN RHEE, WAR, AND THE ARROGANCE OF POWER

To the outside world, especially the United States, Syngman Rhee symbolized Korea. Insofar as any Korean had international stature, it was Rhee. A leader of the fight against Japanese colonialism all his adult life, in his old age he had finally witnessed Japan's defeat, his life-long ambition.

Within Korea, however, his stature was quite different. There had been many other anti-Japanese leaders, especially those Koreans in the provisional government in unoccupied China, such as Kim Ku, and there were patriots at home. Rhee was one of many. Out of touch with Korean reality, and with a foreign wife, he was perhaps too foreign and too conservative for the needs of that society at that time, especially in the heady period following liberation and before the Korean War. He was opposed by an increasingly large body of influential politicians. His life in the United States had not made him into a democrat; he was determined to manipulate the political and economic system to further what he regarded as Korean interests. He was ill served by the sycophantic rightist group with which he increasingly surrounded himself. Before 1950, he assiduously subdued the Left: peasant unrest; the massive Cheju rebellion that resulted in tens of thousands of deaths and which devastated that poor island; and the Yosu-Sunch'on military uprising, which resulted in some five thousand deaths and the purging of 10 percent of the commissioned and noncommissioned officers of the army.

Bellicose toward the North, he publicly called for an invasion to unify the peninsula under his leadership. For this reason, the United States, which helped to supply an army of a hundred thousand essentially for internal security, provided no offensive weapons. When the North did attack the South, there were some who believed that Rhee had somehow engineered the invasion. However, subsequent evidence indicates incontrovertibly that the North did plan and initiate the attack. In a lightning thrust, spearheaded by Soviet-built tanks, the North Koreans attacked the South on June 25, 1950. The lightly armed South Korean troops were no match for the North; Seoul was occupied on

June 28. The South Korean government had moved south to Taejon the previous day, then later to Pusan, where it was to remain for much of the war.

The United States had considered South Korea within the perimeter of its containment policy toward the Soviet Union but had withdrawn its troops in June 1949. That same month, the U.S. Joint Chiefs of Staff, motivated by reduced U.S. resources and worldwide commitments, had secretly approved a policy under which the United States would not intervene if North Korea invaded the South. In January 1950, Secretary of State Dean Acheson publicly seemed to indicate that Korea was outside the U.S. Pacific defense perimeter, although he noted that such excluded countries should rely on their own resources and the UN umbrella. The immediate reaction in the United States to the invasion was to treat it as a major Soviet attempt to determine U.S. resolve in the cold war. The confrontation also was considered the first major international test of whether a "limited war" was possible in an age of atomic weapons. Later studies show, however, that the Korean War was more of a civil war. Although it engendered international support for each side and served broader geopolitical purposes, it was locally planned and instigated. Kim Il Sung had approached Moscow for approval, and the Kremlin agreed only after Beijing did not object.

The UN Security Council met on June 25 (June 26 in Korea) and called for a cessation of hostilities and a North Korean withdrawal. The resolution was passed because of the inadvertent absence of the Soviet delegate, who would no doubt have vetoed the measure. On June 27, the Security Council recommended that member nations assist South Korea, and over the course of the hostilities sixteen nations provided troops under a joint UN command that was, in fact, led by the United States.

On June 30, President Truman ordered General Douglas MacArthur, commander in Japan, to defend the South, and the first U.S. engagement with North Korean forces took place south of Seoul on July 4. The U.S.–South Korean troops were no match for the North Koreans, who continued their swift southerly advance, completely occuping the country with the exception of the "Pusan Perimeter," the southeast corner of the nation that included Pusan, the city of Taegu to its north, and the Naktong River to the west. There the North was finally stopped. In a brilliant and controversial tactical movement that many thought impossible because of the deep tidal character of the Yellow Sea, General MacArthur landed U.S. forces at Inchon near Seoul and outflanked the bulk of the North Korean army. Seoul was retaken in ten days after heavy fighting had virtually destroyed it.

As the North Korean forces retreated north of the 38th parallel with UN forces in hot pursuit, the UN troops captured Pyongyang and continued north until advance forces reach the Yalu River on the Manchurian border. U.S. policy had quietly changed from one of containment to one involving the rollback of Soviet influence. The UN troops might have stopped their advance at the 38th parallel, where the war had started; instead, they proceeded northward, in spite of what in restrospect seem clear indications of Chinese intent to become involved, which General MacArthur chose to ignore (he stated that UN troops would be home by Christmas). Chinese communist "volunteers," numbering almost thirty divisions, attacked the UN troops, splitting them and hurtling the UN divisions back down the peninsula in a major U.S. military defeat. Seoul was reoccupied in January by the North, the battle lines fluctuated, and then Seoul was once again retaken by slowly advancing UN forces. A line was drawn that wavered marginally for the next two years but ended close to the 38th parallel.

Although Syngman Rhee was against any truce that left the peninsula divided, the United States entered into negotiations with the North. These ended on July 27, 1953, and resulted in an armistice signed by the North Koreans, the Chinese, and the United States. Seoul would not sign. Rhee unilaterally released North Korean and Chinese prisoners who did not want to go home, contravening the negotiations, and finally agreed to the cease-fire only on condition that the United States sign a bilateral defense treaty with the South and that the South's forces be expanded and properly armed.

The war was devastating. Among more than 6 million casualties, the majority were civilians on both sides. Almost 300,000 North Korean troops, 200,000 Chinese, 227,000 South Korean troops, and 57,440 UN troops, of whom more than 33,000 were Americans, were killed, and about 105,000 Americans were wounded.[2] North Korea lost over 11 percent of its population; in the South, there was massive dislocation and death.

The physical destruction on a national level was perhaps unparalled. There was scarcely a major building left unscathed in North Korea. In the South, the cost was $2 billion the first year alone. In Seoul, 80 percent of industry, public utilities, and transport and three-quarters of office buildings and half of the dwellings were destroyed. Gross national product (GNP) fell by 16 percent, agricultural production declined by one-quarter, and the meager standard of living deteriorated.

The war demonstrated U.S. resolve to stand up to communist expansion, but any victory was a pyrrhic one. The situation was more that of a stalemate. No power was prepared to use nuclear force; nor was the United States willing to enlarge the conflict by bombing the

Manchurian bases of the Chinese or by bringing the Chinese Nationalist army from Taiwan into Korea, both of which tactics MacArthur advocated. The effects in Korea were long-lasting—a hardened border and implacable hatred between the regimes. The war did not seem to deter other international communist adventures, perhaps because the Eastern bloc viewed the conflict as a civil war, whereas the West believed it to be a Soviet test of U.S. resolve. The war indicated that even in a time of nuclear weapons and confrontational politics, massive retaliation might be unnecessary as well as undesirable—although the threat of the use of atomic weapons was ever present. The war was an important factor in Eisenhower's election as U.S. president in 1952, as the promise to go to Korea and end the struggle had been a major part of his platform. The war also reinforced the constitutional primacy of the civilian president over the U.S. military: Truman dismissed General MacArthur for ignoring the civilian orders of the president, an action met by considerable public outcry. In Korea, the war made the subsequent economic progress of both South and North all the more remarkable, because the disaster that had befallen the peninsula lowered the economic base.

The First Republic was a sad commentary on democratic principles. Overt and covert suppression of leftist and any other dissent took place continuously, starting with the subduing of the 1948 Cheju peasant rebellion and Yŏsu-Sunch'ŏn military uprising as well as of general peasant discontent throughout the country. Opposition leaders from various parties were arrested and assassinated. Elections were rigged, the votes of legislators bought and sold, and public opinion thwarted; a cynical corruption pervaded the state. It was a sorry democratic beginning in a state in which democracy was a textbook concept, unrelated to a long, indigenous authoritarian tradition.

Syngman Rhee manipulated the National Assembly by strong-arm tactics, forced through legislation that facilitated his retention of power, and revised the constitution to allow his continuation in office (the president was limited to two terms, totaling eight years). The result was a travesty for the United States, which had fought in Korea to protect the "free world," a concept that was clearly undermined by the political regime in the South.

Yet, there was dissent, and the formality of the elective process was necessary, both to satisfy internal Korean demands and to present a veneer of international respectability to the outside. Rhee rigged the presidential elections to some degree in 1952 and again in 1956, but in 1956 he could not prevent Chang Myon (also known as John M. Chang), the opposition candidate for vice president, from being elected, nor could he completely prevent the opposition candidates from obtaining considerable representation in the National Assembly.

The ultimate crisis came in the March 15, 1960, presidential election, when Rhee once again ran. Even by previous standards, this election was exceptionally corrupt. The body of an opposition student who had been murdered by the Masan police in the south was found floating in Masan's harbor. Student demonstrations quickly erupted and spread to Seoul. On April 18, students from Korea University rose in revolt, and they were joined on April 19 (which has become the anniversary of the student revolution) and in the following week by both students and faculty. They could not be contained in spite of many deaths. Rhee had no other recourse; he announced his resignation, on the advice of the U.S. Embassy, and left Korea on April 26. He died in exile in Honolulu in 1965. Vice President Lee Ki Bung, a hated Rhee sycophant, committed suicide. Ho Chong, former acting prime minister, was chosen as interim president.

There had been some economic growth (approximately 4 percent per year) in the Rhee period, largely a result of U.S. economic assistance, and agricultural production was again at prewar levels (see Chapter 10). The legacy of the Rhee period, however, was not enviable: autocratic leadership; a political process that could stand little careful scrutiny; only a modicum of international credibility; lack of economic management—indeed, almost no interest—from the top; a record of extreme corruption; and pent-up frustrations that were later to result in the fall of democracy.

THE SECOND REPUBLIC: THE DEMOCRATIC INTERREGNUM

The ebullience created by the overthrow of Rhee by the people, and especially by the role of the students, the nascent literati who were traditionally the self-styled guardians of political morality, was a heady mixture that could not be controlled. In July 1960, in what was the only really free election in Korea until that time, a new National Assembly was elected, with a new House of Councillors added. Yun Po Son was elected president under a system in which presidential power was much diminished, and Chang Myon became prime minister.

Chang Myon came from the North as a refugee, but his political strength was in the southwest (Cholla) region, the seat of power of his Democratic party, which would undergo various permutations to become, in later times, the opposition party of Kim Dae Jung and of Kim Yong Sam. Chang was a Catholic, a political liberal, and a leader who could be considered strongly influenced by the new democratic political wave. His government, however, was plagued from the beginning by the frustrations and unfulfilled aspirations left by the suppressive policies of the Rhee period and the inability of his regime to meet intensified demands for political and economic progress. Probably no government could have satisfied these needs, and neither the elective process nor the economy could cope with them. In little more than one year, until the overthrow of the Second Republic by the military, there were some 500 major demonstrations by university students and 45 by the trade unions. In all, there were more than 2,000 demonstrations with 900,000 participants. The press was free, often given to license and irresponsibility, even blackmail. The hope that had initiated this period gradually deteriorated into dismay.

THE THIRD AND FOURTH REPUBLICS: PARK CHUNG HEE AND THE CONCENTRATION OF POWER

On May 16, 1961, in troop movements that contravened the regulation that required UN Command approval, the military executed a coup against the popularly elected government of Chang Myon. It was efficient and carefully accomplished, remarkable in that U.S. military advisors, who permeated the Korean military down to battalion level, knew nothing of these plans.

Chang To Yong, army chief of staff, was named chairman of the Revolutionary Committee, and a Supreme Council for National Reconstruction was established. However, Park Chung Hee quickly became the chairman of the council—and, in fact, the head of state—although Yun Po Son was kept on as titular president until March 1962.

The ostensible reasons for the coup were to purify a corrupt government and save the country from national disintegration in the face of the continuing threat from the North. Students had talked about reunification and holding direct discussions with the North Koreans, and there was clearly increased liberal or leftist sentiment among the youth, not surprising after the repression of the First Republic.

The United States was exceedingly displeased with the coup. The coup had overthrown a popularly elected (if ineffectual) government, which the United States supported. The change established a precedent of which the Americans disapproved (both of coups and of the unilateral movement of Korean troops), and its leader—Park Chung Hee—was suspect. Park had been involved in the leftist Yosu-Sunch'on uprising in 1948, and his political leanings were unclear.

Park obviously wanted to distance himself from the United States in this early period. He stopped joint economic planning, engaged unilaterally in an ill-conceived currency reform, and together with his relative and colleague, Colonel Kim Jong Pil, began to build up centralized power. Park and Kim founded the Korean Central Intelligence Agency (KCIA), thereby planting the seeds of Park's destruction. The KCIA was to have a profound influence on the society for the next generation by merging executive and judicial functions informally into one organization responsible only to the president. They manipulated the Korean Stock Exchange to raise money for the government political party; founded a dubious resort for the U.S. military from which, it was rumored, payoffs to key government institutions were made; and garnered massive donations and confiscations of "illegal" wealth from prominent individuals associated with previous regimes. Park restructured the executive branch of government so that he could exert centralized control and implement economic policies; he controlled the judicial branch and suspended the legislative branch and elections for a period, until U.S. pressure forced him to reconsider.

The first two years following the coup were difficult for the new military government because of the estrangement of the United States. Although a referendum was held in December 1962 to reconstitute the presidential system of administration, Park preferred to rule by fiat, and it was only pressures from the United States that forced his acquiescence to holding elections. He was also of two minds about personally running in any such election and at first publicly refused, reversing his position a few days later. He and his military colleagues, many from the Eighth Class of the Korean Military Academy (KMA), founded the Democratic Republican party (DRP), which remained during Park's regime the government's major tool for mass mobilization, although other, less-obvious political programs were also used for this purpose.

In October 1963, Park defeated Yun Po Son in a presidential election in which there were charges that *sakura* played a role (the Japanese term for "cherry blossom" is used in Korea to designate opposition candidates paid by government to split the opposition vote). In the election for the Sixth National Assembly in November 1963, the government won sufficient seats to ensure support for most of its programs. When tempers flared in the National Assembly, strong-arm tactics were sometimes used, as in the 1965 passage of legislation approving the normalization of relations with Japan.

In May 1967, Park ran against Yun Po Son once again for the presidency, this time barely beating him with 51.4 percent of the vote. This was to have been the last term for Park, who under the constitution he had promoted could not run a third time. But in September 1969, Park engineered a constitutional amendment allowing him to run for a third term. It was endorsed by 65 percent of the vote in a national referendum in November. Given the political and economic mobilization resources available to the government, this was a significantly small margin of victory.

In April 1971, another presidential election was held. This time, Park, in an election that probably reflected the beginnings of a transition from electoral form to real electoral substance, almost lost to a young opposition congressman, Kim Dae Jung. In the general election that followed the next month, the Democratic Republican party fell short of the two-thirds majority the government wanted so that it could manipulate the constitution. The New Democratic party of the opposition won 89 seats to 113 for the government.

Park was faced with a serious political problem. His support had badly eroded, even in rural areas, where the population was disadvantaged but government influence was strongest. In the cities, government sur-veillance was less compelling. There the opposition could win more votes because the government was less able to manipulate the better-educated urban vote. At this juncture, on December 6, 1971, President Park, playing on pervasive fears, declared a national emergency on the basis of the continuing, undeniable threat from the North—a threat that was omnipresent but also convenient for stifling domestic or foreign opposition to any action that the government cared to make. On October 17, 1972, Park declared martial law, which essentially gave him unlimited power. Although this action was justified on the basis of strengthening the South in its, at first, secret, then public, dialogue with North Korea, it was not unrelated to the fact that three weeks earlier, without public U.S. objection, President Marcos in the Philippines had also declared martial law. It is said that President Park had his staff monitor the U.S. reaction to that move, and when Washington did not object, Park felt free to follow his own inclinations.

President Park promulgated the T'ong'il Chuch'e Kungmin Hoeŭi, the Autonomous Council for Unification, by which the president would be indirectly elected. One-third of its members were to be appointed by the president and two-thirds elected by the public. This gave the government the virtual certainty of controlling the election.

President Park then announced the Yushin Constitution, called the "revitalizing reforms," the Korean equivalent of the Meiji Restoration of the emperor in Japan in 1868. It concentrated all power in the hands of the government. This, then, became the Fourth Republic, the most centralized, autocratic, and dictatorial Korean regime in history. These "reforms" were ratified in November 1972 by the usual national ref-erendum, a technique that Korean governments had continuously used to legitimate their actions.

A set of draconian laws followed that established an effective police state. A series of emergency decrees were promulgated. Decree number one banned all activities opposing or slandering the Yushin Constitution, including press reports on such events. Number two established a special court-martial system to try those who violated edict number one. The Park government brooked no opposition and even attempted to assassinate Kim Dae Jung, whom it kidnapped from Japan in August 1973. He was saved by quiet U.S. intervention. During this period, the United States made few public statements questioning the regime, although in individual cases, behind the scenes, it attempted to mitigate the worst excesses of the government.

During the Third Republic, economic growth, personally monitored by Park, proceeded apace. In the Fourth Republic, although exports expanded and national income rose, Park—concerned about the Nixon Doctrine, improved U.S. relations with China, and the continuing U.S. disillusionment with involvement on the Asian mainland as a result of the Vietnam War—undertook a massive program of military self-sufficiency and heavy industrial development that placed major strains on the economy. He improved the lot of the peasant, as an immediate response to the rural political problems evidenced in the election of 1971 and as a reflection of his own rural background. Over the span of both republics, Japanese economic assistance and investment became important factors in Korean growth, as did the Korean commitment of troops to Vietnam and the resulting procurement of the commodities, services, and financial support provided by the United States. To ensure the diversification of its oil supply and the generation of foreign exchange, Korean firms under government guidance undertook major construction and other contracts and provided Korean personnel and laborers to projects throughout the Middle East.

As the Korean economy staggered under the weight of Park's imposed defense initiative, massive foreign borrowing was required, wages rose, inflation increased, and major structural adjustment of the economy was required. In an assassination attempt in August 1974 by a North Korean agent, the president's wife was killed, and he narrowly escaped. Even stricter security was the result. During this period, demonstrations were increasingly held against the dictatorial and autocratic government. Park was advised by his close associates to control them with a firm hand. There was also growing evidence of anti-U.S. sentiment, and U.S. cultural centers became targets for demonstrators as Washington was perceived to be a supporter of the Park government.

The demonstrations spread in the south in Masan and Pusan as the president became convinced that the government should take a harder line toward the demonstrators. On October 26, 1979, Park Chung Hee, attending a dinner with some of his closest associates, was assassinated by his colleague, Kim Jae Kyu, the director of the Korean Central Intelligence Agency. It is ironic that the KCIA, the organization most closely associated with Park's control over the society, wanted a more conciliatory posture toward the demonstrators.

THE FIFTH REPUBLIC: CHUN DOO HWAN AND THE TRANSFER OF POWER

The death of Park Chung Hee, like the fall of Syngman Rhee, released social forces that had been bottled up for almost two decades. There was an outpouring of vitality and a sense of liberalization and euphoria so long held in check. Choi Kyu Ha, a senior figure who was without political power, became interim president. Efforts began to reform the constitution and liberalize its provisions.

These activities were cut short on December 12, 1979, by what may be described as a coup carried out by General Chun Doo Hwan against other military elements whereby Chun arrested General Chung Sung Hwan, head of the Martial Law Command, and others for complicity in Park's assassination. He gradually took over power, (although Choi Kyu Ha remained titular president for eight more months), inheriting an economy that was rapidly disintegrating because of the dislocation related to Park's death, overly heavy expenditures in defense and heavy industries leading to inflation, and later, in 1980, because of the failure of the rice crop.

With Park's death, Kim Dae Jung, whom Park had sentenced to death, regained prominence. Demonstrations against Chun spread, this time centered on South Cholla Province, the home of Kim and the area that traditionally had been subject to economic discrimination under both Rhee and Park; Park and, later, Chun (and most of Chun's entourage) came from the Kyongsang provinces to the east. On May 18, students in Kwangju demonstrated, and the populace joined in. Martial law was declared. The government sent in special forces, which brutally put down the rebellion in an orgy of killing (the government claimed almost 200 people were killed; the opposition said the number was 2,000). The citizens drove out the troops on May 21, held the city, and attempted to negotiate. On May 27, regular troops were dispatched, retook the city, and dispersed what became known as the Kwangju Rebellion, or Incident, the most serious and traumatic event in Korea since the Korean War.

The Kwangju Rebellion may have started as demonstrations by students expressing solidarity with other demonstrators in Seoul and elsewhere, but it quickly became a popular rebellion that transcended age, class, and occupation. It was lacking in ideological coloration and was essentially a massive, classless response to specific government abuses and to a general sense that the Cholla region had suffered repeated discrimination under all governments (except the short-lived Second Republic) for some twenty-five years. The U.S. ambassador suggested that the government apologize for these excesses, but the regime refused. The issue remained unresolved until 1988.

The Kwangju Rebellion seriously impaired any sense of legitimacy that the Chun regime might have hoped to have. The United States was severely damaged by it as well, for the popular impression was that all Korean forces were under the control of the UN Command and, thus, under U.S. leadership. Although this was (and is) legally incorrect, as the special forces and certain other troops were excluded, it has become increasingly apparent that there are dangers inherent in any system under which a foreign power, lacking real authority, may be held popularly responsible for actions or tension. Some say the populace had fully expected the United States to intervene and force negotiations and were astonished when it did not do so, further attributing U.S. inaction to support for the Chun government.

On August 22, 1980, Chun retired from the military (after being promoted to the rank of four-star general) and was elected president on August 29 through a continuation of an indirect (manipulated) election system. On October 23, 91.6 percent of the electorate voted in the usual plebiscite in favor of a new constitution for the Fifth Republic. The constitution limited the president to one seven-year term, but retained indirect elections for that office. In January, martial law was lifted. Chun was reelected by indirect voting under the new constitution, and in the March elections for the National Assembly the government's Democratic Justice party (DJP) won 151 of 276 seats.

Following his inauguration in January 1981, President Reagan invited President Chun to be his first official foreign guest, a singular invitation that saved Kim Dae Jung's life. Kim was once again under sentence of death for allegedly instigating the riots that led to Kwangju, and the price paid for his life (at Washington's insistence) was the legitimacy that such an invitation might convey. The Reagan administration wanted to make a major effort to improve relations with the Republic of Korea. During the Carter administration a coolness had developed because of Carter's pressure on human rights issues and his advocacy, as part of his campaign platform in 1976, of withdrawing U.S. troops from Korea.

Complaints against the Chun government rose. Political suppression was the main theme, along with lack of legitimacy, but economic issues surfaced, especially those related to the pervasive role of the chaebŏl, the large conglomerates that came, as a matter of policy under Park, virtually to control the economy.

Anti-U.S. sentiment, traditionally surprisingly small, began to rise among the youth. There was increasing collaboration between students and the emasculated labor movement. Students, expelled from classes for political activity and denied positions commensurate with their training by a government that could control all public and ostensibly private sectors of the economy, infiltrated the labor movement by hiding their educational attainments (otherwise they would not have been hired) in order to help organize workers. Some of these intellectuals who were Christians promulgated a type of radical theology called *minjung* (mass) theology, or theology of the people (which had Latin American origins), to provide justification for more equity in the society. Overt North Korean slogans were heard in the rapidly increasing numbers of demonstrations.

As these student incidents, as well as a few labor demonstrations, became more frequent, for a period in the spring of 1984 the police refrained from entering campuses, allowing demonstrations to be confined to the schools. Over time, the policy changed, and the government took harsher measures to subdue these incidents. Although the radicalized students in such demonstrations seemed relatively few in comparison with those opposing the regime, the spectre of North Korea always loomed behind the scenes, the government used that spectre to justify ever harsher measures to limit public displays of disapproval. In 1985, there were 3,877 on-campus demonstrations.

These demonstrations, and those that were to follow, have been quite different in character from those in other societies in which civil violence, looting, and general destruction of public and private property reflect broad social anomie. In Korea, violence has been focused, directed at symbols of central government authority—police boxes and police buses or vans. No shops were looted and no indiscriminate violence against spectators perpetrated, thus demonstrating the singular target of the demonstrators rather than vague social unease.

In spite of a government that was increasingly severe toward its opposition, National Assembly elections had to be held and were held on February 12, 1985. The New Korea Democratic party, created only a month before the elections and led by Kim Dae Jung (who was under house arrest for much of this period and was not allowed to run for office) and Kim Yong Sam, made surprising major inroads on government power. The government's Democratic Justice party received only 35.3 percent of the vote, gaining 87 seats, whereas the new opposition received 29.2 percent, or 50 seats. A complex proportional system for allocating seats gave the government 148 seats to 67 for the opposition. The government lost in the five largest cities in the nation: Seoul, Pusan, Taegu, Kwangju, and Inchon. It is clear that elections had become more than a necessary ritual for external consumption but were now a vigorous element in the growth—slow and unsteady but sure—of pluralism in Korean society.

Although the press was allowed more leeway under the Chun government, and news from foreign sources was more widely available and less grotesquely censored, the strong hand of government was felt in the press, in politics, in the articulation of dissent, in occupational purges of intellectuals, and in the economy. To "purify" the society, in the period following the Chun takeover, some 5,000 officials were dismissed, as were several hundred journalists (many from the private sector); 172 "harmful" periodicals were closed, 611 teachers and principals fired, and 57,000 "hoodlums" rounded up. Some of the harsher suggestions for control were not implemented, such as "reeducation centers" for dissident students. Political tensions mounted as the Olympics neared and the question of the transfer of power from President Chun to his successor remained unresolved. Under the constitution, Chun was unable to run again and had sworn not to do so.

The opposition wanted direct election of the president and mounted a nationwide signature campaign calling for a referendum on this subject. The government declared the campaign illegal (Washington supported the concept of petition) but eventually said it would negotiate with the opposition. On April 13, 1987, President Chun, after a year of fruitless discussions, unilaterally cut off negotiations with the opposition on new constitutional provisions to replace the indirect election of the president, a system that was generally thought to be inappropriate as it could ratify any government in power. The government suggested a parliamentary system, while the opposition pushed for the direct election of a president. Neither had marked intellectual underpinnings in Korea. Each group seemed intent on pursuing its formula in the belief that this would bring victory to its side.

President Chun was determined to transfer power to his chosen successor in the Democratic Justice party, former General Roh Tae Woo. This was to be the first such transfer in Korean history (but similar to changes in leadership in Japan and Mexico), and as such it was a welcome democratic precedent. Democracy, however, may be defined in part as the peaceful transfer of power between competing political parties, not just between factions of the same party. Yet Chun seems to have believed his gesture sufficient for democratic progress. The populace did not agree. Popular demonstrations intensified in response to increased police brutality—specifically, the death of a leading student under police interrogation—and a general sense of frustration with the political process, as members of the middle class joined in. The movement became the broadest expression of public discontent with government, probably in that respect exceeding the demonstrations that led to the fall of Syngman Rhee.

The climax came between June 10, 1987, when President Chun formally held a party convention designating Roh as the DJP candidate, and June 29, when Roh announced a sweeping liberalization program. Public expressions of sympathy with the demonstrators grew, and even government party legislators backed away from the executive branch decisions. Rumors spread about military intervention through martial law or garrison decree, or even a coup against Chun by disaffected military who were wary about further troop confrontations with the populace and falling military prestige.

In a move that stunned much of the government and its entourage as well as the opposition, Roh announced on June 29 that the government would agree to the direct election of the president and that political liberalization would take place, with stringent laws terminated, political prisoners released, and the political rights of Kim Dae Jung restored. Two days later President Chun endorsed this plan. In fact, he had no choice. Although Roh probably received critical support from some key figures in the military, the plan may not have been directly discussed with the president. Roh thus distanced himself from an increasingly unpopular leader. It was a move both respected and politically astute.

What role, if any, did the United States play in these events? On February 6, the assistant secretary of state for East Asia and the Pacific gave a strong speech, calling for conciliation and placing emphasis on the government's special responsibility. It was the strongest public statement on Korean politics that the United States had made in years. Later, the U.S. ambassador warned the government against storming the Seoul Catholic cathedral, where students had taken sanctuary, and he delivered a letter from President Reagan asking Chun to compromise and negotiate. The assistant secretary visited Seoul a few days before the June 29 announcement and probably informed the administration that Washington would publicly indicate its disapproval of any troop movements, should the government decide on martial law or garrison decree or if some elements of the military should stage a coup against Chun. This left the government in a dilemma. If it moved troops, the U.S. public disavowal would probably induce larger and more intense demonstrations, and the government might be overthrown. In a brilliant political move, Roh used the situation to his own personal advantage and to that of his party. The period following the June 29 liberalization pronouncement resulted in widespread social ferment, expected in periods following repression and similar to the situations in 1960 and 1979.

Even before June 29, the clutch of the government's hand on the press had weakened. The press had begun to exhibit far more autonomous reporting than at any time since the Chun coup of December 12, 1979, but after that date most restraints were lifted or simply disappeared. Newspapers rehired many staff who had been purged in 1980 and reported on opposition activities and controversial topics long hidden from the public (except through the pervasive rumor mills that are the antidote to official silence in closely controlled societies).

Labor, long dominated and fragmented into government-authorized and business-controlled unions, began to demand its rights in the most strident terms heard since 1960. Workers struck the largest firms, such as Hyundae and Daewoo, as well engaged in thirty-five hundred demonstrations and strikes in all sectors of the economy and parts of the country, in wave after wave of protest in the three months following liberalization. Although some violence occurred, these strikes were remarkably free of destruction. At the time, there was considerable concern that the export drive might be halted and that the resulting economic distress could threaten a nation that lived on exports to manage its large foreign debt.

For the first time and in many cases, the government interceded with management on behalf of the workers, essentially forcing reluctant companies to meet many of the workers' demands. The shudder that passed through the government and the expanding middle class, both of which feared that progress might retrogress, was relieved, the workers felt that their needs were assuaged, even if all their demands were not met. Worker benefits improved, and wages rose by over 20 percent. By September, exports had increased once more.

Politics, however, was the primary field of liberalization. Not all political prisoners were released, and more were detained throughout the fall as demonstrations and incidents marred the political process, but the government essentially kept its promise. The National Assembly reached agreement on a new constitution, which was approved by over 93 percent of the electorate in a national plebescite in late October. The constitution called for the direct election of a president for a single five-year term and restricted the president's right to dissolve the National Assembly, which gained more oversight authority. The military was to remain neutral. Both the government and the opposition groups compromised. The opposition wanted the voting age lowered (as educated youth were largely antigovernment) and explicit restrictions included on the role of the military. They also wanted an apology for Kwangju. Although the opposition did not get these provisions, the new constitution set forth an enhanced legal base for a wide range of freedoms and provided new underpinnings for the political process.

Despite these new underpinnings, the presidential campaign began in earnest almost immediately after liberalization and, before the elections scheduled for December 16, 1987, well in advance of the one-month formal campaign the constitution allowed. Roh Tae Woo, leading the government's Democratic Justice party, was the only candidate heading a party he had not founded to further his political ambitions. He attempted to downplay his military role and involvement both in Kwangju and in the Chun coup, distancing himself from the incumbent president.

Although Kim Yong Sam and Kim Dae Jung both held leadership positions in the Reunification Democratic party—and they held long negotiations to agree on a single candidate to oppose Roh—their individual presidential ambitions took precedence over opposition unity. Kim Dae Jung split and formed his own Peace and Democracy party. These two parties formed the nucleus of opposition hopes, but other opposition candidates formed parties to further their (unrealistic) presidential aspirations. The only important contender was Kim Jong Pil, running for the New Democratic Republican party (the reincarnation of President Park's group). Three other candidates registered (Kim Son Jok, the United Democratic party; Shin Jong Il, the Hanism Unification Korea party; and Hong Suk Ja, a woman and the head of the liberal Social Democratic party); all but Shin dropped out.

The regional origins of the major candidates reflected and played upon primordial loyalties within ethnic homogeneity. Roh was from North Kyongsang Province (as had been Park Chung Hee). Kim Dae Jung came from South Cholla Province and had the loyalty of many from the Cholla region, who were scattered around the nation. Kim Yong Sam was from South Kyongsang, and Kim Jong Pil was from South Chungchong. Reminders of economic progress in some areas, allegations of past economic discrimination in others, and references to Kwangju intensified rallies and campaigning. The result was an increasingly disturbing level of violence.

Roh campaigned on the basis of government economic accomplishments, which were considerable, and an appeal for stability. Kim Yong Sam, an unimpressive public speaker, ran by appealing to the middle class and responsible opposition. He received the support of former general Chung Sung Hwan, the martial law commander ousted by the Chun coup (Chung served three months of a seven-year sentence for not taking sufficient action against Park's assassin). Kim Jong Pil essentially ran to clear his reputation and that of the former administration. Kim Dae Jung, unquestionably the most dynamic speaker, appealed to liberal elements, especially youth and labor, and voters from his region. In widespread rumors, it was alleged that senior members of the military ardently opposed his candidacy.

In such a fragmented campaign, with regional loyalties so strong and emotions so intense, no candidate could expect to win an absolute majority. Many Koreans who wanted to see a peaceful transfer of institutional (in addition to individual) power were frustrated by the inability of opposition candidates to allow the national interest to transcend individual aspirations.

Some of the opposition charged the government with attempting to manipulate the electoral process, paying voters, and using the impressive state resources to influence the results. The government announced a 17 percent increase in the producer price for rice, thus garnering farm votes. It dismissed some opposition demands for an interim government until the elections and for a new supervisory group for the elections themselves. Kim Dae Jung announced that Roh could only win through corruption of the campaign, thereby increasing the likelihood that the new head of state would inherit an unstable political situation.

The vigorous campaign ended with the voting on December 16. Over 22 million people voted, with Roh winning about 36 percent of the vote, followed by Kim Yong Sam with 27 percent, Kim Dae Jung with 26 percent, and Kim Jong Pil with about 8 percent. In spite of charges from the losers that there were irregularities—especially in the military votes, most of which are cast by absentee ballot—the margin of Roh's victory indicates that such charges, even if proven, would not invalidate the basic results of the election. Roh legally won, but it is perhaps equally accurate to say that the opposition lost. Because of the intransigence of the two leading opposition candidates, who had they united could have had a clear majority, the government was able to maintain itself in power.

As important as the overall vote were the regional differences, which reveal deep political animosities. The opposition normally wins Seoul, and Kim Dae Jung received 32 percent of the vote there, compared to Roh's 29 percent and Kim Yong Sam's 28 percent. Roh won handily in Kyonggi (40 percent); Kangwon, where many of the military are located (58 percent); Cheju (48 percent); North Chungchong (46 percent); North Kyongsang, his home province (65 percent); and in his home town of Taegu (70 percent). Kim Dae Jung swept his home province of South Cholla (88 percent); North Cholla (81 percent); and Kwangju (93 percent). Kim Yong Sam won in his province of South Kyongsang (50 percent) and in Pusan (55 percent). Kim Jong Pil only won in his province of South Chungchong (44 percent).

THE SIXTH REPUBLIC: ROH TAE WOO— A NEW BEGINNING?

On February 25, 1988, Roh Tae Woo was sworn in as president. Although he may not have been the choice of the majority, he was inaugurated with a sense of promise. Although the opposition leaders acted in a manner that may be termed petulant—and later resigned from the leadership of their parties—the general population, if not the students, were clearly ready to give Roh a chance.

The first major task of the Sixth Republic was the preparation for the elections to the National Assembly, which were scheduled for April 26. The opposition parties once again failed to merge, and although there was considerable debate over the complex issues of election districts and slates of delegates, a formula was agreed upon.

The problems for Roh were twofold: how to distance himself from Chun and the negative image of Chun and his regime and how to establish himself as a national leader of the majority of the population when a majority did not elect him. Roh's easy manner during the first months were viewed as a welcome change over the stiffness of Chun. On April 1 Roh publicly expressed regret (but stopping short of an apology) over Kwangju, the first government admission that its action may not have been right, and he promised compensation to the relatives of victims of the massacre. Although Roh retained many members of the Chun cabinet (to the chagrin of some), he scheduled the National Assembly elections to follow the inauguration—in opposition to Chun's purported wishes. Chun could have played a major role in the choice of delegates had the elections been held while he was still in power. On April 13, one year after his announcement that negotiations with the opposition on a new presidential system were over—an announcement that led to the momentous events of 1987—Chun resigned from his role on the Advisory Council of Elder Statesmen and as honorary president of the DJP, thus officially ending his ties to government and politics. He did this to take the blame for his brother's involvement in a *saemaŭl* scandal. This eventuality gave Roh his needed distance from Chun.

The National Assembly elections were held on April 26. The results and format were different than previous such elections. The voting was in single delegate constituencies, a departure from the recent past, and the results followed the presidential elections, but only in part. Although there were charges of vote buying, the close results indicate a great degree of freedom. Out of a total of 299 seats, the government Democratic Justice party received only 33.6 percent of the popular vote and were able to obtain a total of 125 seats, including 38 as a result of a proportionally derived formula. Kim Dae Jung's Peace and Democracy party received 19.1 percent of the votes, and Kim Yong Sam's Reunification Democratic Party 23.6 percent, while the New Democratic Republican party of Kim Jong Pil garnered 15.3 percent of the vote. Thus the total opposition gained 174 seats in the new National Assembly.

The government did well in Kyonggi and the Kyongsang provinces, but came in third in Seoul. Kim Dae Jung won a plurality of seats in Seoul and essentially swept the Cholla provinces and Kwangju. Kim Yong Sam took Pusan and came in second in Seoul and South Kyongsang Province. Kim Jong Pil won his home province of South Chungchong and did well in Kyonggi.

This election created several precedents. For the first time in Korean history the government has a minority in the legislature, although they are the largest single party. The DJP will attempt to woo opposition legislators from their political affiliations and increase DJP representation in the Assembly as well as to form coalitions through various inducements. The Sixth Republic will be in a very weak position, and political turmoil is likely following the Olympics.

The continued surge of regionalism was the single most important aspect of the election after the government's defeat. Kim Dae Jung virtually swept his Cholla region, Kim Yong Sam his home base of Pusan, Roh the Kyongsang provinces and Taegu, and Kim Jong Pil his provincial base. Past patterns of assembly voting have demonstrated that the opposition usually is strong in urban areas, but in this election this is the first time that the opposition has succeeded in major wins in rural areas, and it is apparent that regional loyalties were more important than the urban-rural split.

An unstable political situation is thus likely, with much vying for loyalties than may well shift over time. The pluralism of the Korean political system has been demonstrated. What remains problematic is (1) the ability of the society to coalesce internally on critical issues, and (2) the development of the concept of the loyal opposition(s). The Sixth Republic has established its political legitimacy; it must demonstrate its capacity to function effectively.

The panorama of Korean politics through the formation of six republics points out lessons from the Korean political process that will be discussed in more abstract terms in Chapter 8, but more practical conclusions may also be reached. Forces in Korean society have gained the strength to move Korea from merely exercising the trappings and forms of democracy to allowing some of the content associated with it. As Korean society changes, more stress on plural values and institutions, less hierarchy, and broader representation are likely. The pace of change seems to be quickening, partly as a result of the forces that have brought about a measure of economic prosperity. Modern international forces are coming into more open conflict with traditional elements from Korean culture. It is now appropriate to look at some of those elements in the culture that affect Korean attitudes and then at the political culture in broader perspective.

7
Korean Society and Culture

Korean culture is a unique, vibrant contribution to world civilization. Its art, especially ceramics, is prized among international cognoscenti. Its society today is the most economically dynamic in the world.

Foreigners, however, have sometimes regarded Korea as being on the periphery of the great East Asian tradition, as a pale reflection or imitation of its more powerful neighbors—China and Japan—and thus unworthy of serious study or consideration. If analogies were drawn from the European experience, the absurdity of ignoring Korea would immediately be apparent: Because France and Spain were strongly influenced by Rome, or Rome by Greece, are they not unique and important?

In part, this attitude stems from the orientations of those in the academic community who study Asia; they take on the coloration and prejudices of their major interests—China or Japan. In part, the attitude is related to centuries of Korean self-imposed isolation at times when China and Japan had implanted enduring impressions, not always of the greatest accuracy, in the Western consciousness.

Even today, perceptions of Korea are likely to be distorted. In the United States, attitudes of both young and old are often a complex of Korean War and popular television ("M*A*S*H") memories of dubious relevance to understanding a culture of world significance and a transformed society and economy. As Korean automobiles, computers, appliances, and textiles inundate U.S. markets, as Korean grocery and convenience stores dot U.S. cities, and as Korean students receive top honors in national U.S. competitive examinations, a different Korea has become apparent and palpably important. We cannot comprehend this present without exploring the past—the nature of the society that has produced these changes. Korean society, while in the midst of unprecedented transformation, retains much of its heritage.

69

Hyangwon Pavilion in Kyongbok Palace in winter

ELEMENTS OF KOREAN CULTURE

The gradual amalgamation of a series of Altaic-speaking Tungusic tribal groups, whose origins were probably Siberian or central Asian, into what has become the Korean people, was a process tempered by more than a millennium of internecine tribal struggle. Superimposed over this amalgamation were some four hundred years of Chinese control of varying but diminishing intensity during the Lolang period. In spite of the imposition of linguistic, administrative, and technological advances during this time, probably with a considerable admixture of Chinese colonists, cultural remnants from the pre-Chinese period before the second century B.C. remain imbedded in the Korean fabric. The influence of this Siberian or central Asian memory is illustrated and retained in such material remains as the gold Silla crowns that have clear reindeer antler motifs. The dolmens (burial stone slabs that are also found in western Europe and are prevalent throughout North and South Korea) are considered to have originated in that same region.

Relevant today is the myth of the founding of the Korean people—the mating of Tan'gun, descendant of the gods, with a bear transformed into a woman. The bear also figures prominently in Ainu aboriginal myths in Japan and is considered to be a Siberian influence. There is a growing interest in this myth in Korea (even the assertion that Tan'gun was real) with the rise of Korean nationalism and the emphasis on things particularly Korean. Most important are three enduring social elements: the role of shamanism as the indigenous religion of Korea, the strong influence of social class, and the particular emphasis on clan and family, only the last of which was reinforced by Confucian overlays.

Shamanism is generally thought to have Siberian origins, and it is still extensively practiced throughout Korean society. It involves the spiritual possession of a person, today usually a woman called a *mudang*, who propitiates the spirits, which must be placated to prevent loss or injury. The role of women in shamanism is particularly important in Korea in comparison to China or Japan. There are also spirits associated with mountains, streams, animals, and other natural elements. The tiger is an important motif in Korean folk art. The eclectic nature of Korean society and religion is illustrated by the inclusion of shrines to the mountain and other spirits in Buddhist temples, which also incorporate Chinese Taoist elements. Shamanistic ceremonies become prevalent when illness occurs within the family or when someone moves to a new house. Absolute dichotomies between religious beliefs and social ceremonies, or even within religious rites themselves, are not necessary conditions of Korean life; these are perhaps more Western distinctions or analyses. One may pay Confucian homage to one's parents or one's

Hwagwan-mu performance (flower-crown dance)

ancestors and be considered a good Christian at the same time. Funerals often combine elements drawn from Confucian, Buddhist, and Christian rituals. Shamans have adapted elements of Confucian ancestor worship to their practices.

Even more important to Korean society has been the concept of rigidly defined social class, a pre-Confucian inheritance. Noted as early as the Silla Dynasty, for which records are quite good, hereditary rank at that time was defined minutely in a system that had almost a caste structure, more inflexible than what normally is called a class; "bred in the bone" is perhaps the English equivalent of the Silla "bone rank." Rank was a product of birth, and the lines were quite rigid, as far as we can determine. Rising in rank was quite rare, falling in status more frequent. This sense of absolute social hierarchy was later mitigated as Confucian, Buddhist, and other influences spread. Rigid class distinctions were then tempered by the desire for social and economic mobility, which occurred in some undefined but significant proportion, at least during the Yi Dynasty. The *yangban*, or gentry, however, were later able to continue their social control because they essentially limited access to the bureaucracy (and thus access to their own ranks) to their own social class, perpetuating their hegemony. This was markedly distinct from the Chinese model on which the Korean system was based, which theoretically was far more open.

Korea, however, was not composed simply of *yangban* and *sangmin* (the commoners). At least by the time of the Yi Dynasty, there had evolved a middle clerk, artisan, or technocratic class, the *chung'in*, which would seek to rise within the Korean social system. The *chung'in* became critical to the administrative functioning of the kingdom. In addition, there were large numbers of slaves. Some were captives, a result of war, others more equivalent to a type of indentured servant, both personal and to the state. Slavery rapidly disappeared in the later days of the Yi Dynasty, and that outcast population, which may have been as large as one-third of the total in some areas, was absorbed into the lower reaches of the society.

The *yangban* could perpetuate itself through access to education and money. Although the rigid class structure eroded, and then was officially eliminated, remnants remained, especially in social situations such as marriage. Marriage is still in general arranged, between socially appropriate families, as it is more a union of groups than of individuals, even among the highly educated. The traditional structure has become modernized, however, in that socially appropriate potential spouses are introduced through the parents, with their children retaining veto power. Social cohesion through marriage is strong. In 1986, only one-half of 1 percent of the population was divorced.

In all Asian societies, with the single exception of the Burmans in Burma, some elements of the traditional elites were retained under colonial rule. In Korea, such elites were able to maintain their comparative positions in regard to the rest of the Korean population under the Japanese overlords in spite of the elimination of legal class distinctions.

Following liberation, however, the rigidity of class distinctions began to be blurred. The extensive migration from North to South and the destruction caused by the Korean War all contributed to social mobility. Since 1961 and the economic progress that Korea has made, mobility at various levels may be attributed to the military channels, the rise of smaller entrepreneurs, and the vast expansion of higher education, long a preserve of the gentry. The military expansion of higher education may have been prompted not only by a need to expand the trained labor force but by the intent to continue to break down traditional class distinctions. Some say that government-sponsored village programs were in part designed to replace the traditional village class structure. The growth of the middle class, however defined, and the self-inclusion of over half the population in it is one of the salient changes in Korean society over a single generation. Whereas a small middle class was previously dominated by the bureaucracy, the bureaucracy is dwarfed in numbers, prestige, and wealth within the expanding middle class by greater numbers of businesspeople and professionals.

In spite of some neo-Marxist comments that traditional Korea was "feudal," this term is technically not applicable on the peninsula. Although Japan did evolve into a major feudal society, and China did so as well for a period in the first millennium B.C., Korea never developed the autonomous centers of local power under vassals of the king nor the specialized systems of rights and obligations inherent in a feudal society. Korean society was, rather, as some scholars argue, a patrimonial structure with rewards distributed through a complex system of hierarchical, essentially morally based, obligations.

Class structure was reinforced by the Confucian tradition, which conceptualized society as a family with strong hierarchical roles. Authority, however, imposed moral obligations on the part of each member of the group; power was never to be arbitrary. Paternalism on the part of government or business management (family control is still the basis of most Korean businesses, including the largest conglomerates) was an extension of the familial concept that had its origins and philosophic rationale in Confucian thought. Any government had extensive rights but had to maintain a moral basis for its exercise of power to be considered legitimate.

In North Korea as well, class and hierarchy is reflected in what theoretically was to be a classless society. The concept is a moral one; stratification is based on *sŏngbun*, or one's inherent nature or background (as determined by the leadership). To have high status, one should have sprung from an appropriately oppressed class in society. Some comrades are thus more equal than others. Even the term "comrade," ubiquitous in North Korea, has two usages, one more respectful than the other. Some maintain that North Korea may have a more pronounced class structure than does the South.

The concept of a sociopolitical vortex, pulling all into the center in an upwardly mobile spiral, has been used to describe Korean society. In some sense in modern Korea we have witnessed the *"yangban*ization" of society, which also took place in the later Yi Dynasty. Such status is claimed by more and more Koreans as social and economic aspirations rise in tandem.

In Korea today, all official personal identities are determined by the patrilineal family register, a residual Confucian institution that is the basis on which identity cards, passports, and other official documents are issued. In contrast to Western individual birth certificates, the register graphically illustrates the importance of the patrilineal family in the Korean social structure. Only a change in this generation allows women legally to become heads of households in the register.

The basic social institutions are the clan and family. The paucity of surnames makes the origins of one's particular branch of a common surname especially important. Ceremonies honoring clan ancestors are still held in some important clans. The function of the clan, especially in consanguinous villages, was to take care of its members in a type of social security, to protect them from the state, and, in the premodern period, to provide education for the promising sons and thus ensure the perpetuation of clan prosperity. There were few institutions between those connected with the clan and family and those controlled by the state. Increasing urbanization, however, has diminished clan solidarity and functions. This is evident in a high, constant rate of admissions of babies into orphanages; such children once would have been cared for through the clan system. Family control is illustrated by the fact that until 1977 men under twenty-seven years of age and women under twenty-three needed permission to marry; both men and women may now marry and vote at age twenty.

THE ROLE AND STATUS OF WOMEN

The strength of the Korean family system, the analogy for governance and the basis on which group loyalties are built, rests with the male line. Not only is registration patrilineal, but marriage is traditionally patrilocal. The wife exits from her family register and is transferred to her husband's. The following poem illustrates the attitudes of a daughter-in-law toward her husband's family:

> Although it is difficult to pass another
>   on a single-track bridge,
> My husband's father is more difficult
> Although the tree's leaf is green,
> Greener with anger and envy is my mother-in-law's face.
> My husband's brother's wife is like a bird who gives
>   me dirty looks,
> My husband's sister is a bird who always complains,
> My husband's father is a pompous bird,
> And my husband,
> He's plain foolish.[1]

The status of women in Korean society historically has been low. In the traditional multigenerational family compound, women were essentially servants. They gained identity in general insofar as they had children, but especially the sons necessary to perpetuate the family ancestral offerings. It is significant that jokes about mothers-in-law in the United States are usually about the wife's mother, but in Korea they are invariably about the husband's mother. Even today, a woman is usually known as "so-and-so's mother" (a husband is sometimes known in a similar way but more often by his title) and not by her own personal name and surname, which she maintains even after marriage. Traditionally, a woman's life was rigorous and unpleasant, and even when she was of high status, she was vastly subordinate to her brother or husband.

> My mother shouldn't have borne me,
> She should have borne a pear she could have sold.
> My father shouldn't have given me life,
> He should've made a mat seat instead of lying on the
>   mat with her.
> Why did they give me life that I must bear this
>   hardship?[2]

Korean women of lower social groups sometimes were forced into or sought the role of *kisaeng*, the Korean demimonde equivalent of the Japanese geisha. Traditionally, in a system where marriages were arranged and few women were literate, *kisaeng* were the male's companions, often educated and accomplished in the arts and music. The maintenance of the *p'ansori* vocal musical tradition, now popular in the revival of scholarly interest in things Korean, was in the hands of *kisaeng*, and such scholarship, socially impossible several decades ago, is now highly respectable. The classic poem by Korea's most famous female poet, Hwang Chin-i (1506–1544), illustrates the talent of the *kisaeng*.

> I cut in two
> A long November night, and
> Place half under the coverlet,
> Sweet-scented as a spring breeze,
> And when he comes, I shall take it out,
> Unroll it inch by inch, to stretch the night.[3]

The traditional place of women who had achieved family status was of course high within the compound walls, which higher-status women were not supposed to leave, although lower-class women were free to come and go and were involved in petty trade. Today, there are constitutional guarantees for the rights of women, but these are often ignored in lower laws and in practice. Women do not inherit equally with men and normally do not receive custody of children if there is a divorce or separation, both of which are still relatively rare but growing in incidence. No matter how high her educational attainment, a woman is generally expected to give up work upon marriage or the birth of her first child. Women in factories (of more than ten persons) are paid about 46 percent the salary of men, basically a supplementary family salary or enough, if there are factory dormitory facilities, to accrue a small dowry for marriage. Although 21.4 percent of all civil servants are women, only 1 percent are in managerial posts. There have been five female cabinet ministers since independence, three before 1954 and only two after 1979. Since 1948, only fifty-five women (2.1 percent of total assembly membership) have served in the National Assembly, twenty-five since 1971; of these, thirty-nine were appointed.

The foreign missions' role in improving women's status may have been the missionaries' single greatest achievement. The founding of schools and higher educational institutions for women, such as Ewha Women's University, was critical to their advancement. Today, women are not discriminated against in schools. By 1980, primary and secondary male-female enrollment ratios were about equal; among older children, 97.1 percent of males and 92.1 percent of females attend middle school. Women are a minority at university level, however, not because of institutional discrimination, but because parents put their limited resources into the education of their sons. Because they are retained on the family registers and have higher income potential, sons become parents' social security for the future. The average number of years of education for the group of twenty- to twenty-nine-year-olds in 1980 was 10.3 years for males and 9.4 years for females. Women teachers constitute about 40 percent of teachers in primary school, 37 percent of those in middle school, 20 percent in high school, and 17 percent of college and university staff.

Koreans have always regarded the informal influence of women as powerful—the ch'ima param ("the wind of the skirts")—and the character of women as strong and outspoken. But to be p'an gwan, or "henpecked" (in Seoul slang), is still a potent male insult. Perhaps one of the most important elements of progress in Korea, although the distance to travel to equality is still great, is that of the status of women. Their political influence is likely to grow.

EDUCATION, THE LITERATI, STUDENTS, AND THE PRESS

There is a constant affirmation in both Eastern and Western circles of the general connection between Confucianism and scholarship. Although this is indeed true, the link in Korea between the two, and with literacy and the role of the literati, may be more intense than in China. Korea may have the only major armed forces in the world that are completely composed of high school graduates. The Korean overall literacy rate (98 percent in the Korean script) is, and has been for three decades, far in advance of that of most other nations with a similar, or even higher, per capita income. It may be significant that the Korean autonomous region of Manchuria has an educational level double that of China as a whole. In 1986, Korea published 145 million books, including 65 million reference books and 27 million children's books, indicating the importance of education. Monthly literary magazines have circulations in the hundreds of thousands. In 1985, over 37 percent of the population subscribed to at least one magazine, and over 62 percent read newspapers, almost half of these daily.

The general Confucian tradition stresses scholarship and respect for learning, but the peculiarities of the Korean environment have intensified these values. Perhaps as a "minority" or peripheral nation in the Sino-centric world order, Koreans felt it necessary to be more Confucian than their mentor. Perhaps the small size of the nation and the *yangban*, at least in the earlier period, strengthened these attitudes. Perhaps the minority status of Koreans in Manchuria or in the United States added intensity or another dimension. Until the recent rise of the Korean bourgeoisie, the pinnacle of social prestige was to be a professor, and the most prestigious universities were almost by definition *yangban* enclaves. Today, in South Korea intellectuals are paid well (with supplementary income from government "research" grants), but they are probably the least well rewarded element of society in comparison to their former status. In North Korea they are co-opted into the political system and are recognized for their contributions to the state.

Linguistic problems emerged early in Korean history as a result of a court system based on a foreign model that conducted official (written) business in classical Chinese. Chinese characters were used phonetically to write native Korean words, called the *hyangch'al*, as well as for Chinese loan words, and the system was cumbersome, evolving through several stages of adaptation. In 1443–1444, however, under the aegis of King Sejong, scholars evolved a specialized alphabet, the first and most scientific invented worldwide until the introduction of the modern international phonetic script. Evolved from the position of the tongue in the mouth when producing certain sounds, and composed of seventeen consonants and eleven vowel symbols, it was simple and exceedingly logical. It was, in fact, so simple that it had the potential to revolutionize literacy in the society. *Han'gŭl*, as it was called (Chinese characters are called *hancha*), was downgraded to a script of the kitchen, suitable for women and not for sophisticated, and especially court, use. Because *han'gŭl* had no precedent in China, conservatives downplayed its importance. The literati might have lost their monopoly on power if it had spread, for access to Chinese equated to access to power. *Han'gŭl* did eventually play a role in poetry and other literary forms, but it was not used in the bureaucratic mainstream.

Suppressed by the Japanese and reintroduced immediately on liberation, in North Korea *han'gŭl* has completely superseded the use of Chinese characters. In South Korea, it is used in all works: for the inflections required in the Korean grammatical structure, for native Korean words, for some Chinese loan words, and exclusively in publications intended for those with limited education—youth, farmers, and workers. Literacy in *han'gŭl* is virtually universal. Because newspapers, magazines, and books are written in a combination of *han'gŭl* and Chinese characters, and names are normally given in Chinese as well, and because these Chinese characters are not introduced until the fourth grade, a middle-school education is virtually required to function effectively in South Korean society.

Confucianism may have bred centralized control but not, as is sometimes thought, intellectual or technological stagnation. The first metal movable type was invented in Korea, before Gutenberg lived in Europe and before similar type was developed in China. A seventh-century Korean astronomical observatory still exists, as do ice storage facilities from the same period. Korean ceramic techniques were both aesthetically important and innovative, in some cases surpassing some wares of China. The world's first ironclad warship was invented in Korea and defeated the Japanese fleet in 1592. Radiant heating has been a traditional form of survival in Korea's cold climate since the beginnings of recorded history. Evidence exists that Koreans sent as envoys to the Chinese court took strong and continuing interest in all forms of technology, which they reported back to their government.

The literati were traditionally replenished through the scrupulous attention paid to the education of their sons (thus the importance of clan schools). If a family did not produce a graduate of the examination system in several generations, and if no family member held official position, the *yangban* status of the family would gradually be lost. Individual scholars or clans established schools, called *sŏwŏn*, throughout the country to provide the best possible training to the sons of the rural elite. The Confucian Academy in Seoul, now Sŏnggyungwan University, was the site since the early fifteenth century of official student training.

Students, as the nascent literati, were often the watchdogs of political morality. Student demonstrations, against what they regarded as undue Buddhist influences or unorthodox Confucian behavior, may be traced to the fifteenth century and were sporadic thereafter. Students today continue to regard themselves as the political conscience of the country, although on occasion that role is disputed by elements of the society at large.

Contemporary student activism dates from the success of the student revolution of April 19, 1960, that overthrew Syngman Rhee. Since then, significant numbers of students have continuously protested some of the actions of all governments. At times, these demonstrations have been massive, such as those in 1965 against normalization of relations with Japan and in 1987 concerning the presidential election system and police brutality. At other times, they have been confined (by police or military force) to demonstrations by small minorities on individual campuses. The increasing stridency of demonstrations since 1980 was largely a reflection of Kwangju, political frustration, the lack of alternative legal political options, and changing educational and economic circumstances, plus the growth of internal and external communications.

Each government since independence has sought to expand the opportunities for education, which are now universal. Even in the period of extreme poverty following the Korean War, primary schools dotted the Korean rural landscape. In 1945, there were 2,834 primary schools with 1.3 million students; in 1980, 6,479 schools and 5.6 million students. The development of rural roads and other infrastructure has expanded access to middle-school and high school education, generally located in the towns. These schools are now within the economic reach of most families. It is significant that education as a percentage of household expenditures in rural areas was 13 percent in 1985, compared to half that for urban areas and double the percentage for rural areas in 1970. These figures indicate the extent of educational demand and expectations; they may also be a surrogate indicator of rural-urban income inequalities.

In the past twenty-five years, the government has vastly increased access to higher education, both by encouraging the development of postsecondary technical and general schools and universities and by expanding the number of public and private school entrants, which number had been (and still is) rigidly controlled by the government. There were fewer than 8,000 students in higher (including junior college) education before the Korean War; in 1960, there were about 101,000, in 1980 more than 611,000, and in 1986 about 1.3 million (see Table 7.1). More engineers are trained in Korea than in India, and Korea has the second highest percentage of students, of that age group, in higher education in the world, after the United States. About 41 percent of students in college study science, and 45 percent study humanities and social sciences. Eighty-four percent of the population expect to see their sons go to college, and 70 percent their daughters.

This expansion has provided a trained elite that can staff businesses and growing industries, but it also resulted in the loss of literati control over education and will thus contribute to the more rapid breakdown of the traditional class structure. Because Korea has followed the Japanese

TABLE 7.1
Educational Statistics, 1945-1985

a. Number of Students (in thousands)

school level	1945	1960	1965	1975	1985
Primary	1,366	3,621	4,941	5,599	4,856
Secondary	350	792	1,177	2,674	4,049
Vocational	33	99	172	474	885
Higher	8	101	140	238	1,260

b. Percentage of Cohort Group

school level	1960	1983
Secondary School	27	80
Post-secondary (20-24 yrs.)	5	24

c. Percentage of Household Expenses
Spent on Education

Area	1970	1985
Urban	8.0	6.7
Rural	6.8	13.0

Source: Derived from Economic Planning Board statistics.

model of rigorous college entrance examinations, resulting in what the Japanese call "examination hell," entering a university has been very difficult but staying in has been easy. The government has thought that students had too much time for demonstrations and paid too little attention to study. In 1980, the Chun government increased enrollment by one-third but decreed that one-third of the students could not graduate. The order was rescinded after public outcries.

Employment opportunities for youth have been cyclical. Before the expansion of export industries and businesses, there were few employment possibilities outside of a limited number in government and the banking system. Appointments were based on competitive examinations, and there was extensive unemployment for skilled and unskilled workers. The growth of the Korean economy then produced widespread labor shortages at all levels, with a general and rapid rise in wages (because of the shortages, not government policies) and virtually full employment by the mid-1970s, at which time the pool of unemployed labor was absorbed. As the number of university and technical institute graduates has increased, however, jobs commensurate with their training and self-perceived status have become more difficult to find. (Unemployment is also widespread among those who have retired from the military or civil service but want or need jobs.) Korean wage rates have made labor-instensive industries less competitive on world markets, and the move to higher technological products and services may result in fewer jobs and increasing frustration of youth, who by now have come to expect rising standards of living and increased mobility in a society in which such progress may well become more difficult to obtain.

The press, and by extension the media, in Korea has been considered as a kind of adjunct of the literati. The first real press dates from the last two decades of the nineteenth century. Leading newspapers, such as *Dong-A*, were founded in 1920 but were subject to rigorous Japanese supervision through registration and censorship.

Under the various republics, with the exception of the Chang Myon period, all governments have attempted to control the press to varying degrees. Information is regarded as power. In the earlier period, anti-government or North Korean stories were blacked out by hand in all foreign newspapers and journals entering Korea (except through diplomatic or U.S. military channels). Prior to 1980, the mass media were characterized by independent (albeit controlled) ownership. President Chun in 1980 forced mergers and restricted the media to bolster political integration and to maintain an orientation to state-defined national goals. News agencies were pooled, and the Korean government became critical shareholders in various radio and television stations, controlling four of the nine national-level institutions. KCIA staff at various periods sometimes sat in the editorial offices of the newspapers; senior staff were purged. The publication in *Mal* ("words") of government directives to the press on what was not permissible to print caused acute government embarrassment and a trial in 1987 of the offenders who had released the materials. The government used many other methods to control the press: It discouraged advertisers; it minimized, laundered, or left unprinted stories about events that put the government in a bad light; and foreign stories that established dangerous internal political precedents received similar treatment. The state viewed the control of information as a legitimate element of governmental power.

Increased urbanization and technological sophistication, however, have significantly diminished the capacity of any government for such control. In June 1987, as part of the road toward greater political liberalization, the government promised to abolish the restrictive press laws and allow press freedom. In part, this is simply a reflection of a diminished government capacity to control the press, as well as a response to public pressure.

THE KOREAN ARTISTIC TRADITION

The dynamism of the Korean artistic tradition was largely unknown to the West until this generation. The Korean arts were ignored, partly because of the country's isolation and partly because better-known cultural traditions, such as the Japanese, overshadowed that of Korea.

This error is now being rectified. The world recognizes the role of Korea, and especially the Kingdom of Paekche, as the funnel through which early Chinese influences, such as Buddhism, came into Japan. The art of that period straddled the Tsushima Straits, creating a Korean-Japanese culture that modern political and emotional boundaries obfuscate. Korean cultural exhibits that have traveled to major cities in the United States and Europe have spread information on the long, remarkable tradition of Korean art.

Perhaps the greatest Korean achievement in the arts has been in ceramics. Ceramics were produced for use even at the highest levels of court by artisans of the lower social order—by indentured servants or slaves of the state, peasants, and other socially lower groups. The architectural forms, the subtlety of the glazes, the spontaneity of the designs were and are much admired, even in wares made for the lower classes. The rise of the Japanese pottery industry may be traced to potters introduced into Kyushu from Korea as war prisoners in the Imjin Wars of 1592–1598. Some types of Japanese pottery are still clearly influenced by the Korean tradition, and some towns, such as Karatsu on Kyushu, are noted for maintaining a tradition of Korean-type wares made by descendents of Koreans.

Starting in the fifth century in the Silla period, Korean potters produced a high-fired, grey, unglazed type of ceramics of high aesthetic and architectural quality. Peasant Korean ceramics of the Yi Dynasty have a freedom and spontaneity that sparkles with unaffected vitality. They are much admired, especially in Japan, with its more rigid and circumscribed social and aesthetic sense. Many ceramic wares illustrate the Korean search for openness and freedom in a "tightly structured" society characterized by traditional Confucian rigidity. The low social status of potters may have contributed to this verve. In a sense, the sponteneity of the wares reflects the mercurial temperament and individuality of Koreans today.

Of all Korean ceramics, those with universal appeal are the celadons, a name derived from a classic French drama in which a character of that name wore a grey-green cape. Of a blue-green-grey color at their finest, celadons have an unctuous and translucent quality and a subtlety of tone that distinguishes them from those Chinese works from which they originate. Fired in a reducing atmosphere (with little oxygen so

Celadon
teapot
from the
late Koryŏ
dynasty

that the glaze is of ferrous oxide, not ferric oxide, which is brown), of
at least 1,832 degrees fahrenheit (1,200 degrees centigrade), celadon
required the highest skills and was most expensive to produce. It was
introduced from China in about the tenth century (the first dated proto-
celadon in Korea is from that era) and flowered until the thirteenth
century, when it gradually evolved into a different ware. The Koreans
invented a means to inlay under the celadon glaze—an innovation that
escaped the Chinese. They also incised, molded, and painted under it.
Chinese histories of the period commented on the excellence of the
Korean product. A modern Korean poem describes celadon:

Bluish green with subtle lines,
O supple smooth curving,
Like the bodhisattva's shoulders,
Grace and elegance combined . . .
Depth of color, softly shaded;
Irridescent kingfisher;
Blue sky glimpsed through autumn clouds
As the rain squall passes on. . . . [4]

In contrast to pottery, Korean traditional painting and calligraphy, which in East Asia are inseparable, were court and literati traditions with close links to their Chinese origins. Thus, in the Yi Dynasty a court-sponsored Academy of Art, the *Tohwasŏ*, produced, among other types of painting, genre portraits of officials. This was regarded as a type of artisanry, beneath the dignity of a *yangban* painter. Although important artists sometimes drew or painted charming scenes of everyday life, the traditional landscapes, flowers, and portraits dominate, as in China. Perhaps the oldest extant depiction of pure landscape in world art is on an early seventh-century Paekche temple floor tile.

Some argue that Korean Buddhist sculpture reached its apogee in the Koryŏ period, the time of the flowering of Buddhism. It may be argued that the greatest of the sculptures were created in the United Silla era, when the Buddha images radiated an aura of transcendent tranquility, perhaps unequalled in Buddhist art. These figures, also found in Japan but made by Korean artisans, have elicited a universal sense of admiration and wonder.

Korea seems different from either China or Japan in not having produced a distinct corpus of aesthetic theory about art and in lacking either royal or *yangban* major collectors and patrons. Korean painting, at least in the later Yi period, bears distinctive Korean characteristics. Both color and composition in many of these Korean landscapes express an enhanced element of sentiment that seem lacking in Chinese landscapes.

Closely allied with calligraphy was literature, which has had a continuous record for more than a millennium. Korea evolved its own poetic forms, which were written first in classical Chinese and later in *han'gŭl*. Probably the most famous is *sijo*, which generally had forty-five syllables and was most popular in the classical period. It was also written to be chanted or sung. Poetry has probably been the most admired of the written art forms in Korea. Although fiction was early produced in Korea (in 1435–1493, Kim Si-sup wrote a collection of short stories called *The New Tales of the Golden Turtle*), it never gained the popularity of that genre in China or of comparable works, such as *The Tale of Genji*, in Japan.

Cats and sparrows, by
Pyon Sang-byok (late
17th century, ink and
color on silk)

Temple with Buddha statue

The most touching story, the quintessential Korean literary piece, which exemplifies much of the nature of traditional Korean society, is that of *Ch'unhyang Chŏn*. Ch'unhyang, the daughter of a *yangban* and a *kisaeng*, secretly marries the son of an official in the town of Namwon. When he is called to Seoul, an evil high-ranking official tries to seduce her, as she is of lower status. Even in jail, she remains loyal to her husband, and he returns as a secret emissary of the king and punishes the would-be seducer. This story, in song and literature, now in opera as well, exemplifies the Confucian virtues of fidelity and loyalty and subtly illustrates the issue of class status.

THE ROLE OF RELIGION IN CONTEMPORARY KOREAN SOCIETY

The worldly focus of Confucian thought should not obscure the traditional importance of religion in Korean life, nor its emerging renaissance in contemporary society. Whether Confucianism is considered as a religion or as an ethic, it pervaded society, so that Confucian customs and attitudes were assimilated by avowed Buddhists or Christians or atheists. The majority of Koreans, however, are not formally affiliated with any religion.

The Roman Catholic cathedral in Myong-dong, Seoul

The growth of Buddhism from its introduction in 372 A.D., its adoption by the court as the state religion in 517, and its eventual replacement by state Confucianism at the beginning of the Yi Dynasty are reviewed in Chapters 3 and 4, as is Confucianism's splendid artistic, sculptural, and architectural accomplishments and the introduction and influence of Christianity, both Catholicism in the seventeenth century and Protestantism in the nineteenth. In this chapter, more contemporary religious issues are the topic.

The remarkable flowering of religion in modern Korea transcends sects or creeds, internal or foreign. Religion has grown metaphorically as the Korean economy has expanded, although no causal relationship is implied. Religious interest and affiliation have mushroomed, including the Tan'gun myth adherents; Ch'ŏndogyo, the syncretic religion that arose out of the Tonghak ("Eastern Learning") peasant revolts of the nineteenth century; a seeming myriad of "new religions," including the sect of Reverend Moon Sun Myung; Buddhism; Islam (through the Koreans working in the Middle East and funds provided by some of those governments for the construction of mosques); and various forms of more traditional Christianity. The growth of Christianity in Korea in the past generation, from perhaps 10 percent to 25 percent of the population, is the single greatest explosion of this cluster of faiths in Asia in modern times.

Although all religions have an increasingly important place in Korean society (perhaps in response to rapid social and economic change, the erosion of traditions, the rise of the nuclear family and the decline of clan solidarity, and the absence of intermediate institutions between the family and the state), the growth of Christianity has been exceptional. Between liberation and the Korean War, many northern Christians fled south. Protestantism had its center in Korea in Pyongyang, where one-sixth of all Christians in the country lived. The expansion of Protestant and Catholic churches is not simply a product of the elite or the middle class, even though such groups are proportionally better represented in these churches. It is a pervasive phenomenon that reaches to villages and smaller towns as well. Nor can Christianity be explained simply as a means of social protest, although it is evident that in certain groups and on certain issues church-related activism is influential and deemed threatening by government. Both Protestantism and Catholicism are now accepted as indigenous elements in Korean life rather than as foreign institutions, as they once were considered in Korea and still are in other nations. It may be that Christian groups continue to attract large segments of the population because they have offered the most articulate overall leadership, provide a regimen of services and activities, and espouse a clarity of faith (and perhaps because they espouse democracy and are considered modern). Other factors in the resurgence of religion in Korea may be the role of religions in general as cohesive social institutions in periods of internal and external migration, the decline (indeed, in some cases the intentional replacement) of traditional village clan leadership, and the anonymity of urban life.

INTERNATIONALISM AND TRADITION

A modern Korea has emerged, its people as internationally oriented and sophisticated as any people on the world scene. Contemporary Koreans are far better acquainted with Western artistic and intellectual traditions than are Western literati with Eastern cultures. Such Koreans see no dichotomy in being both international and Korean. They feel no necessary conflict, for example, between acquiring a doctorate degree from a U.S. or Western university and getting married in a modified traditional manner. They may prefer *ondŏl* heating or Korean food but go to concerts of Western classical music and have their children educated in the Western classical music tradition. Newspaper editorials on contemporary Korean problems may quote Western philosophical classics or refer to the most modern intellectual trends. Translations of Western works are exceedingly popular, as are modern Korean novels and essays. Younger people may be seen wearing the latest international fashions, bought by the rich in boutiques and by the poor from pushcarts.

Yet, at the same time, there is a growing interest in things Korean and in the values of the traditional society. These are often advocated by the young, who see the changing culture inundated by foreign, especially American, values and modes. A more nationalistic sense of identity is likely to grow and intensify, as it has in periods when the culture seemed threatened, but it probably will not significantly challenge the trend toward internationalization that has so quickly become so deeply imbedded in Korean society.

8

The Nature of Politics
and Administration in Korea

The King is father,
And Ministers are loving mothers.
Subjects are foolish children;
They only receive what love brings.

The People are slow, often they live idly;
But once feed them love, and they thrive.
No one will desert the familiar land,
This is the way to govern a country.

Peace and prosperity will prevail if each—
King, minister, subject—lives as he should.
—Master Ch'ungdam (c. 742–765 A.D.)[1]

The interwoven yet conflicting factors that influence concepts of governance in contemporary Korea illustrate the eclectic nature of political and social life. The profound effects of more than a thousand years of Confucian political thought (which the quotation, still relevant, from Master Ch'ungdam illustrates); thirty-five years of Japanese colonial rule; forty years of strong military influence; and an equally long period of U.S. involvement, which aroused an interest in democracy, combine to form a complex, sometimes dissonant, and heterogeneous political culture.

That discordant mix reflects the stresses inherent in Korean politics and administration. It makes Korea difficult to encapsulate with a single, memorable phrase. Traditional Korea was described as an "agrarian bureaucracy"—a Confucian bureaucracy based on class status conferred through classical scholarship and with wealth from landholdings providing the leisure for such study. Contemporary Korea has been characterized as a "bureaucratic-authoritarian regime," "state capitalism," a "mercantilist" system, "command capitalism," or a "corporatist regime." All of these descriptions are in part germane, for they describe the interventionist tendency and capacity of the state to control the economy and the importance of the bureaucracy. Such descriptions, however, lose in nuance and accuracy what they make up in terseness. Entrepreneurship and *dirigiste* (state) influence are not unique to Korea but are common to many societies. Their historical and modern influences, their mix and relative changing weights, at any time give Korea, and any of its governments or opposition movements, its particular flavor.

The forces that seem most germane to understanding the Korean political and governmental scene are perhaps better analyzed if clustered along a series of abstract continua, polarized only for the purposes of more clearly defining the tensions, degrees, and trends in the society and anticipating future developments. These continua are those related to hierarchy and egalitarianism, centralization and pluralism, collectivity and individuality, infinite and finite concepts of power, and issues of orthodoxy and heterogeneity, including both law and morality. The sequence and origins of these forces are less important than their traits and their relative, constantly changing, prominence. Although such generalizations may be useful to describe broad societal differences, Koreans singularly or collectively are not rigid in their views, nor does any particular tendency produce any necessary result. If Korean society may be considered eclectic, so may individual Koreans who maintain, like most modern peoples, a broad spectrum of supportive and conflicting concepts.

First, however, it is important to note that the political structure is dependent on a bureaucracy of quite limited size. The bureaucracy in 1945 totaled 90,000, of whom half were Korean and half Japanese. They worked mostly in Seoul. In 1980, the executive branch of government totaled 389,000, of whom 199,164 were career officials, including those in local government. These figures represent only a 59 percent overall increase since 1953 in executive branch personnel and a 62 percent increase in executive branch bureaucrats. This increase is remarkably small, considering that GNP during this same period grew by about 2,500 percent. Government-sponsored research institutions (from economic planning to science and culture) have proliferated in the past generation, and although their staff are not included in these figures and contribute to the public sector of the GNP, as do state-run industries, they hold no line functions in the bureaucracy. Admission to this bureaucracy is normally by examination. Between 1960 and 1980, about 2.5 percent of those who took the examinations for administrative and diplomatic positions passed; about half that percentage passed in 1981–1982. During the same two decades, the rate of success for those who took the lower examination, who included technicians, was only about

5 percent. Whatever their numbers and how these may have changed, they operate within a cultural milieu that helps shape their efficacy.

HIERARCHY AND EGALITARIANISM

Hierarchy is integral to the Confucian tradition and exceptionally pervasive. Ideally, the ruler treats his subjects as a father would his children, and the bureaucracy must do the same. The king's role and rule are unquestioned. The wife is subordinate to her husband, the younger brother to the elder brother; there are no equals. Friends are termed elder or younger brother or sister. "Elder brother–younger brother" is often used to describe the U.S.-Korean national relationship. Age is equated with superiority, and age and higher authority are evidence of greater moral virtue, with the highest such virtue residing with the ruler. This sense of hierarchy is reflected in the Korean language itself, which like Japanese (but unlike Chinese) requires a complex system of grammatic and lexographical honorifics that explicitly designate the relative status of each person referred to or involved in a conversation.

Hierarchy creates strong ties of dependency that flow from those morally superior to those subject to them. In turn, these superior-inferior relationships determine who has power and give the government a legitimate, formal monopoly on it. Those in power are to act according to established norms and to become examples of conduct for others, thus influencing both the behavior of others for good or evil and the very fertility of the land and the tranquility of nature.

The pre-Confucian social order was, in fact, more hierarchical than the Confucian ideal. Early Korean states were organized along rigid class differentiations based on "bone rank," or a hereditary system that eventually evolved into the *yangban* system. In this class of both civilian and military gentry, the civilians dominated. The *yangban*—the backbone of the political, governmental, moral, and social order—originally claimed status on the basis of aristocratic lineage, and then on their scholastic, and thus bureaucratic, standing. China maintained that even the poorest person could theoretically pass the imperial examinations and thereby secure the social and economic rewards available within the bureaucracy. This was not true in Korea. In Korea, only the *yangban* were eligible to take the examinations (and thus to enter the bureaucracy). As in all such systems, there were exceptions—one might buy one's way into the bureaucracy. The result was a self-perpetuating but expanding upper class, which protected itself by limiting access to the lucrative perquisites of office, weeding out other *yangban* competitors through vigorous and continuing factional strife.

Any colonial system maintains and reinforces concepts of hierarchy, but in the case of Japanese rule the hierarchical structure seemed especially strict. Although the Japanese eliminated the Korean monarchy, and some of the highest-status Koreans, still considered supreme patriots, refused to collaborate with the Japanese, many of the *yangban*, the only educated group in the country, did become minor officials in the colonial government, sometimes in the later period rising in position to become governor or, as was more common, *kunsu* (county chief). Some of these officials' children went to universities in Japan.

If we maintain that the colonial era destroyed the traditional class structure in Korea by providing a modern sector of the economy, encouraging migration, and eliminating Korean traditions (and there are arguments that this is at least partly accurate beyond the formalistic legal sense), then it may also be argued that the Japanese system reinforced more abstracted concepts of hierarchy and allowed at least some of the *yangban* to retain their traditional roles vis-à-vis other Koreans, if not the Japanese themselves.

Class status has been maintained through judicious investments: in modern education for children (the contemporary equivalent to passing the imperial examination is a doctorate degree from a U.S. university) and in urban real estate. Wealth allowed the family to obtain private tutoring (now illegal but still widespread), thus admission into good secondary or even primary schools, and then entrance to the highest class of university, which in turn gave access to the bureaucracy and other, quasi-governmental institutions, such as banks.

Although the military system, by its nature, obviously reinforces the concept of hierarchy and pervasively exploits it in its internal operations, both military regimes have either consciously or unconsciously attempted to eliminate the traditional class structure by increasing social mobility. The military itself is the primary avenue of social mobility for the very poor, allowing bright young men access to a good university-level education and lateral mobility after high military service into prestigious civilian and governmental positions. The government recruits military officers into the mid-levels of the bureaucracy on a regular basis.

The government has further attempted to break up special educational advantages of the wealthy by outlawing private tutoring and by enforcing admission to high schools by lottery and location. Prestigious schools, to which upper-class children were sent, virtually guaranteed admission to prestigious universities and then to government positions. The state regulates the number of students in tertiary education, but it has vastly expanded higher education so that it is no longer the province of the elite. Once the prerogative of the wealthy, universities now admit a much broader spectrum of society. In expanding the numbers of trained workers for higher-technology industries, the state has also explicitly broken the inherent monopoly of the upper class. But the Korean desire for social mobility is not necessarily destructive of hierarchy. We do not know whether and to what degree those who succeed in gaining entry to a higher social class adopt the attitudes toward hierarchical authority of their new peers, although such attitudinal transference seems likely.

U.S. influence, so strong in other fields, and stress on egalitarian principles seem marginal to the issue of hierarchy. During the occupation, the U.S. military government did attempt to democratize the educational system, but the effects were very short-lived. Korean education stresses traditional Confucian values, especially loyalty to the state and, by implication, to its ruler. The degree to which a U.S. graduate education alone produces an egalitarian democrat is questionable. Education may have little relation to breaking down strongly imbedded vertical structures. The election process, although firmly established in Korea, may not have had any marked effect on social or bureaucratic attitudes.

The effectiveness of the Korean bureaucratic machine, which has been a remarkable performer in the context of economic development in transmitting instructions for nationwide compliance, may be attributed to some unknown degree to traditional concepts of hierarchy, as well as to a modern military command system and contemporary concepts of public administration. Replication of the Korean experience in other nations will be difficult.

CENTRALIZATION AND PLURALISM

The tendency to keep control of the process of government has its counterpoint in efforts to prevent alternative centers of power or authority from developing. Thus, the concept, central to the U.S. system, of a series of checks and balances—among branches of government, between federal and local authorities, or within the structures of organizations from businesses to universities and nonprofit organizations— is in Korea a traditional conceptual anathema. There has never been an independent judiciary in Korea, and no government law or edict has been declared unconstitutional. The Constitutional Committee, the supreme organ of judicial review, has been dormant, and no case has been referred to it or decided by it in more than fifteen years. Attempts to have an independent legislature, although far more visible, have normally failed on critical issues on which the government would brook no interference, although a certain amount of critical debate was allowed as a minor outlet for frustration. At various times, such debates were censored from the press, but there has been increasing vitality in the National Assembly since the elections of 1985.

Government has viewed any autonomy as inherently destabilizing, diminishing governmental power, and, in fact, subverting the moral order, of which it alone was the guardian. Autonomous power may not always have been viewed as a threat, but it was considered suspicious; thus, it had to be neutralized. In the traditional period, any individual or faction out of favor in the endless internal strife was exiled to the literal or figurative social periphery.

Governments have thus tended to be interventionist, whether through regulation, economic power, legal control, the political process, or the intelligence networks (Yi Mong Nyong, the husband of Korea's premier literary heroine Ch'unhyang, rescues her in his role as a secret royal inspector (*amhaeng osa*) and punishes the corrupt governor). Intervention cannot solely be attributed to military "tidiness" or attempts at bureaucratic compliance. In the United States, government intervention, if sanctioned, is generally considered a last resort; in Korea, it may be the first move. The existence of an autonomous private sector in Korea, whether it be in education or in business, is arguable; nongovernmental or quasi-governmental might be a more accurate description of this sector. Public-private collaboration, with government in the lead, is the more usual form of action.

Local government, with rare exceptions, has been centrally appointed and local officials not allowed to develop strong local ties, which might diminish the power of the center. Royal officials could not serve in their home areas (perhaps more to prevent collusion than rebellion) and were constantly transferred. The lack of primogeniture in Korea not only resulted in the fragmentation of landholdings but allowed the state to maintain control by effectively discouraging very large accumulations of wealth in land. The state retarded the development of any commerce that was autonomous from the court; in the modern period, commerce has been channeled through government-controlled financial or business institutions. Thus, families and organizations could not accumulate major reserves of capital without government sanction. In the republican period, local government was elected until 1958, when President Rhee had a constitutional amendment passed allowing him to appoint governors and mayors of major cities. During the time when local government was elected it functioned poorly, representing personal or factional interests more than regional concerns.

Even under planned decentralization or devolution of power, the initiative rests with government, and its tendency is to prevent pluralism rather than encourage it. Thus, following his coup, Park Chung Hee centralized almost all institutions, including cultural and education groups, under various umbrella organizations that allowed governmental control and simplified state surveillance. The single exception was the student movement, which he forced to be fragmented so that it could be more effectively controlled. Chun Doo Hwan in 1980 broke up labor organizations so that they would have less power, effectively ensuring that authority would remain at the center. But he centralized the media and press institutions. The state may reinstate a modicum of local government in 1989, through local councils, in the belief that local elections for these offices will pose little overall threat, given the state's power over appointed officials and its control over most organizations and economic institutions. That assessment may prove wrong, and the government may discover that it has neglected the changed mood of the nation.

The U.S. military government, through its dicta and its massive support to education during the occupation, had as one of its three primary goals the decentralization of the educational system away from the prewar Japanese example. It failed, and the system became even more centralized than it had been. The elimination of effective local elected government, the monopolization of institutional credit, rural mobilization systems, and urban block meetings sponsored by the Ministry of Home Affairs are, among other methods, all indications of consistent government attempts to maintain control of power and prevent power from accruing to other centers of potential influence.

Not only have external forces been excluded, but government decisions have been handled only at the apex. For example, since 1961, the State Council (the highest executive branch authority under the president, composed of selected economic ministers) has passed without modification perhaps 90 percent of all bills proposed by separate ministries, as the council with the president determined policy. Other ministers could not voice opposition, even privately. Executive branch bills or budgets may be vigorously debated in the National Assembly, but that body's control over such matters is severely circumscribed, although the new constitution of 1987 broadens the scope of that review. The trepidation with which executive branch officials regard legislative review may be a product of concern more for how the Blue House (the Korean equivalent of the U.S. White House) would react to such criticisms than for any material changes that might be made in the legislation.

CONCEPTS OF POWER

Concepts of power and its legitimate and illegitimate use are central to discussion of the nature of culture, the state, and economic development. The multiple external and internal influences on Korean society have complicated understanding of how power functions. Power is, of course, intimately involved in issues of hierarchy, which is one of its manifestations, and with morality and orthodoxy, which are its philosophical bases.

The concept of the finite or infinite nature of power is an issue in contemporary society, as is the zero-sum game or limited good in peasant communities. The implications of each inchoate approach are extraordinary. If power is considered infinite (and thus the stock of it may be increased), sharing it, devolving it, or delegating it may, in fact, accrue more power to the giver. If, however, it is thought of as finite, sharing or delegating power diminishes the limited stock one has and thus causes a decline in authority and in personal and public perceptions of the efficacy of one's institution or position. Perhaps only in some modern societies, and then only in part, does this concept of shared, infinite power take hold.

In Korea, and in many non-Confucian cultures in the region, power is generally considered finite, an integral part of the position one holds in the hierarchy, whether that be family or state. Thus, to share power is to diminish one's own power and one's position; to delegate it is to lose it. The implications for institutional and personal relationships are profound. The leader cannot easily delegate authority to subordinates; the central government will not willingly allow power of any significant nature to accrue to local government and institutions, and thus the concept of pluralism, which inherently concerns the shared nature of some power, becomes difficult. Shared power implies institutional or personal trust, which is low in many societies. It is significant that the Korean government sets standards, professional qualifications, admittance requirements, and numbers of entrants in fields that many developed societies have left to private or nongovernmental organizations.

Contemporary Western influence, concepts of public administration, and even modern military usage (within well-defined limits) have made inroads on this traditional view. Yet, much of U.S. technical assistance advice in the earlier period of economic development was geared to sharing power: in the schools and in the cooperatives; between public and private institutions, central and local authorities, and branches of government. These suggestions were rarely heeded. More acceptable was advice that called for centralization for more efficient management. Perhaps one reason for the continuity and strength of family institutions is simply that power shared within the family is not power shared beyond; it remains concentrated within a small (and trusted) group. This may help account for the continued family nature of even the largest businesses.

This conceptual struggle continues as the society evolves. Because of other contradictions in the society, and the changing nature of both economics and politics, the forces for more institutional pluralism are growing, and some types of power are more frequently shared. This trend is likely to accelerate.

COLLECTIVITY AND INDIVIDUALITY

The relative strength of clan and family varies among Confucian societies, but in all of them these institutions are far more important than in most Western contemporary cultures. Perhaps the family retained more importance in Korea because Korea lacked the Japanese system of setting up new family hierarchies through the adoption of sons and involvement of sons-in-law in family affairs.

The strong emphasis in Confucianism on the family as the intellectual and ideological analogy for state governance and the institution of primary loyalty reinforced earlier Korean emphasis on family and clan. With few intermediate institutions between the state and family, the family protected the individual against the outside world. This preeminence of the family also retarded the development of other institutional loyalties. The result, reinforced by Confucianism as a form of ancestor reverence, has been the submerging of individual identity within the familial context. This collectivity is a pervasive phenomenon and is illustrated linguistically by the use of the Korean "we" when the American would normally say "I" ("our house," "our country," even "our wife").

This phenomenon has not, however, produced uniformity among Koreans nor a lack of personal initiative. In fact, the Korean educational system, which is still exceptionally Confucian, hierarchical, group-oriented, and traditional, graduates children with a highly developed sense of personal efficacy, initiative, drive, and entrepreneurial spirit. Some would attribute this seemingly higher risk-taking capacity and interest among Koreans to child-rearing practices. Whatever the causes and however inconsistent individuality and collectivity may seem to be, the system has produced a personal and institutional dynamism, which is the envy of many other developing nations.

Collectivity exists at the national as well as the family level. Constantly buffeted by superior military pressures, Korea has survived as a relatively small nation because of its collective cultural concepts (uri-ism, or "we-ism"), in spite of (perhaps because of) efforts to eliminate them during the latter part of the Japanese colonial period. The degree of government and administrative collectivity, however, is far different from that in Japan. Group consensus in Japan reaches extremes, but in

Korea it is often replaced by strong, often unquestioned, leadership at the top, with subordinate groups bent on implementing top decisions rather than formulating them. Individuality may be far less pronounced in Korea within the family than in the West, but it finds expression beyond the family at the apex of control of nonfamilial institutions such as businesses.

ORTHODOXY AND HETEROGENEITY

The equation of morality with power has produced strong tendencies toward orthodoxy at all levels. In China, the vast distances between the central and local administrations resulted in a degree of geographical obscurity, allowing non-Confucian Buddhist, Taoist, and regional centers—even non-Chinese minorities—to continue to have local influence. There have been no modern Korean warlords as in twentieth-century China, nor even autonomous daimyo, as in earlier Japan. The small size of Korea's territory and restricted elite groups effectively prevented continuous nonorthodox centers from developing after the Yi Dynasty, when the Buddhist temples were stripped of much of their land and power. Korea's ethnic and linguistic homogeneity reinforced these tendencies.

The orthodoxy of the Korean court produced a rigidity that made Korea more Confucian than its mentor, China. Today, for example, scholars have had to go to Korea to study traditional Confucian court music, where it has survived. This rigidity exacerbated factionalism and forced intellectual endeavor into prescribed and accepted areas. Even former officials exiled in disgrace because of their unorthodox ideas or factional alliances played by the established intellectual rules of orthodoxy, attempting in general to prove their loyalty to the center and to accepted precedents, concepts, and canons rather than challenging them.

So strong was this tendency that the vitality of many of the Yi Dynasty arts may be considered as in inverse proportion to the artist's social distance from the court. Pottery, so much admired today, was produced by virtual government slaves or by peasants. The village masked dance, a peasant achievement, was perhaps the only major form of social satire, and the noncourt musical tradition of p'ansori was the province of the demimondaine. Portraits and other painting genres were produced by anonymous individuals, who essentially were government serfs, attached to but not of the court.

The concept of a "virtuocracy," in which rulers were by definition more morally proper than the rest of society, reinforced the concept of orthodoxy; if one did not conform, one was exiled to the geographical periphery in the classical period or was in direct confrontation or went (and stayed) abroad during the republics.

Orthodoxy is closely linked to concepts of purity. Both Presidents Park and Chun came to power and began to "purify" corrupt or dissonant elements in all sectors. The Korean government constantly has called for "social purification" (*sahoe ch'onghwa*), or the elimination of "impure elements" (*pulsun punja*), and guarded against "ideological pollution" (*sasang oyŏm*). These concepts relate to dissent that the state interprets as either internally or externally focused. Even the political opposition has reformed its party to rid itself of "impure elements." Purity is thus the monopoly of those in power.

In the Korean political context, the term "loyal opposition" becomes an oxymoron, because if the opposition is opposed to what authority stipulates, it by nature cannot be loyal. It is significant that the original meaning of the Chinese character used to designate the political opposition (*ya*) is "wilderness" or "wild or uncultivated fields"—beyond the political and even social pale. Thus, compromise is difficult. The June 29, 1987, pronouncement of political liberalization by Roh Tae Woo was not viewed as compromise. To the government, it was a magnanimous gesture; to the opposition, it was a surrender.

Political orthodoxy is in interesting and important contrast to economic pragmatism. In economic development policies, there has been an absence of ideological rigor, from either the Right or Left. The explanation for economic flexibility may lie in the concept of economic development as the means to political legitimacy, the service of economics to the state and the economic successes illuminating the moral superiority of the ruler.

Orthodoxy is also related to concepts of law and legality. The "rule of law" and the idea of equality before the law are not established in Korea, for if the state has control of legitimacy, then law is simply an extension of the role of the state and not of the rights of its citizenry. In Confucian terms, morality was more important than law, and although this dictum may have been overly stressed in Western analyses of East Asia, the general tendency is apparent. Korea has been an "alegal" society, where attitudes toward law were generally negative and where living without law is still considered a moral good by the majority.

The concept that law was a means for a neutral confrontation, either between disputants or between the individual and the state, was not developed. The government had no liability under the law, although it had a moral obligation toward the populace. Reliance on law indicated a loss of morality. The state was assumed to have the authority to control law, and all rights under various constitutions have not been absolute, but subject to law, and thus to state control. Law, rather than a refuge for the individual, is an overt reflection of the moral superiority of the regime and those who hold power.

This does not imply that law, international and local, does not exist; law was always an element of state control, and Korea had to develop contractual law as it became a major trading nation. But law is separated into those areas in which it assists attainment of state goals, such as in economic fields, and internal areas, where it is treated differently. As concepts of human rights became more widespread, legal institutions were established to protect the wronged individual, as long as such problems were not defined by the state as within its purview. A family dispute may be adjudicated without state supervision, but labor disputes or those interpreted by the government as political in nature or implication are subject to intensive government intervention (in the past, usually on the side of management). In the summer of 1987, the government often intervened for the first time to give labor some of its demands and, thus, to prevent spreading social and political unrest. As in many Confucian societies, there are relatively few lawyers, and their status is not as high as in the United States. Governmental control is reflected in the centralized training of all lawyers, judges, and prosecutors in a single state institution, subject to state strictures. The major intermediary between the bureaucracy and the people through law is a group of paralegals called scriveners, who perform notary and other functions.

These tendencies, which have their bases in much that is traditional in Korean society, could not be considered as representative of Korean traits if they did not exist in some significant degree in North Korea as well. The issues of hierarchy, centralization, orthodoxy (to Kim Il Sung's thought), law as the instrument of the state, and power are all reflected in the North Korean regime, as well as in the South. Although the manifestation of any of these particular elements in the North may be quite different from that in the South, the roots of their expression are found in the same cultural elements.

These proclivities in both North and South are likely to continue, although perhaps in diminishing degrees. Within this political context, then, it is possible to understand the role of state intervention in the economy, the nature of the disputes in the political process, and the difficulty of prescribing solutions to particular Korean problems on the basis of non-Korean political patterns, such as compromise and conciliation, that implicitly rely on shared power as integral to their success. Such solutions may play a role, but they are difficult to attain. As more international attention focuses on the Korean political and economic process, the tensions between internal politico-cultural needs and foreign expectations may be expected to grow.

Crossing concepts of centralization, orthodoxy, and personalism is the issue of regionalism within the overall context of national homogeneity. In a sense, regionalism is factionalism writ large, with resources and prebends distributed to areas as well as to individuals under a patrimonial system. Regionalism has been graphically reflected in patterns of leadership as well as in politics and economics. Since 1961 and the rise in prominence of the Kyongsang region under both Park and Chun, more than 31 percent of government ministers came from that area, whereas 13 percent were from the Cholla provinces. (About 15 percent of the population lives in the Chollas; about 16 percent in the Kyongsang provinces.) For vice ministers, the figures are 35 percent from the Kyongsang region and 9 percent from the Chollas; for board directors, 39 percent and 13 percent, respectively. In many societies, including the United States, leaders appoint those they trust (often from their own region) to positions of authority. The issue is the extent to which this occurs and the implications for the degree of trust and mistrust in ruling.

How do these tendencies relate to the perceived legitimacy of the political order and, then, of each regime? In the traditional period, the basis of internal and external political legitimacy was the degree to which the state adhered to the Confucian precepts: the internal role of the sovereign as paternal ruler and the external, tributary role that the state played in relation to China. Each ruler was ratified by the Chinese emperor, and that provided regime legitimation.

In the modern period, the situation has become more complex. In North Korea, the treatment of Kim Il Sung as father (and now Kim Jong Il as son) demonstrates Confucian vestiges, but within the context of legitimacy based chronologically on, anti-Japanese activity, adherence to Marxism-Leninism, and Kim Il Sung–ism. South Korea has moved further away from the articulated Confucian model, although many Confucian atributes are inchoate in state attitudes and actions, and President Park attempted to resuscitate Confucian virtues through education and political mobilization (much as Chiang Kai-shek had tried to do in China in the 1930s). Anticommunism has proven to be a weak national ideology, although at times an effective rallying point. Economic policies have been too pragmatic to provide an ideological base. Democracy has been the theoretical inspiration but not the reality. Legitimation for the state as a whole was weak before economic progress, but democracy (or some Korean version of it) has provided the potential basis for the state and for its past support by foreign donors in times of crisis.

Each South Korean regime must now prove its varied efficacies anew: a measure of pluralism under democratic garb (a foundation that is growing), economic growth that protects hard-won improvements, and the security and international respectibility of the state through global (until recently, U.S.) friendly relations. Strong leadership may be tolerated, for Koreans are aware of the fractious nature of Korean political life, but arbitrary rule will no longer be tolerated for long. No doubt the new configuration will be distinctively Korean and retain much that is politically traditional as well as more modern elements. The political culture of Korea is in the process of tumultuous change. The degree to which all of these factors will continue to be important is uncertain, but they will no doubt color the evolving picture and help delineate major highlights of the scene of governance. They cannot be ignored, but they should not be considered as absolute.

9

The Role of the Military in Korean Society

What a society gets in its armed forces is exactly what it asks for, no more and no less. What it asks for tends to be a reflection of what it is. When a country is looking at its fighting force it is looking in a mirror.
—Lt. Gen. Sir John Winthrop Hackett[1]

No adage seems more archaic in South Korea today than the Confucian one "Good iron is not used to make nails, good men do not become soldiers." This concept, generally more honored in theory than practice, is relevant to understanding East Asia, but it was always part myth, part ideological cant. It was, after all, the literati who wrote the histories. The importance of the military varied by country, era, and class. Because Japan was feudal, in a sense comparable to Europe and unlike Korea and China, the military tradition was more widely honored there. Its importance ebbed and waned in China. The maxim applied to the top literati in Korea during the Yi Dynasty, and the attitude it reflects, held on longer there than elsewhere in East Asia, reinforced by the Japanese military's role in the colonial era.

Both the South Korean and North Korean armies are among the half-dozen largest in the world. More troops per kilometer are spread along both sides of the Demilitarized Zone (DMZ) between North and South than at any other place on earth. South Korea is a state so militarized, where the military and civilian elites have so mingled, that in mufti or uniform the role of the military is inextricably bound with the shorter-term prospects as well as the longer-term future of the society. The same must be said of North Korea.

There was in the 1950s and 1960s a spurt of social science literature on the role of the military in development. Military men were regarded as action- and goal-oriented, modern, managerial, organizationally effective, and with clear concepts of national development. That school

105

of thought lost ground in the wake of a series of bumbling military regimes. It became evident that although such regimes could be as modern or as Western in concept as in their equipment, they might equally be traditional and obscurantist in their policies. The theory neglected a wide variety of influences that affect the efficacy of such governments, including personal leadership within the military, military factionalism, and military-civilian relationships, among others. The roles of Park Chung Hee and Chun Doo Hwan are too complex to be so easily categorized. In addition, there has been in Korea two contradictory tendencies: the military as dynastic or regime founder, and civilian supremacy in state management. These military-civilian tensions continue today.

It is not just the ubiquitous presence of the military that is physically apparent throughout South Korea; the social role of present and former military officers has transformed society and development programs in all fields. The military command structure has been a spur, if not to development, then to the effective implementation and reinforcement of development policies and programs. At a mass level, the military provided early training in some of the technical, lower-level skills that fostered economic growth. Higher military education provided the clearest avenue to real social mobility in society.

Yet, military expenditures often force cuts in development or social programs. With about 6 percent of GNP and one-third of the national budget devoted to defense (about $4.4 billion, compared to North Korea, which spends an estimated $4.2 billion, perhaps 20 percent of GNP), the military also acts as a deterrent to growth. Perhaps this drain, not unproportional to the threat, balances the spur to development that the danger from the North has produced. But if peace came suddenly to the peninsula and the bulk of the military were demobilized, their sudden influx into the labor market could also have important social and economic consequences.

These diverse developmental effects and potentials of the role of the military in South Korea and the military's functions in society are not simply a result of the expansion brought on by the Korean War and the perpetual state of alert along the northern frontier. They are also a product of the migration of northerners to the South beginning in 1945, the interplay of politics and security, the influence of the United States, and social change. Although there are no continuities between the present military and its royal predecessors, governments on both sides of the DMZ use military myth and history to reinforce their roles and mobilize their populations.

THE MILITARY IN KOREAN HISTORY

In 1907, the Japanese demobilized the remaining forces of the Korean army, a decrepit troupe of six thousand men, a shadow of the might that at critical points in Korean history had played an important role on the peninsula. In deterioration through much of the Yi Dynasty, the military in its final, decayed state obscured a checkered record of accomplishment over some fifteen hundred years.

Until the formation of the Yi Dynasty, Korea could be regarded as a series of militarized states. The Three Kingdoms of Silla, Koguryŏ, and Paekche were constantly at war with one another as well as with Kaya in the south and with the forces on the Manchurian frontier in the north. Although details are obscure, each kingdom seems to have organized a communal force, in which the farmer played a military role and the command structure was organized along lines of clan loyalties. The system seems to have been effective. There is no more remarkable feat of arms in Korean history, or perhaps in East Asia, than the decisive defeats by Koguryŏ of the superior armies of the Chinese Sui and T'ang Dynasties in the early seventh century.

Koryŏ was also a highly militarized state. Its population was smaller than that under the Yi Dynasty, which witnessed the nadir of Korean military strength, but Koryŏ supported a military some two to ten times larger, depending on the period, than that of the Yi. In 1552, for example, the Yi army numbered only twelve thousand, one-tenth the size of the Koryŏ army. It was not that Korea was unconcerned with its army or with the new technology of armaments. There were more military than civilian positions open in the court structure, and Korea had a long history of interest in new technologies of many kinds. Factional disputes in a small court certainly caused deterioration in the effective functioning of the military. Yi Korea was also under the titular "military umbrella" of China as its suzerain state and, thus, perhaps did not feel the need for massive forces. But this perception did not match reality. The Japanese pirates; the invasions by Japan in 1592, 1597, and 1894; the Manchu invasions of the seventeenth century; and the peasant rebellions of the nineteenth century all illustrate the folly of relying on China for protection. But stronger armies in the region with greater technologies made Korea a comparatively marginal military actor.

Most nations form their military myths and use them for political and social mobilization. Korea is no exception. North Korea has extolled Koguryŏ and Koryŏ to enhance military fervor, citing their military prowess and claiming their heritage because the capitals of both states fall within North Korean territory. South Korea draws on Silla (Kyongju,

Silla's capital, is a major tourist attraction) and its *hwarang* (an elite, militarized youth corps), which South Korea attempted to reincarnate in a modern version. It has also virtually deified Admiral Yi Sun Sin, the premier military hero in Korea, the inventor of the world's first ironclad ships (the turtle boats of 1592) and the military leader who defeated the Japanese fleet. His memory was carefully cultivated during the Park Chung Hee period, and a shrine was built to him, both to instill a sense of national pride and perhaps to provide legitimacy to military rule in Korea as well as expiation for Park's own role in the Japanese military.

THE MILITARY, 1945–1961

The postliberation military structure, strategy, and tactics in both North and South Korea owe little to the Japanese colonial period, even though the early officer corps of the Rhee regime, unlike that of the North, was largely drawn from those who had been in the Japanese military. In North Korea, 80 percent of the officer corps had served with the Chinese communists. There was a hiatus in leadership and role during the colonial period. Koreans were not drafted into the Japanese army until 1944, and in the last two years of the war there were perhaps three thousand student officers. Only six or seven dozen officers were trained at the Military Academy in Japan during the entire Japanese occupation, and another three or four dozen, from less prosperous economic and social backgrounds, at the Manchurian Military Academy. One of these latter was Park Chung Hee. Part of Japan's policy to incorporate Korea into the Japanese empire was to encourage Koreans to enter the ranks of the Japanese army. This Koreans did in significant numbers—some three or four hundred thousand by 1945—largely to escape the grinding poverty of the rural areas. Park Chung Hee and Chung Il Kwon (prime minister in the 1960s) are but two prominent examples, the former from the south and the latter from the north, where a military tradition seemed more pronounced. Thus, even in the colonial period the military was an avenue, albeit modest, of social mobility.

Korean forces in unoccupied, Nationalist China were not militarily important in World War II, although the Korean Yenan faction with the Chinese communists was to become influential for a period in North Korea. Kim Il Sung and others led anti-Japanese guerrilla activities from Manchuria. Although the end of World War II brought the temporary disbanding of the military, the continued presence of the Japanese-trained police under the U.S. military occupation was deeply resented throughout South Korea. About 30 percent of the Japanese colonial police had been

Koreans, of low social status. Often the link between a subjugated people and their rulers and known as vicious and cruel collaborators, the Korean police were hated. They became the nucleus for both the future police and some of the military, but the former were intentionally built up by the United States to curb social and political unrest, and the latter were kept small by the United States until the Korean War.

The United States feared Rhee's bellicosity toward North Korea. Rhee publicly stated that he hoped to invade the North to unify the peninsula. As Washington was supplying the critical funds for the military (77 percent from 1955 to 1960, 83 percent from 1961 to 1968) and the government, the Koreans were compelled to keep their forces small (about 100,000 troops) until the start of the Korean War, and they were not supplied with offensive weapons.

The war devastated the military, causing both its demoralization and its vast expansion in spite of enormous casualties. (There were 400,000 troops in the Korean army in 1953. This number rose to 600,000 in sixteen divisions in 1954 but was later reduced to 520,000, with an additional 80,000 in the air force and navy; in contrast, there were 360,000 U.S. troops in Korea at the armistice.) Payments to troops were often late and almost always insufficient, so the army was sometimes forced to forage off its own land. Trees were cut to provide fuel for sale to the public as well as for army use. Rations were sparse, and in some areas the military seemed to act like an army of occupation, commandeering food and resources.

In spite of its essential role during the war, the army was still on the social periphery. The draft was pervasive and still exists, although the expansion of the population together with the relatively static size of the military have meant that not all men must serve on extended active duty, and there are now alternative forms of service. A male could not study abroad until he had completed military service. Exemptions from military duty were given to the sole sons in families— a nice Confucian touch, as a male was necessary to continue the family line and perform Confucian rites, and casualties in the military were very high.

To encourage Korean cooperation on U.S. policy issues and military and defense measures, the expansion of the Korean forces under Rhee and modernization of equipment under Park (the Force Mobilization Plan of 1971–1975, calling for $1.5 billion in military aid in return for the withdrawal of one U.S. division, followed by the Force Improvement Plan of 1976–1980 and the Second Force Improvement Plan of 1982–1986), as well as the withdrawal of some U.S. troops, were often used as levers by the U.S. to ensure compliance—from the signing of the armistice to economic stabilization. Thus, in return for Rhee's agreement to repatriate North Korean military prisoners and accept the armistice, the United States provided funds to expand the Korean army from fourteen to twenty divisions. The U.S. role was critical, for the United States effectively paid for the military through military assistance programs and the local currency generated from the import of U.S. agricultural products through Public Law 480 (PL-480), whereby surplus U.S. agricultural commodities were distributed abroad.

Although the military played no overt role in politics in the pre-1961 coup period, military and paramilitary activities were pervasive. Rhee used the military for his own political ends, merging military and political activities by building up paramilitary and political youth groups run by former members of the army. With U.S. encouragement, the Korea National Youth Movement was formed in May 1948; it had 859,000 members. It became the Youth Protector Corps in 1949, with 1,250,000 members. The youth group was tied both to the Rhee political machine and to the army. Prior to the Korean War, the influence of the small military had been marginal, although its activities have been described as almost exclusively political.

The coup of 1961 was not the first planned military response to civil unrest. Some elements of the military had wanted a coup against Rhee, but they were upstaged by the student revolution. Whether Chang Myon's efforts to reduce the military by 100,000 men was a further cause for the Park coup is unclear.

THE ROLE OF THE MILITARY SINCE 1961

In 1988, the presence of the military is overwhelming in numbers, influence, and budgetary resources. More than 30 percent of the annual government budget ($4.6 billion in fiscal year 1985) and about 6 percent of GNP is devoted to the military. In addition to 598,000 personnel under arms (including an air force of 33,000, 20,000 marines, and a navy of 23,000) (see Table 9.1), there is a regular army reserve of 1.4 million, a civilian defense corps of 3.5 million, a Student Homeland Defense Corps of 600,000 (the last two organized in 1975), and an additional Homeland Defense Reserve of 3.3 million men. Perhaps two-thirds of all males from eighteen to forty-five years of age are thus associated directly with the military. From 1966 to 1972, some 340,000 Korean troops had direct combat experience in Vietnam.

The military's importance is not measured only in funds or troops. Its influence is far more broad. In contrast to the Rhee regime, when conditions allowed little mobility through the military, under Park the rapid promotion of the officer corps was actively fostered, thereby ensuring the officers' loyalty and preventing a coup (similar to Park's own) by

TABLE 9.1
Korean Military Forces on the Peninsula, 1987

	North Korea	South Korea
Total Active Armed Forces (exclusive of reserves)	838,000	598,000
Ground Forces a		
Personnel	750,000	542,000
Infantry divisions	25	19
Armored divisions	0	0
Motorized divisions	1	2
Armored brigades	15	1
Infantry brigades (incl. motorized)	30	2
Special Forces Brigades	20	7
Medium/light tanks	2,700/300	1,200/0
APCs	1,500	700
Field artillery	6,000	3,000
MRLs	1,800	few
SSMs	54	12
AAA	8,000	580
SAM sites/MSLS b	45/800	34/210
Air Forces		
Personnel	53,000	33,000
Bombers	80	0
Jet fighters	680	440
Transports	270	30
Helicopters	170	275 c
Naval Forces		
Personnel	35,000	23,000
Attack submarines	20	0
Destroyers	0	11
Frigates	4	7
Corvettes	0	10
Missile attack boats	25	11
Coastal patrol types	370	50
Mine warfare types	15	9
Amphibious craft	100	28

a-Includes Marine forces for South Korea
b-Does not include SA-7 handheld SAMs that probably number 5,000+
c-Including army helicopters

Source: U.S. Department of Defense, 1987.

younger, frustrated officers with no hope for advancement. (It is said that from 1961 to 1970 there were sixteen abortive coups planned against Park.) Senior and well remunerated posts were found for high-ranking retired military. They became members of the cabinet, governors of the provinces, and ambassadors abroad. As economic growth occurred, some became key executives or advisors in corporations, both public and private.

In the military period of 1961–1963—before elections but after the coup—more than 55 percent of cabinet-level officials were former military officers (from the Third through the Fifth Republics, this proportion was one-third). Although only 15.8 percent of the National Assembly members had formerly served in the military, a significant 42 percent of committee chairmen in the assembly came from that background, as did all of the Defense Committee and three-quarters of the Home Affairs Committee. The military dominated ministerial committees where large amounts of money were spent: transportation, 55 percent; construction, 45 percent; and agriculture, 36 percent. Equally important, 39 percent of board directors (equivalent to vice ministers) of the central government ministries were from the military, as were over 18 percent of vice ministers themselves. In addition, mid-level officers were brought into the bureaucracy each year; by 1986, they totaled 686. The result has been a permeation of civilian life by the military. But there has been less infiltration into the military of civilian concepts. The system, although continuing, has begun to produce a large number of retired senior military on modest pensions (and, because of late marriages, with children to educate) who must seek additional income and employment, which is not currently available. The government often eases their transition to civilian life by providing "research" grants.

In an era when mobility was dependent on education and higher education was rigidly restricted in numbers and in the public's ability to pay for it, the military gave the bright, impoverished male an opportunity to acquire a good college degree and prestige in the community. The Korean Military Academy (KMA) for officers has played an important role in shaping the leadership's social and political attitudes. It was started in December 1945 as the Military English Language Institute, producing 110 graduates before April 1946, when it was replaced by the South Korean National Defense Officers Training Academy. For recruits, military service was the sole chance to learn skills that would be eminently useful in a postmilitary career. Drivers, electricians, mechanics, and other blue-collar workers often received their initial technical training in the military. Military training probably broke down regional isolation more quickly than did the later development of rural infrastructure.

Group loyalties have been important factors in military affairs. In contrast to the British system, where loyalty is to the regiment or unit, in Korea loyalty is to fellow classmates from the academy. For example, the First and Second Classes each had sixty officers: twenty from the Japanese army, twenty from the Japanese Kwantung (Manchurian) forces, and twenty from the Chinese Kuomintang "Restoration Army." Included were Park Chung Hee, Kim Jae Kyu (who killed Park), Chung Il Kwon (who, as prime minister under Park, is said to have saved Park from execution during the Yosu-Sunch'on uprising in 1948), and Chang To Yong (titular coup leader). The core of the Park coup, however, was the Eighth Class of the academy; the core of the Chun group was the Eleventh Class and, as important, a sufficiently junior group from the Seventeenth Class that was not a threat to Chun. These bonds have proven significant not only in political terms but also in business, where military associations provide the personal glue for financial relationships and links between military in key government positions and civilian entrepreneurs. When the elite was quite small and hereditary in Korea, such relationships were more commonly built on family alliances through marriage or, later, by class attendance at prestigious secondary schools and universities. With the expansion of the elite, the military provides focus in a society that seems to require some personal, alegal, relationships to cement internal transactions.

If the military has played a beneficial social role by fostering mobility, its economic predominance has had both positive and negative effects on the capacity of the state to engage in development. On the positive side, the reinforcement of a managerial structure that reaches down into and pervades the society as a whole results in excellent implementation of central government decisions; but the allocation of significant resources to the military cuts what might otherwise be provided for developmental or social welfare activities. In neither case is the result always uniform.

The military command structure perpetuated and strengthened the traditionally strong authoritarian and hierarchical tendencies inside Korean society that were exacerbated under Japanese colonial rule. This fostered a remarkably effective level of implementation that is the envy of many nations. This structure had, however, two major defects: First, it was destructive of mechanisms allowing the center to learn from the periphery, for there were few incentives, and many deterrents, to positive criticism or suggestions for change from below; and second, if the decisions at the top were inappropriate, then an effective command structure exaggerated these problems. Koreans have written that an essential difficulty with the saemaŭl movement, the rural development and mobilization effort begun by President Park in 1971, was its top-heavy command; and the failure of the rice crop of 1980 was a result of inappropriate decisions effectively implemented (see Chapter 10).

South Korea has engaged in a massive buildup of its defense productive capacity. In reaction to the Nixon Doctrine of 1969, it has been determined to become more self-sufficient militarily. In 1970, the government created the Agency for Defense Development, which ranges in scope from data collection to planning and production. Through special legislation and massive loans for corporate involvement, the private sector, including many of the largest *chaebŏl*, was heavily engaged. The public also paid for this buildup, through a National Defense Tax (a 10 percent income and sales surcharge) as well as through "voluntary" donations. Defense surtaxes were 3.8 percent of total revenues in 1975, 15 percent in 1982. Research and development expenditures among military appropriations increased from .2 percent in 1971 to 5.1 percent in 1976.

By the mid-1980s, Korea was completely self-sufficient in conventional weapons. It produced twenty-three types of munitions, aircraft, tanks, armored personnel carriers, naval vessels, and several varieties of missiles. Korea became the fifth largest Third World exporter of arms: 8.8 percent of the Third World total in the 1975–1982 period. Although Korea has continuously requested U.S. permission for third country sales of U.S.-owned technology, only a very small percentage has been approved—a source of some quiet tension between the nations.

Extensive military expenditures may have resulted in a type of economic triage where choices were made in favor of the army and to the detriment of economic growth or social welfare. The results, however, were rarely clear-cut. Although the military budget was essentially sacrosanct and was virtually unaffected by National Assembly budgetary debates (it was, instead, limited by the Blue House), with the result that social programs came last, if at all, military and security considerations had important, sometimes positive impacts. The decision to expand defense industries in the 1970s, based on the perceived need to be freer from dependence on the United States, resulted in uneconomic excess industrial capacity, inflation, and the need for a major structural adjustment program in 1979 and thereafter, but it also accelerated Korean heavy industry exports and improved the status of higher technology, which was then available for other developmental purposes.

The penetration of Korean society by the military—Korean social attitudes now regard military careers as not only respectable but desirable—has given the military a pivotal and unprecedented role in the culture. Whereas the authority of the military in revolutionary China was tempered by the Communist party, as was the case in North Korea, in the South ideological or political influences have been subservient to military structure. No other governmental institution has yet been able to balance the influence of the military in Korean society. The intelligence apparatus is also pervasive and is second in subtle influence, but the two are often intimately connected. Although the military may not continue directly to dominate the political process at the apex, it is likely to have veto power over it for the future. As the society grows more affluent, a military career may appear a less attractive option, as families can increasingly send sons to good universities. If this becomes the case, the military leadership may again be drawn mainly from the working class, this time—as Korea has become urbanized—from the cities.

The military should not be considered monolithic, for age, rank, regionalism, experience, and personal interests and loyalties affect its cohesion. There was, for example, a plot against Chun in 1982. If the military is treated as a unit, it is for convenience, without implications of ideological, factional, or political solidarity. There are significant differences within the military as to its proper role in the society, especially in politics. Some feel the need for broader social programs; some are concerned with the plight of the rural population; others are suspicious of the *chaebŏl*; some senior military abhor members of the opposition; some younger officers are avowedly socialist. If there are diverse military views, these are united in their nationalism. And, in spite of these differences, there is more organizational unity in the military than in any other single major institution in the society. Its importance should not be underestimated.

The military's contribution to Korean economic development may lie most obviously in its command structure, which has enforced and implemented economic change, but its internal diversity may have made it more economically pragmatic and, thus, more successful. The personal role of President Park should also not be underestimated. In retrospect, however, the era beginning in 1961 may well be remembered as much for the social mobility encouraged by and through the military as for remarkable economic progress.

THE ROLE OF THE U.S. MILITARY

The U.S. military role in South Korea is vast and varied. It is pervasive and provides both deterrence and the balance of power on the peninsula, yet it has little political effect. It has command responsibility yet little control. There is hardly an area of military training, strategy, equipment, or policies it has not influenced, yet the Korean military has continuously exhibited its penchant for autonomous action.

The U.S. presence, following the withdrawal of U.S. forces in June 1949 after the formation of the First Republic but before the Korean War, stems from the hostilities. A United Nations Security Council resolution established the UN Command on July 7, 1950. All allied troops on the peninsula, including Korean and third-nation forces, were placed under this command. That command still exists and is supplemented (but essentially replaced except for armistice issues) by a Combined (U.S.-Korean) Forces Command formed in 1978, the only such command outside of NATO. South Korea is the only one of the five Asian allies of the United States with which the United States would automatically be involved in combat in the event of war. The purpose of the Combined Forces Command is to integrate the U.S. and Korean forces, and one of the cardinal elements of U.S. military policy is still that all such forces should be interoperable—that there should be some form of single command and that their equipment should be compatible.

With the growth of Korean nationalism, anomalies in the command structure that are becoming increasingly disadvantageous to the United States are likely to be sources of intensified U.S.-Korean tension if they continue unchanged and eventually engender more anti-U.S. sentiment. All troops in South Korea were theoretically under the UN Command established two weeks after the start of the Korean War. This effectively meant that all allied forces, including those of the Koreans, were under U.S. control, as the United States headed the UN Command. Troops could not be moved internally without approval, although later this ruling was changed to apply only to certain combat forces.

Thus, Park's coup of May 16, 1961, was an unauthorized or illegal deployment of forces, for troops were moved without the permission of the UN Command against a government that Washington supported. The coup was also engineered without U.S. knowledge, in spite of the presence of U.S. advisors down to the battalion level. Under the 1978 agreement for the Combined Command (the deputy commander of which is Korean), approximately 50 percent of Korean troops in normal times, and 90 percent in times of war, are under this control. The Koreans normally may move their troops but must notify the U.S. commander, who may protest if he feels such moves might affect the command's capacity to deal with North Korea. The mechanism for resolution of any disputes is unclear.

Thus, in the Chun coup of December 12, 1979, Chun notified the command two days after the event, without public U.S. protest. Later, the Koreans ordered their Special Forces into Kwangju in 1980, resulting in mayhem to the population. These initial forces were not under the Combined Command, but the regular army troops who finally put down the insurrection were, and the U.S. commander (who is reported to have felt that the regular army would be less rapacious) did not object to deployment to suppress the insurrection. Although the U.S. action may not have been intended as supportive of Korean policy, a large segment of the Korean population so interpreted it.

Despite the legality of the first Korean Special Forces move and the U.S.-condoned follow-up, many of the public still charge the United States with connivance in this disaster. U.S. influence is effectively limited to an explicit or implied threat to make public U.S. disagreement over such movements, which would undercut the credibility and indeed legitimacy of the government, as the public still regards the U.S. sanction as important. Washington's opposition may have been one factor in the government's reluctance to invoke martial law in June 1987. More important was the memory of the hatred engendered by Kwangju and concern, felt also by some in high military circles, that such a move would once again risk massive bloodshed and test the trustworthiness of the troops.

The United States maintains a major presence in Korea (40,000 U.S. troops in 1986), which reinforces the Korean-U.S. Mutual Defense Treaty of 1954. At the time of the armistice, three U.S. infantry divisions were stationed there; one was withdrawn in 1954 and another (the 7th Infantry Division) in 1971. In 1987, the major elements of the U.S. services in Korea were the 2nd Infantry Division, the 7th Air Force, and the 2nd Engineer Group. In addition, a substantial U.S. offshore presence is critical in any assessment of the military balance. This includes major sea forces and an unknown nuclear capacity, as U.S. policy is neither to confirm nor deny the presence of nuclear weapons. There are also said to be some seven hundred to a thousand tactical nuclear weapons in and about Korea, including 203mm and 155mm nuclear artillery shells and atomic demolition landmines. Eight-inch artillery shells of the neutron bomb variety were to be introduced in 1979. The armistice agreement of 1953 stipulated that only replacement weapons could be introduced into the peninsula, a provision that has been ignored on both sides of the DMZ.

The purposes of the U.S. military presence have included the tasks of ensuring the integrity of the Republic of Korea against North Korea and the Soviet Union (earlier, against China), as well as the general protection of Japan. To this end, the United States wishes to maintain its numerous bases in Korea, to continue its command over substantive Korean forces in the event of hostilities, and to encourage a greater Korean contribution to its own defense (the United States earlier had suggested the 6 percent of GNP spent on defense as a minimum), as well as to provide more financial support for U.S. troops in Korea. The Koreans maintain that they already provide more per soldier than does either Japan or West Germany, but a great deal of their contribution is in services.

As Korean military levels reach self-sufficiency on the ground, Washington has begun to redefine and justify the U.S. presence as more regional in scope (it is also for the defense of Hokkaido Island in Japan), rather than peninsular. The United States is also interested in expanding the role of Korean troops to include responsibility for regional defense, including that of Japan and the sea-lanes. How the Combined Forces

Agreement would work under either approach is unclear. A strong Korea also contributes to delaying the rearmament and potential militarization of Japan, which many in the region fear.

Although Korea acknowledges its defense dependency in air and naval matters, as well as in military technology, it is increasingly unhappy over aspects of this dependency. Thus, many Koreans want the republic to be self-sufficient in deterrence capacity, self-reliant logistically, have full control over its forces, have a clearer defense treaty, and have greater defense production and rights to sell to third countries under U.S. licensing arrangements. In 1987, Roh indicated during his visit to Washington that the Koreans desired changes in the Combined Command structure, which is viewed as not in keeping with new nationalistic attitudes.

Some Koreans argue that Washington is interested in stability on the peninsula rather than the security of South Korea per se; a stronger South Korea might upset the balance with the North and this stability. The improvement of South Korean military technological capacity (such as the addition of F-16 aircraft) has lead to North Korean procurement from Russia of MIG-23 planes. South Korean economic success has led both the Korean and U.S. governments to rethink the nature and scope of the defense partnership.

Other factors affecting the relationship include the growth of anti-U.S. sentiment as a result of the obvious presence of U.S. forces, although some say that the mere presence of U.S. troops could give the Korean government leverage over U.S. actions in the region. The U.S. military presence is blatant, occupying a major tract of Seoul real estate (a golf course and other recreational facilities are open also to the senior Korean elite), as well as more discreet camps and bases in less-obvious areas. The usual unsavory as well as more orthodox entrepreneurial activities have grown up around such bases, exacerbating social tensions. More than five thousand well-educated Korean troops (known as Korean Augmentation to the U.S. Army, or KATUSAs) are assigned to U.S. units, and cultural discrepancies in living standards and life-styles between the two groups further augment tensions. In addition, both sides display normal bureaucratic vested interests in continuing the relationship. For the United States, the command provides some of the more senior posts available for the army, posts that are increasingly in short supply.

The purpose in stationing many of these troops along the frontier is to have them serve as a "tripwire," so that North Korea will think more than twice about any overt aggression against the South, which would then force an immediate U.S. response. A U.S. National Security Decision of 1970 that would have redeployed these forces away from the DMZ area was never implemented. Because the Mutual Defense

Treaty calls for military support in accordance with the constitutional provisions of each nation, in the event of an invasion U.S. forces would likely be hit before Congress could act. Thus, these troops, which no Korean administration or major opposition party wants to see withdrawn, are the visible and immediate security that a treaty could not guarantee. Critics argue that the tripwire concept is an effort both to prevent North Korean aggression and to circumvent congressional intent: A tripwire confrontation would force U.S. casualties, whose emotional impact would necessitate an extra-congressional presidential decision to defend Korea.

U.S. strategy is based, in addition, on "tripwire plus escalation"— the threat of nuclear retaliation to a conventional North Korean invasion, as the United States could not mobilize the four to six divisions in time to stop the North Koreans before they could reach Seoul. Whatever the past effectiveness of the nuclear threat as a deterrent, in a period of heightened Korean nationalism, given Korea's ethnic homogeneity and with millions in the South having extended families in the North, there would likely be strong, understandable protests even from the South Koreans about the use of such weapons. Thus, U.S. strategy, insofar as the nuclear option is paramount to that policy, may be detrimental to longer-range U.S. interests on the peninsula and might indeed be opposed by some future South Korean government.

There is bipartisan support for the continuation of the defense commitment, but this support is not contingent of any particular level of troop presence. Thus, it is likely that these issues may be negotiated following the 1988 Olympics. When President Carter advocated troop withdrawal from Korea in his 1976 presidential campaign (President Ford had earlier talked about troop reductions), he contributed to a severe freeze in official U.S.-Korean relations. Other major issues in the freeze were concerns over human rights issues in Korea, growing internal repression under the Yushin Constitution, the KCIA's kidnapping of Kim Dae Jung from Tokyo, U.S. embarrassment over "Koreagate" (the attempts by the Korean government to influence through bribes and other illegal activities U.S. policy toward Korea) and the unwillingness of the Korean government to collaborate effectively in exposing the scandal, and post-Vietnam concerns over the U.S. ground commitment to defend Asian states.

The planned phaseout of U.S. forces, personally supported by President Carter, gradually and painfully changed over time under congressional, U.S. military, and Korean pressures toward a reduction in forces. A 1979 upward reassessment of North Korean troop strength and armaments conveniently allowed a graceful postponement of the issue. To temper criticism, the Korean government began to contribute about $1.2 billion, or half, of the costs (calculated in terms of facilities and services, as well as funds) of maintaining U.S. troops in Korea.

Since 1978, Korean and U.S. forces (including some from outside Korea) have conducted an annual spring exercise called "Team Spirit," in which the combined forces of up to 118,000 men carry out maneuvers. The North Korean government has continuously regarded such exercises as provocations and has denounced them, but the South and the United States have insisted that they represent a deterrent to North Korean action.

If conventional warfare on the peninsula has been quiescent since the 1953 armistice, unconventional warfare has ebbed and flowed. In 1961, Kim Il Sung called for a Marxist-Leninist party in the South, and in 1964 an underground Revolutionary Party for Reunification ostensibly was formed there. It followed the North Korean party line. Northern infiltration along the DMZ and by ship along the whole South Korean coast was in various periods widespread, and underground spy networks existed. There were hundreds of incidents, internal and external, over these years. The most blatant demonstration of infiltration was the attempted assassination of President Park in January 1968, when a North Korean team got within a short distance of the presidential mansion. Gunshots aimed at President Park in 1974 killed his wife; two U.S. soldiers were axe murdered along the DMZ; a number of tunnels have been dug by the North under the DMZ with the seeming intent of infiltrating troops through them; and, in addition, just before the Asian Games in 1986, there was a bombing at the Seoul airport. Outside of Korea, the most dramatic event was the Rangoon bombing of 1983 that missed President Chun but killed seventeen Koreans and four Burmese. In January 1968, the U.S. intelligence ship, the *Pueblo*, was seized by the North in international waters; and in October 1969, a U.S. reconnaissance EC-121 aircraft was shot down along the North Korean border.

In 1988, Korea can produce about 70 percent of its military needs, including (under license) some tanks, F-5E fighter aircraft, and various helicopters. Perhaps the greatest U.S. contribution has not been in hardware, as important as this assistance may have been, but in military training, with the resultant influence on tactics, strategy, and policies (see Table 9.2). Through 1984, the United States had trained 35,539 Korean officers. It continues to assist in such training and in fiscal year 1985 allocated almost $2 million for the training of 286 officers. Military training, however, has no necessary influence on political practices. In 1986, Korea spent approximately $1.3 billion to purchase foreign military equipment, of which $1.05 billion was for equipment procured from the United States.

TABLE 9.2
U.S. Military Assistance to Korea (totals for fiscal years 1950-84)

	(millions of dollars)
Military Assistance Program (excluding training)	5,400
Military Assistance Program (excess defense articles delivered, including acquisition costs)	663.7
International Military Education and Training Program (students trained: 35,539)	163.2
Foreign Military Sales:	
agreements	4,300
delivered	2,600
FY1985	301
FY1986	652
FY1987	none

Source: U.S. Department of Defense, Foreign Military Sales, Foreign Military Construction Sales, and Military Assistance Facts as of September 30, 1984.

The United States has become increasingly concerned with the Soviet military buildup in the region, as well as heightened Soviet influence in North Korea since 1984, when the Soviets began providing more advanced military technology in return for overflight and port visitation rights. The United States is also suspicious of Soviet use of the Vietnamese port of Cam Rahn Bay.

The U.S. military commitment seems secure in the face of a mercurial North Korea and its uncertain behavior toward the South, as such postures may be affected by internal North Korean power changes. A change in North Korean leadership and a lessening of bellicosity and more Soviet attempts at conciliation in the area, if accompanied by a major worsening of political conditions in the South and continuing trade tensions, might prompt U.S. congressional concern of legislation for troop reductions. Conversely, a more belligerent North Korean stance could have the dual effect of encouraging repression in the South and increasing U.S. involvement. Under either circumstance, the basic security commitment would likely remain. Whatever the scenario, the Korean military will remain a vital, pervasive force in Korean society for the forseeable future, and the increasingly delicate relationship with the United States will slowly evolve into one more suitable to meet new needs in the region.

10

The Economic Development of Korea: 1953–1986

"Increase production and export"
"Build the nation on exports"

—National slogans of
President Park Chung Hee

The growth of the Korean economy since independence and after the vast destruction caused by the Korean War is the most remarkable instance of national economic developmental success in the contemporary world. Even Japan's reemergence as an economic superpower is of a different magnitude, and less surprising, for Japanese economic progress and modernization predates this contemporary period and, indeed, this century.

Void of natural resources, Korea has created an economy, if not yet a political system, vibrant with internal hope—an example to which other nations now aspire. From the dark nadir of 1953, progress of this magnitude was virtually unthinkable; few Koreans radiated self-confidence; few foreigners realized Korea's potential. There were valid reasons for pessimism. South Korea suffered perhaps a million casualties and damage estimated at more than $2 billion during the Korean War. Per capita income for 1953 was only $67, lower than before the war and one of the lowest in the world (see Table 10.1). Some 40 percent of all structures in the nation had been destroyed or damaged, as was two-thirds of industry. Agricultural production was 27 percent below that of prewar years; without help, many in Korea would have starved.

There was in Korea, moreover, a sense of despair and hopelessness, as well as a "mendicant mentality," a reliance on foreign patrons, especially the United States, for military, economic, and political support. Korea was at that time a U.S. client state. Aside from its participation in the UN Command, essentially managed by the United States, it was

TABLE 10.1
Per Capita and Total GNP, 1953-1990

(current dollars)		
	Per capita GNP	Total GNP (billion dollars)
1953	67	n/a
1960	94	n/a
1965	114	3.7 (66)
1970	248	8.0
1975	590	20.9
1980	1,589	60.3
1981	1,719	66.2
1982	1,773	69.3
1983	1,914	76.0
1984	2,044	80.6
1985	2,032	87.0
1986	2,296	95.1
1987	2,813	118.0
1989	3,065 (estimated)	139.1 (estimated)
1990	3,396 "	155.9 "
(Per capita income is estimated to have been about $50 in 1948.)		

Source: Economic Planning Board, various publications.

virtually isolated from the rest of the world. Its modest diplomatic relations with other nations, in which it was in direct competition with North Korea, were perfunctory, its trade nonexistent. Formal relations with Japan were anathema to Syngman Rhee.

In the Yi Dynasty, reliance on a great power had been termed *sadae juŭi*, literally (and positively) the philosophy of serving the great; that is, hierarchy operated in international affairs as well as in government and in the family. At that time, the term referred to relations with China. In a pejorative sense, as the term has been used more recently, such reliance is considered toadyism. In modern times, as the attitude toward reliance changed, and as Korean nationalism grew, the term was resurrected and used to characterize relations with the United States.

The influence of the United States in the early period of the republic was dominant in many spheres, yet anomalously it was limited in others, such as the distribution of power. Still, Korea had to rely on U.S. foods and funds, weapons and training, and economic and diplomatic advice, not all of which were necessarily sound or suited to Korean requirements or potential, for few Americans knew much about Korea. Not only did the U.S. public sector respond to self-evident Korean needs, but from private and voluntary organizations worldwide, mainly from the United States, came an outpouring of materiel and goodwill. All types of assistance at that time were essential to the survival of the state. Sometimes these resources were used with cynicism both by the Korean government, which could manipulate exchange rates and assistance for its own political ends and for the personal rewards of its key staff, and by the private sector. It was an era when managing an orphanage, of which there were necessarily an abundance, could be a lucrative business.

There was cynicism in the United States as well. The Korean War had not been popular, although disaffection with it never reached the intensity that disaffection with the U.S. involvement in Vietnam did. Evidence of Korean political corruption was manifest (and later became evident in the United States in the 1970s as Koreagate); official U.S. studies indicated that assistance was not used as wisely as was desirable. Put bluntly, some called Korea a "rat hole" down which funds were endlessly poured without effect. Efforts to cut the foreign-aid budget proliferated. Korea was perceived to have been too great a drain on the United States for too long with too little result.

The economic transformation of Korea has been so spectacular that much of this distressful past is forgotten or ignored. Korea is now regarded as an economic model to be emulated by other nations. As such, it is intensively and extensively studied. Academic articles and theses have mushroomed; policymakers in Korea and abroad have credited various reasons for this progress; donor agencies—multilateral and bilateral—have invoked the Korean experience to show the success of foreign aid to demonstrate their own efficacy; Korean regimes have used the economic success to support their political legitimacy; and the popular press has spouted simplistic explanations for such dramatic changes.

Such intense, diverse, and continuing interest has spawned development myths. The spectrum of these myths encompasses explanations ranging from revolutionary red on the Left to imperial purple on the Right. Growth has variously been attributed to foreign aid or its absence; the vitality of the private sector or the efficiency of the public sector; sound economic policies or excellent implementation; exploitation of Korean labor or its productivity; education, export promotion, authoritarian rule, the Confucian or post-Confucian society; and to a host of other causes.

As with most myths, these assertions contain elements of truth but tend to be obscured—by a lack of balance, comparative perspective, or understanding of the importance of sequential and parallel timing; or by inadequate comprehension of the complexities and interrelationships of these factors within the Korean societal fabric. To understand the reasons for Korean growth, it is important not only to estimate the strengths and fragilities of the Korean economic system—thus, more accurately to predict its future—but also to analyze Korea's relevance as an economic development model. The startling economic progress of Korea cannot and should not be denied or underestimated, but whether

Korea is sui generis or a generic development model, or what elements of the Korean development experience are transferable or adaptable, are important contemporary policy issues often only loosely considered.

Economic development must first be defined. As used here, it refers to substantive and sustained increases in aggregate economic indicators as well as to improved equity. These are also the ostensible goals of many bilateral and multilateral donors. Growth is the expansion of gross national product in real terms in the aggregate and on a per capita basis. It also subsumes increases in the productivity of land, labor, and capital; mobilization of savings for investment; and the effective allocation of these resources. Growth is also concerned with increases in the rates and types of technological change, the capacity of the state to generate foreign exchange, and the volume and changes in the composition and direction of trade.

Equity is more culture-specific. It disaggregates growth. Equity in developmental terms may be defined as participation in and shared access to the resources, benefits, decisions, and costs associated with the development process in economic, social, and cultural spheres and the potential mobility to partake of social and economic change. Equity is, thus, not limited to income distribution, which it subsumes, but is more akin to an admittedly ill defined—or perhaps more accurately stated, culturally definable—concept of social and economic fairness.

To understand equity is to estimate under what conditions income can be enhanced and who controls those conditions, what types of social and economic mobility or stasis exist in the society, who benefited from and who paid for progress, and what kinds and degree of access individuals have to the social services generally included under the rubric of basic human needs. Equity involves access to the market, as well as to services. The concept disaggregates growth not only at the family level but at the level of its individual components, for development may affect differently male and female, adult and child. The effects of development may also differ by region, class, and urban or rural location. In many societies, ethnicity could be a critical variable, although in the Korean instance it is not relevant.

The economic development of the Republic of Korea following the Korean War may be somewhat arbitrarily classified by political eras, as critical economic policies received different emphases under each regime. Thus, this discussion is divided into three parts: import substitution and foreign-aid maximization under the First and Second Republics (Syngman Rhee and Chang Myon); Park Chung Hee and rapid export growth (the Third and Fourth Republics); and Chun Doo Hwan and the Fifth Republic.

IMPORT SUBSTITUTION AND FOREIGN-AID MAXIMIZATION, 1953–1960

The Rhee era was marked by a poor record of growth, a virtual absence of economic planning, an intense effort to manipulate the foreign-aid program on which Korea relied, rapid inflation, and unrealistic multiple exchange rates that deflected entrepreneurial talents from production and exports, turning them toward speculation. It was also the era of an overall import-substitution policy, which restricted imports and protected and perpetuated many fledgling and uncompetitive Korean industries.

The causes for a lack of sustained growth during this period were not only the result of trauma brought about by wartime devastation (North Korea, which had suffered even more damage, grew faster in those years). Syngman Rhee's political legitimacy, for the period in which he had any, rested on his anticolonial—later, the anti–North Korean—struggle. Economic development was of secondary importance as long as he could rely on U.S. assistance, the arguments for and quantity of which he manipulated with considerable dexterity, playing off one U.S. agency against another. Rhee also did not want overall economic planning, because he unrealistically looked forward to the time when the whole peninsula would be united under his leadership, when the heavy industry of the North would complement the light industry and agriculture of the South. He avoided consideration of industrial formation that might be competitive with a unified Korea. Immediately following the war, maximization of U.S. assistance was critical to his survival as leader and to Korea's survival.

U.S. aid was massive. It provided more than one-third of the total Korean government budget, about 85 percent of imports, and 75 percent of total fixed capital formation, as well as 8 percent of GNP. The last figure might have doubled had the calculations been based on a realistic exchange rate, but such rates were multiple and were manipulated to maximize such support, not encourage growth. In addition, constantly undulating black market exchange rates were more realistic indicators of the value of the limited goods and services available.

Yet, Koreans have charged the United States, as the primary donor during this period, with neglecting to help build up the industrial infrastructure, while instead supplying consumption goods (such as food and tobacco) and raw materials (such as cotton) for existing Korean light industrial plants; the sales from all such imports helped support the Korean treasury. The charge is correct, as investment goods were less than 14 percent of all imports under the aid program from 1953 to 1961; yet, the record shows that even those industries assisted were plagued by systemic problems based on favoritism and rewards outside of economic efficiency. More of such assistance probably would not have substantially aided productivity.

To ensure coordination, a joint Korean and U.S. economic planning commission was established during the Korean War to deal with economic desiderata. Although the two nations were allied in security, they often reacted as enemies on questions of economic policy, such as stabilization. This period was characterized by tension and hostility.

In spite of critical and extensive assistance from the United States, and the virtual identification of the two nations in foreign eyes, there seemed to be little agreement between the two governments on anything beyond the survival of the Korean state. Arguments about the level of foreign aid were epidemic, with the Koreans attempting to expand the government's role without internal resource mobilization, while the United States sought to ensure fiscal responsibility and stability, as well as to limit its own expenditures within the overall priority of maintaining an effective military and security establishment. Economic development was not the primary objective of either party.

Syngman Rhee maintained autocratic authority over much of the economy, demanding personal control over such issues as the exchange rate, relations with Japan, and foreign assistance. Rhee wanted more industrial support, but the United States suspected it might be used for political purposes. Yet, excess industrial capacity was created that could not effectively be exploited under the political institutions that Rhee manipulated. Rhee did not want too much assistance in agriculture, which he feared might invigorate his political opposition, which had a rural base in the southwest. Rhee (and Park, for the first decade of Park's rule) pauperized the rural sector by keeping producer prices, especially for rice, low—often below the costs of production. Rhee relied instead on U.S. PL-480 food assistance to bridge the gap and keep the urban population quiescent. This era, in sum, was one in which foreign assistance was essential to the survival of the state—but it was poorly used, planned without imagination and for short-term effects, and ineffectively administered.

There were institutions within the Korean government even then that were economically rational and which attempted to make sense out of a situation that was essentially nondevelopmental. These included the Ministry of Reconstruction and nascent planning and economic units, which had well-trained staff (but rarely employed on critical issues) and with whom U.S. advisors worked.

Although the era may accurately be called one of import substitution, for the overriding industrial issue was the balance of payments and the need to cut imports by producing more, export promotion was not completely ignored. It was, however, far easier to exploit political contacts in the use of imports or to speculate on exchange rates than to produce. But some progress did occur. Agricultural growth averaged 4.1 percent (high by worldwide standards), although rice production remained relatively constant. Industry grew, even if it was inefficient. The population was educated, and universities were upgraded. Workers received modern, specialized training in skills needed for development. To claim, however, that such economic aid was "successful" because a later regime, under substantially different economic motivation, policies, and incentives, effectively built upon and used some of the fruits of previous assistance is somewhat disingenuous. There was modest economic progress under Rhee, who built upon and expanded infrastructure created during the Japanese colonial period for Japan's purposes. But to take advantage of the potential latent in the society, what was required was different political leadership, more productive economic policies that encouraged fiscal stability and released indigenous entrepreneurial talent, and a new relationship with the private sector, one demanding performance and not simply political loyalty.

The period of the Second Republic (1960–1961), from the overthrow of Syngman Rhee by the student revolution to the coup of Park Chung Hee, was an economic limbo. The release of pent-up tensions and frustrations resulted in strikes and demonstrations that disrupted the economy and effectively prevented anything more than regime maintenance. There were no changes in economic planning or progress of a magnitude reflecting the political revolution that had occurred.

The first, but abortive, effort at economic planning started three months before Rhee's overthrow. It was resurrected under Chang and then by the Park government as its first economic plan. The plan was essentially import substitution in focus, with exports largely devoted to traditional primary products. The political institutions were not in place, nor was political will sufficiently evident to encourage the economy to perform.

PARK CHUNG HEE AND RAPID EXPORT GROWTH, 1961–1979

The motivations for and the early strategy of Park Chung Hee's determined economic drive are a complex of internal needs coupled with external threats and perceived dangers. Although it is not uncommon to charcterize an era by its leader, in the case of Korean economic growth under Park the portrayal is particularly apt. Park personally led the drive for exports and then for heavy and defense industries; met regularly with the economic leadership of both the public and private sectors to review achievement of planned targets; ensured that economic technocrats were employed, insulated from external pressures, and allowed to function; and then, when he became convinced that it was necessary to concentrate on the agricultural community, used exactly the same methods for that sector. Korea during the Park Chung Hee period illustrates the salient importance of political leadership in economic policy formulation and implementation, as the Syngman Rhee era demonstrates that lack of such leadership can be a major factor in economic malaise.

Park initially had an overwhelming problem. He was politically suspect on several grounds and had no leadership legitimacy in the Korean social order. He lacked the anticolonial credentials of Rhee, having been in the Japanese army. He had no *yangban* status, and the military at that time still suffered from a stigma established more than two millennia ago by the Chinese Confucian literati and later imported into Korea. Barring a war he could win with North Korea, his only possible claim to legitimacy was through economic progress, an end to which he devoted himself with intense energy and drive.

His internal needs reinforced his external requirements. The United States, toward the close of the Rhee period, had warned Korea that its economic assistance would decrease. Initially, Washington did not support Park, who was suspect on four grounds: He had been involved in but later pardoned for participation in the communist-inspired Yosu-Sunch'on uprising of 1948, and his political loyalties seemed questionable; he had overthrown a democratically elected government of which the United States approved; he engaged in economic measures, such as an ill-conceived currency reform and monetary expansion, without the normal consultations with Washington; and he was at first intransigent in his opposition to holding elections and was only forced to do so in 1963 when the United States threatened to terminate economic support. Korean-U.S. relations were severely strained. Park's need for internal and external legitimacy eventually coalesced into a strategy calling for priority in economic development but less economic reliance on the United States, to be achieved through a policy of diversification of foreign assistance and export promotion. Park expected continuing U.S. security support but knew that a decrease in economic dependency was inevitable in any case.

After the Park government had assumed its mufti role, elections were called, and relations with Washington improved, the U.S. posture became supportive, backing Park's economic policy through encouraging exports, continued economic assistance for economic stabilization, and providing technical assistance for economic planning and export promotion. In addition, the United States publicly encouraged and approved of Korean normalization of relations with Japan (U.S.-supported negotiations between Syngman Rhee and the Japanese had proved abortive) and engaged in a campaign to instill confidence in the Korean government, and in the public, that Korea could succeed in its plans. The Park program suited the United States, which wished to loosen the economic strings of the donor-recipient relationship while keeping the military and security ties tight. It is ironic that those ties became closer as the aid relationship became marginal and as trade became paramount. Now, a new set of economic tensions exist between Korea and the United States.

As Park formulated and began to implement his policies and apply his personal attention to those ends, he created the means through which to achieve his goals, means that many nations hoping to emulate Korea lack. There was a reservoir of economic talent; some industrial infrastructure; an indigenous business community lacking political power but ready to be mobilized (and to which Park owed no political debts); and, especially important, a strong bureaucratic capacity for effective implementation of any proposed policies.

Following the coup, as part of his consolidation of political power, Park had concentrated all political, economic, and social forces under his command. Owing nothing to the previous regime and power elite, he could mold these forces to his will. He attempted to control both internal and external sources of information. He had nationalized all banks; formed the Economic Planning Board, combining both planning and budgeting in one office headed by the deputy prime minister; gave the Ministry of Finance control over the central bank; consolidated the cooperatives and the agricultural bank; formed the Federation of Korean Industries and installed his hand-picked leadership; and merged agricultural research and extension services (known in Korean as "guidance," a more realistic term there).

Park forced the formation of a single, umbrella labor union and then controlled it through the KCIA, which he also formed (one head of which became prime minister; another later assassinated him). He formed and manipulated the leadership of a variety of social and professional organizations, including those of teachers, cultural leaders, doctors, pharmacists, certified public accountants, newspaper owners, and newspaper editors. He eliminated elected local government, substituting instead a highly centralized, appointed command system emanating from the Ministry of Home Affairs—which also controlled the police—through the province, to the county (kun), and down to the township (myŏn). The provincial governors were often former high military officers, reinforcing the tautness of the command structure and its timely response to central directives. Few governments in the world had so effective, pervasive, and controlled a hierarchical system reaching down so far into the society, one that was augmented by Korean social patterns.

Diversification of foreign assistance, allowing the United States to assume a less quantitative role, as both Park and the U.S. Congress wanted, was high on Park's agenda. The first World Bank loan to Korea (for railroads) was signed in 1962, the same year that the Federal Republic of Germany began its assistance. Of primary importance, however, in ways that are sometimes difficult for Koreans to admit, was the role of Japan in that process. In 1965, maneuvering with dubious legality, the government pushed normalization of relations with Japan through a reluctant Korean National Assembly. Legislative apprehensions about acceding to government pressures reflected widespread public concern about Japan, concern that was articulated through massive student demonstrations. These demonstrations, which perhaps also reflected questions about the regime's legitimacy, resulted in the imposition of martial law. The treaty with Japan declared invalid the annexation of Korea and included recognition of the Republic of Korea (in accordance with the 1948 UN resolution) as the only legitimate government in its territory, but not over the whole peninsula. Japan, however, agreed not to establish formal relations with the North.

Japanese normalization initially brought with it $800 million in grants, loans, and commercial credits over a ten-year period and was the precursor of an investment program that totaled some $1.4 billion by 1985,[1] or more than half of the $2.65 billion in foreign investment in Korea (the United States had $771 million invested there, excluding foreign subsidiaries of international firms). Total Japanese economic assistance through 1982 reached $4.4 billion, of which $1.9 billion was in loans, grants, and technical assistance.

Japan also supplied technology that was to be critical for Korean growth; one-third of all sales and royalties paid on technology came from Japan. Japan also became the most important market after the United States for Korean products ($5.4 billion in 1986), and Korea became a major market for Japanese goods ($10.9 billion in 1986), especially industrial components that were later incorporated into Korean export products. Japan not only was Korea's largest importer but was also an unacknowledged model for various economic policies that were later followed by the Korean government. In the first few years after normalization, Japanese capital contributed 10 percent of gross domestic capital formation in Korea.

Both the colonial era and fiscal reality intensified the Japanese economic repenetration of Korea. Japan needed to move out of labor-intensive industries, which was what Korea (with excess, low-paid labor) required at that time, as well as out of pollution-intense manufacturing. The proximity of Japan reduced shipping costs and travel of industrial and technical assistance personnel and of management as well. The

Television factory workers

Automobile factory assembly line (Korea produced about 800,000 vehicles in 1987)

colonial residue meant that all educated Koreans over forty could speak and read Japanese (even if many preferred for nationalistic reasons to negotiate in English, a neutral language), as they had gone to primary school in Korea but had been taught in Japanese, and many of the elite had, in addition, been educated at Japanese universities. Trade with Japan was critical. Korea's total deficit with Japan between 1965 and 1985 was $31.4 billion, or 81.6 percent of Korea's total trade deficit during that period.

If normalization of relations with Japan was a critical component in the Park program, the Vietnam War was a fortuitous economic bonanza for Korea. Korean participation at the request of the United States brought with it many economic benefits supportive of Korea's development plans, in addition to enabling the Korean military to train two combat divisions. It also provided the Koreans with a real sense of pride, for if in the past they had continuously been on the receiving end of foreign largesse, for the first time they perceived themselves as donors rather than recipients of aid. As many Koreans openly admitted, as Japanese development had been spurred by the Korean War, so would Korea grow because of Vietnam.

It may never be possible to calculate accurately the amounts of foreign exchange from all sources, formal and informal, earned by the Koreans as a result of the Vietnam War and from offshore procurement as well. Estimates range from $660 to $926 million. The total foreign exchange accruing to Korea from normalization of relations with Japan and the Vietnam War has been estimated at one-third to one-half of all such funds during the period 1965–1973. Earnings from Vietnam alone have been calculated as contributing about 20 percent of foreign-exchange holdings and between 1.5 and 4.4 percent of GNP between 1965 and 1970.

The boost to Park's program from these foreign involvements was calculated and important, but equally relevant was the worldwide re-ceptivity to an export drive in the 1960s. The first oil crisis had not yet disrupted the world economy (and Korea was utterly dependent on oil imports), and there was considerably less protectionist sentiment in the industrialized world than there would be two decades later. It is fortuitous that Korea embarked on its export role at the most advantageous time. Other nations that have hoped to emulate Korea have started under much more unfavorable international conditions.

Whether Korea could have succeeded in its export promotion campaign without Japanese involvement or without the foreign exchange generated through the Vietnam War is still debated, as is the question of whether Korea had earlier essentially set in motion the export mechanisms. Prior to normalization, however, Korean determination was clear, policies were in place, and methods for implementation established. Korea could certainly not have proceeded so far so quickly without Japanese involvement, and funds from Vietnam provided an economic cushion but not (as in some other countries that had foreign-exchange bonanzas) a disincentive to growth. Both Japan and the Vietnam War provided needed capital and technology (and in the case of Vietnam, training for a construction industry that in 1981 reached $13.7 billion in the value of contracts signed) that accelerated Korean growth. Korea probably could have succeeded in its export drive even without the formal Japanese normalization; there would have been extensive trade, and perhaps some investment without it, just as Korea now trades with the People's Republic of China, with which it has no diplomatic relations. Korean residents in Japan provide a significant portion of Japanese investment in Korea. Vietnam was economically important but not critical to Korean plans at that time.

South Korea was not bound by economic ideologies that set objectives or priorities, in contrast to North Korea or other states. It could utilize the public or the private sector and intervene or influence industries or fields in accordance with its perceived national interests. Throughout Park's rule, this flexibility of Korean economic planning policies—which were quickly adjusted to new circumstances or perceived failures untrammeled by ideological considerations from the Right or the Left—contrasted sharply with the rigorous enforcement of such policies and the rigidity of the political system.

The president met monthly with business and government leaders, during which export targets were discussed and bureaucratic impediments to achieving those targets summarily removed. Rewards of public recognition were provided to successful firms, and economic incentives promulgated; conversely, failure resulted in economic or bureaucratic sanctions. If government-designated priority industries met their export targets, the government would make institutional credit available on most favorable terms (sometimes negative real interest rates), would authorize liberal "wastage allowances" that enabled exporters informally to syphon off export-designated goods to the lucrative local market, and would allow imports.

Because the government had a complete monopoly on all institutional credit, firms that failed to fulfill government-set objectives could lose access to bank credit, forcing them to seek credit on the curb, or informal, market at double or more the interest rates and, thus, making them uncompetitive. The government intervened to influence, sometimes to control, the private sector. It could force firms to fire or hire key executives, require companies to merge or to move from family to public ownership, and stress critical industries. The government built up a special Korean phenomenon, the *chaebŏl*.

The *chaebŏl* ("conglomerates," similar to the Japanese *zaibatsu*) were in essence the creation of the Park regime; their origins may be traced to a Japanese model. Although a variety of these corporate entities predate the Park era, and some individual entrepreneurs got their start under the Japanese occupation, during the Park regime they became the chosen instruments of industrialization and the export drive. They owed their expansion to Park's use of them to achieve national economic goals. Because the *chaebŏl* were in debt to government-sponsored or approved institutions for more than four times the value of their equity assets (much higher than the debt of average Korean concerns and far higher than that of most comparable firms in other countries), state direction and intervention, culturally reinforced by traditional Korean and Confucian concepts of state power, were pronounced. The *chaebŏl* were also relatively efficient; compared to smaller firms, they had better marketing facilities worldwide and more-skilled, higher-paid workers.

Because of a limit on the availability of institutional credit, however, these firms soon virtually controlled the modern sector of the economy. They were growing at rates far in excess of the growth rate of the national economy: in 1975–1980, at 42.7 percent in value added, compared to GNP growth of 24.5 percent; during 1980–1983, at 32 percent, compared to 16.2 percent of manufacturing shipments. In 1983, three firms' sales shares in manufacturing markets totaled 62 percent. In the Park era, three circumstances distinguished the *chaebŏl* from the Japanese *zaibatsu:* the more domineering, less consensual, role of the Korean government; the maintenance of family control over the major *chaebŏl;* and their lack of independent access at that time to banks (although the *chaebŏl* did control some insurance companies).

It is sometimes assumed that a liberalization of an export economy implies internal liberalization of imports. This is not necessarily true and was not true in the Korean case. As exports rose, imports rose faster, leaving Korea until 1986 with a negative trade balance. These imports, however, were geared to the supply of components for finished export goods, energy, machines, and raw material for special export processing zones. In 1981, 23.9 percent of imports were for export use; by 1986, the rate was 40.3 percent. Food and feed grains were also important, as was oil, absent in Korea. High tariffs were constructed around nascent Korean industries to protect them from competing imports. Korea became a mercantile economy, one that was devoted to exports but restricted imports as well.

Foreign investment in Korea was virtually nonexistent before 1962, when a new law to encourage it was enacted. Continuous efforts since that date have resulted in cumulative investments of more than $2.6 billion—a very small amount given the size of the Korean economy (a GNP in 1987 of $115 billion) and the amounts that foreign firms have invested in other nations. As might be expected, about half of the investment has come from Japan (or Koreans resident in Japan, such as the Lotte group). U.S. economic investment has been surprisingly far less than U.S. security and political interests might imply. Both economic and political factors were responsible: Korean government restrictions and economic uncertainties because of business cycles, constant international tension along the Demilitarized Zone, and fear of internal political unrest or violence.

The importance of foreign investments in the 1980s was not in the funding generated, for such funding was marginal given Korea's good credit rating and capacity to borrow commercially. Nor was technology the only critical concern, although perhaps one-third of all new technology introduced into Korea came from such investment. The bulk of technology came from trade. (Koreans have relied on foreign buyers for product-design technology, but they have been innovative in production, or process, technology.) Such foreign investments are important for the security they provide to the state as a whole; they may be viewed as the economic equivalent of the U.S. troop tripwire along the DMZ. They may guarantee, in Korean eyes, foreign intervention to protect the republic should North Korea ever attack. They are also evidence of world acceptance of Korea and thus contribute to the government's political legitimacy.

Although it is essentially correct to characterize the Park period as one of export promotion, there is no necessary Manichean dualism inherent in the dichotomy between export promotion and import substitution. At the same time as exports were an obsession, major efforts were directed at import substitution for two products—arms and rice. (Rice production will be discussed in the next section.) Following the formulation of the Nixon Doctrine calling for the withdrawal of U.S. troops from Vietnam and the shock of improved U.S. relations with the People's Republic of China in 1972, the Park government felt that it could no longer rely completely on the United States for its supply of sophisticated arms for its defense. It also believed that if it could manufacture arms, it could also export them. The government perhaps did not fully appreciate the complexity associated with the granting of required export licenses for such trade, nor that the United States was unlikely to grant licenses for exports that would undercut the U.S. market.

In the mid-1970s, in an effort to become more self-reliant militarily, the state under President Park's personal direction began to commit extensive funds to develop heavy, chemical, and defense industries. This major policy decision and the intensity with which it was pushed was, at least for a decade, perhaps the single most critical economic policy mistake since 1961. Implementation required extensive borrowing from abroad, and it created excess industrial capacity that could not be gainfully used at that time. Financial institutions were saddled with debts at impossibly low interest rates (in some cases at negative real interest) for which there was little or no economic return. Excessive inflation returned, and by March 1979, the Korean government and the president personally recognized the need for a painful economic stabilization program in these industries and in other government expenditures. In October 1979, however, before this program could be implemented, Park was assassinated, causing further economic dislocation and necessitating major structural adjustment in the economy, for the subsidies to heavy industry and to agriculture could not be sustained. There were also errors in the process. By attempting so much so quickly, the government created skilled labor shortages, thus driving up wages. Also, the chemical industries were dependent on Middle East oil, financed by Korean construction contracts there, which declined precipitously when oil prices receded in the early 1980s.

There were also systemic problems in the Korean economy. Protectionism was high (and tariffs increased in the heavy and chemical industries); technology transfer was proceeding too slowly; the internal market was comparatively small for the type of products produced, and purchasing power was unequally distributed; and Korea was beginning to experience diminishing labor advantages as wages rose because of labor shortages. Much of Korean skilled labor was working in the Middle East generating foreign exchange and protecting Korean sources of oil. In addition, international oil prices were having a severe impact on the economy.

It is significant, however, that Park chose the private sector for much of this economic expansion, when he might have given the assignment to the efficient public sector. Korea was able to overcome these problems during the Chun period, assisted by stringent structural adjustment measures, a drop in oil prices, and a decline in international interest rates.

The legacy of Park's policy is now less negative. Although Korean defense industries operate at some 40 percent of capacity and the decision to develop heavy industry markedly increased Korea's international debt, this massive push enabled the country to produce an array of automobiles for export, operate the most efficient steelmill in the world, and in general increased Korean competitiveness on world markets. Overall, this policy may eventually be reassessed as positive, in spite of the negative economic consequences in its first decade.

CHUN DOO HWAN AND THE FIFTH REPUBLIC, 1980–1988

The intellectual and social ferment that marked Park's assassination in 1979 was reminiscent of that following the overthrow of Syngman Rhee. Like each regime since Syngman Rhee, the Chun government publicly dedicated itself to "social purification," the elimination of the corrupt, and the effort to retrieve for the state (perhaps also for the new political process) the ill-gotten gains of unscrupulous leaders in the business community or their unpaid taxes.

Political uncertainly was exacerbated by economic trauma. Not only was there an urgent need for structural adjustment in the economy because of the heavy industry policies, but agriculture was in disarray because of the rice failure. In 1980, for the first time since the Korean War, there was economic decline. The GNP dropped by 5.2 percent.

The government attributed the failure of the rice crop to cold weather. Although an unseasonable cold spell did hit Korea before the harvest, the weather was merely the precipitating element in a complex set of political decisions that pushed a particular variety of rice, t'ongil ("unification," symbolically a potent Korean political designation), beyond its known limits. To achieve quickly the political goal of rice self-sufficiency—a target of both Park and Chun—the government encouraged growth of this variety beyond its optimum quantity (as too great a spread of the same variety increases the likelihood of blast, a fungus disease) and in unsuitable areas. The rice crop failure, the most important error in an otherwise successful, if highly *dirigiste*, rural development effort, may be attributed to bureaucratic success: The wrong decision was pushed effectively through a responsive bureaucracy, beyond its inherent bounds, resulting in failure.

The Chun government confronted a difficult first year. Unpopular because he had overthrown a lilberalizing regime, but buoyed by his invitation to the White House before his election under the new constitution, President Chun faced a variety of difficulties: the crisis of Kwangju; financial scandals, including those involving his wife's relations; and economic adjustment as a consequence of higher oil prices and a world recession that effectively lowered the Korean standard of living by some 10 percent. Rigorous new labor legislation in 1980 almost halved labor union membership in the Federation of Korean Trade Unions, the umbrella organization. The opposition demanded more government support for small and medium industry and subjected the *chaebŏl* to severe criticism for their exploitative economic control.

To finance growth and adjustment, and to maintain full employment, major foreign borrowing was required. The debt burden for Korea reached $46 billion in the mid-1980s, the fourth largest debt among developing

Transplanting rice mechanically

Transplanting rice by hand

TABLE 10.2
External Public Debt, 1965-1986

Year	Debt (million dollars)	Debt as a % of GNP	Debt as a % of Exports	Debt Service as a % of Exports
1965	0.2	--	--	--
1966	3.3	10.7	156.6	3.2
1970	2.3	27.7	254.5	21.0
1975	8.5	40.6	168.8	12.1
1977	12.6	34.5	125.9	13.9
1978	14.9	28.9	116.6	16.3
1979	20.5	33.1	138.0	16.0
1980	27.4	44.6	222.5	18.5
1981	32.5	48.4	156.9	20.1
1982	37.3	52.4	177.6	20.6
1983	40.4	53.1	174.0	18.8
1984	43.1	52.3	163.5	20.4
1985	46.8	55.9	176.9	21.7
1986	44.5	46.8	131.3	22.7
1987	35.6	30.0	75.3	n.a.

Sources: Economic Planning Board/ Ministry of Finance/ World Bank,
various publications.

TABLE 10.3
Trade Account Balances of Korea, U.S., and Japan, 1979-1986

Year	Korea Overall	Korea Bilateral w/Japan	Korea Bilateral w/U.S.	Japan Overall	U.S. Overall
1979	-4.9	-3.3	-0.2	1.7	-27.5
1980	-4.3	-2.8	-0.3	2.1	-25.5
1981	-3.6	-2.9	-0.5	20.0	-28.0
1982	-2.6	-2.0	0.2	18.1	-36.5
1983	-1.8	-2.8	1.9	31.5	-67.3
1984	-1.0	-3.0	3.6	44.3	-112.5
1985	0.0	-3.0	4.3	56.0	-112.1
1986	4.2	-5.4	7.3	92.8	-148.1
1987	6.3	-5.2	9.6	n.a.	n.a.

Sources: Economic Planning Board, Major Statistics of Foreign
Economy, 1986; Korea Development Institute, Major Indicators of
Korean Economy, May 20, 1987.

nations, and larger per capita than Brazil's (see Table 10.2). Because of
Korea's export success, foreign bankers did not regard this burden as
untoward but were skeptical of higher levels. Opposition politicians,
however, severely criticized the government for mortgaging the nation
for the benefit of the *chaebŏl*. With the first current account surplus in
1986 of $4.6 billion, the government began to reduce the size of the
debt, perhaps more for political than economic reasons (see Table 10.3).

The rise in value of the Japanese *yen* against the U.S. dollar in 1985 and 1986 made Korean goods more competitive on the world market, even though a substantial percentage of some exports had essential Japanese components. Korea continued to have a major trade deficit with Japan of approximately $6 billion but had a simultaneous trade surplus with the United States of about $7 billion (see Table 10.4). Growth of Korean GNP reached 11.6 percent in 1986 and 12.5 percent in 1987, worldwide records for those years. Korea became the twelfth largest trading nation in the world and the seventh largest trading partner of the United States.

As Korean exports grew, Korea began to be seen, from a simplistic perspective and especially in the United States, as a second Japan, a nation intent on marketing industrialized exports, but which had effectively closed much of its internal markets to foreign goods and services. The Korean government vigorously denied the analogy and took a series of steps to placate foreign critics. It liberalized foreign investment regulations, especially in the service industries, which had largely remained closed to outsiders, and shortened the long list of goods requiring approval for import. Tariffs, however, were still a matter of some foreign concern, even though they were lowered, and were to be more extensively reduced in subsequent years. Although the Fifth Five-Year Plan called for greater reliance on market mechanisms, the pace of government withdrawal from the market was described as "glacial." (See Table 10.5 for an overview of all plans.) Credit provided by a liberalized banking system was still allocated according to government priorities. In addition, in 1980 the state still controlled 34 percent of the GNP.

Trade tensions had long existed between the United States and Korea, with textiles, footwear, steel, color television, and other products figuring in acerbic negotiations on dumping, subsidization, quotas, and orderly marketing agreements. In response, by the end of 1986 Korean firms had invested $212 million in U.S. plants and industries for the production of a variety of household products and had also invested in other countries, such as Bangladesh, where labor was far cheaper, and in industries such as textiles, the export of which from Korea was limited by quotas.

The growing complexity of the Korean economy also prompted many in government and in the private sector to call for less governmental interference in economic affairs. The government liberalized the banking system, ending the state's monopoly. Nonbanking financial institutions, such as insurance and credit associations, were recognized and began to play a major role in credit allocations. Banks were instructed in the

TABLE 10.4
Republic of Korea, Imports/Exports, 1960-1986
(in millions of current dollars)

	Total Imports	Total Exports	Imports from U.S.	Exports to U.S.	Imports from Japan	Exports to Japan
1960	344	33	133.8	3.6	70.4	20.2
1965	463	175	182.3	61.7	166.6	44.0
1970	1,984	835	584.8	395.2	809.3	234.3
1975	7,274	5,081	1,181.1	1,536	2,433.6	1,292.9
1980	22,292	17,505	4,890	4,606	5,857.8	3,039.4
1982	24,251	21,853	5,956	6,243	5,305.3	3,388.1
1983	26,192	24,445	6,274	8,245	6,238.4	3,403.6
1984	30,631	29,245	6,875	10,479	7,640.1	4,602.2
1985	31,136	30,283	6,489	10,754	7,560.4	4,543.4
1986	31,584	34,715	6,644	13,880	10,869.3	5,425.7
1987	41,000	47,300	8,758	18,311	13,656.6	8,436.8

	U.S. Imports as % of total	Japanese Imports as % of total
1966	35.4	41.0
1970	29.5	40.8
1975	25.9	33.5
1980	21.9	26.3
1985	20.8	24.3
1986	20.7	34.4
1987	21.4	33.3

Source: Economic Planning Board, various yearbooks.

TABLE 10.5
South Korean Five-Year Plans, 1962-1986
(annual percentage growth)

	First 1962-66	Second 1967-71	Third 1972-76	Fourth 1977-81	Fifth 1982-86
GNP growth	7.8	9.7	10.1	5.6	5.4
Agriculture, forestry, fisheries	5.6	1.5	6.1	-0.7 [a]	4.5
Manufacturing	15.0	21.8	18.7	9.4	11.2
Social/other services	8.4	12.6	8.4	6.0	4.7
Foreign trade					
Exports	38.6	33.8	32.7	10.5	5.0
Imports	18.7	25.8	12.6	10.3	0.7

a-Largely a result of the failure of the rice crop in 1980

Source: Derived from World Bank data.

1970s to assist smaller businesses, and a general trend toward less government interference could be discerned.

But the liberalization plans were only slowly implemented; the *chaebŏl* were buying into banks and financial institutions, effectively impeding the liberalization efforts. The government's attempt to control the role of the *chaebŏl* through legislation slowed their expansion but did not cut their role. In a period of rising Korean nationalism, U.S. pressures to liberalize both imports and institutions began to be resisted by diverse elements in the Korean government and business sector. These pressures began to contribute to heightened anti-U.S. sentiment, a trend exacerbated by public perceptions of U.S. support for increasingly unpopular Korean regimes; by a concern that the United States (through its corporate structure) was involved in suppression of Korean wages; and, most dramatically, by the issue of Kwangju.

In spite of criticism of Korea's relatively closed internal economy, the growth in the volume of exports and changes in their composition is a remarkable success story. Between 1960 and 1986, exports grew from $33 million to $34.7 billion—an average rate of about 30 percent annually. Changes in the composition of such exports is in some ways even more remarkable. In 1953, only 8 percent of the minuscule exports ($39.6 million) were manufactured goods, and these were mostly handicraft products sold to the U.S. military. By 1961, still only 13.9 percent were manufactures. By the 1980s, however, virtually all of Korean exports were manufactured products, with major shifts from light to heavy industrial goods and from labor-intensive items to products of high technological content (see Tables 10.6 and 10.7). Korean automobiles, computers, microwave ovens, and other sophisticated goods now permeate the U.S. market (see Table 10.8).

As exports have grown, so too have imports. From $316 million in 1961 (mostly as foreign aid), imports increased to $31.6 billion in 1986 (see Table 10.4). This increase was necessary, mainly because of a growing and more affluent population that demanded consumer products, but also because Korea must import much of the raw materials for the goods it exports and components it is unable to produce for other products, as well as items that it is uneconomic to make in Korea. Changing dietary patterns have also resulted in extensive wheat and feedgrain imports and a demand for more beef and chicken for the burgeoning urban population. It is uneconomic for Korea to grow wheat and corn given the limits of arable land, for patterns of rural development have profoundly changed. In 1985, Korea imported $2.8 billion in agricultural commodities (about 10 percent of all imports), including 2.9 million tons of wheat, 3 million tons of corn, and 885,000 tons of soybean products. Korea is only approximately 3 percent self-sufficient

TABLE 10.6
Structure of Merchandise Exports, 1960-1981

	(percent of total exports)	
	1960	1981
Fuels, minerals, metals	30	2
Other primary products	56	8
Textiles, clothing	8	30
Machinery, transport equip.	--	22 [a]
Other manufactures	6	38

Annual Growth of Merchandise Trade (percent)

	1960-70	1970-82
Exports	34.7	20.2
Imports	19.7	9.8

a- 35.7 percent in 1987.

Source: Economic Planning Board, various publications.

TABLE 10.7
Export Shares of Korea's Ten Largest Export Categories, 1970-1986
(percent)

	1970	1981	1986
Textiles	40.8	29.5	25.2
Electronics	3.5	10.6	19.1
Steel products	1.6	10.5	7.2
Footwear	2.1	5.0	6.1
Ships	0.0	6.7	5.2
Automobiles/parts	0.0	2.6	4.8
Machinery	1.1	2.7	3.0
Synthetic resins	1.3	2.9	2.7
Toys/dolls	0.1	1.6	2.1
Metal products	1.5	2.7	1.8
Subtotal	52.0	74.8	77.2
All exports	100.0	100.0	100.0

Source: Korean Traders Association, Export Statistics. Quoted in
   Soogil Young, "Problems of Trade Liberalization in the Republic
   of Korea," 1987.

in wheat, 4 percent in corn, and 29 percent in soybeans (see Table 10.9).

POVERTY AND GROWTH IN THE RURAL SECTOR

As Park Chung Hee began the orchestration of his export-oriented drive in the early 1960s, "spring hunger"—when winter food stocks

TABLE 10.8
Selected Korean Production Figures, 1986, 1987

1986	1987	
5,300,000	5,559,511	Black & white television sets
6,000,000	8,611,000	Color television sets
457,000	795,800	Passenger cars
35,000	57,151	Buses
86,000	106,590	Trucks
165,000	202,221	Pianos

Heavy & chemical industry output: 56% (1967, 33.2%)
Light industry output: 44% (1967, 66.8%)

Industrial Index (1980=100)
1987   227.7
1986   195.0
1975   47.6
1967   10.1

Source: Economic Planning Board, various yearbooks.

TABLE 10.9
Food Production and Imports, 1962-1985
(thousands of tons)

| | Food Production | | | | Food Imports | | |
	Rice	Barley	Wheat	Rice	Wheat	Corn	Soybeans
1962	3,015	1,113	184				
1971	3,998	1,510	205				
1976	5,215	1,755	87	176	1,857	890	119
1980	3,550	811	95	581	1,810	2,234	417
1982	5,175	749	71	269	1,940	2,814	536
1985	5,670	571	13	---	2,996	3,035	885
1986	5,607	453	6				

Source: Economic Planning Board, various yearbooks.

were depleted and the spring crops were not yet available—was common. Farm families could be seen gathering the early wild plants and grasses to provide the nutritional bridge between winter storage supplies, such as *kimch'i* (the staple Korean pickled vegetables) and spring barley. It was a traditional scene, one apparent and pervasive among the poor for centuries. The rural sector, which had greatly benefited from land reform, was still mired in poverty; the essential change was that it was now a shared, equalized state. The only marginal escape from those straits was migration to urban areas that as yet could not gainfully employ most newcomers without skills.

Since the Korean War, the rural population has been quiescent and conservative. Land reform had defused social tensions, earlier government frustration of peasant revolts and unrest had tempered overt dissent, a strong government presence had deterred opposition, and the North Korean occupation of much of the country had soured farmers on radical politics. The result was that modest, local agricultural surpluses were used as a partial subsidy of the urban sector, which was volatile and politically dangerous. During the Rhee period and for almost a decade of Park Chung Hee's rule, agricultural production expanded modestly, slightly exceeding population growth. Government intervention (through the cooperative apparatus) controlled prices through the purchase of a relatively small percentage of the rice and barley crops—the two staples— at less than production costs, calculating the imputed costs of farm labor. There were, of course, few other productive alternatives for farmers at that time.

This situation could continue for almost two decades because the United States, through the PL-480 program that supplied surplus agricultural commodities overseas, tacitly allowed the Korean administration to ignore basic reform in the countryside. The purposes of that program in Korea were manifold. The immediate aim was to provide food for the country (the program also supplied cotton for the spinning mills and tobacco, in the early period, as well). Two short-term objectives were served: The urban population was fed, and the Korean government, through sale of such products on the urban market or their use in the form of food-for-work projects for the subsistence-level rural population, was able to collect funds or complete productive projects. As resource mobilization during the Rhee period was especially poor, this source of income in the form of grants was particularly important. Throughout the life of the program, the value of such commodities totaled about $1.2 billion ($777 million between 1953 and 1971).

The program had longer-range objectives for the United States as well. In addition to supporting economic development, the program was obviously geared to assist attainment of U.S. foreign policy goals. Other objectives included the elimination of U.S. farm surpluses and the creation of future markets for U.S. produce. The program was successful from the U.S. perspective, for surpluses were lessened and markets created (given the security relationship between the two countries, markets might have been created in any case). In the longer term and from a Korean vantage point, the program could be considered detrimental to Korean rural development because it allowed the government to postpone effective action that would fundamentally improve its rural sector, enabling it instead to assist the rural sector on the margin. When the government was prompted to reform rural policies and reduce growing urban-rural income disparities, it was politics, not economics, that essentially brought about that change.

The elections of 1971, which saw Park's support in rural areas (where government had a variety of inducements and incentives to ensure compliance) badly erode in the face of Kim Dae Jung's unexpected near victory, were the essential stimulus for rethinking rural development measures. Also, Park was from a rural background and was sympathetic to farm problems. In addition, in the 1960s, PL-480, which had solely provided grants, now extended loans; although highly concessional, these nevertheless increased Korea's debt. A concerted effort for rural transformation was introduced that combined economic, social, and political incentives with a degree of implicit coercion. Technological, economic, and administrative factors coalesced to make the 1970s the most productive, prosperous period in Korean agricultural history. These efforts, which resulted in real change, were heavily subsidized by the state in much the same way it had fostered exports. President Park devoted himself to the effort, and during the last ten years of his rule his policy statements at press conferences mentioned agricultural issues more frequently than any other topic except for politics and international affairs.

If the 1970s were a period of rural prosperity, they were also a time of rural mobilization, and there are few noncommunist countries where such efforts were more comprehensive. The government plan had four elements, each of which was carefully coordinated and reinforced. These conveyed a central message: to increase production, income, and loyalty to the state. The first, and primary, oversight mechanism for rural mobilization was local government. Appointed by the central government after the coup of 1961, local government was under the strong hierarchical control of the Ministry of Home Affairs down to the level of township, the head of which was also appointed.

The hub of rural activity was the *kun*, the county, with its market town as the county seat. There, the *kunsu*, or county chief, coordinated all local activities of the government, except police, military, and intelligence functions. Reporting to the governor, the *kunsu* was responsible for achieving goals set by the center or the province. Implementation of all policies was thorough, strict, complete, and single-minded. Whether the situation involved rice production, home renovation, latrine construction, or farmer training, the *kunsu* was the nexus of rural activities, delegating some local-level functions to the appointed township officials who reported to him. He was responsible not only for what he accomplished and for reaching his targets but for what went wrong; even events such as forest fires, clearly beyond his control, could cause his dismissal. Moral responsibility for disasters or failures is normally taken by chiefs in Korean bureaucratic circles. In a sense, the *kunsu* was answerable for the well-being of his community (as interpreted by the center) much as the kings had been responsible for the fertility of their lands. Such a system limited innovation, flexibility, and the supply of needed, accurate information back to the center. It was effective, however, in terms of meeting targets (although sometimes in form only; a quota for house renovation might result in new facades on old homes). But the essence of its efficiency may lie as much in the Korean cultural milieu as in the administrative system.

The second mobilization technique involved the cooperatives under the National Agricultural Cooperative Federation, a strong link between the state and the farmers. In 1961, there were 21,042 cooperatives at the village level. They were reorganized in 1969 into 7,525 cooperatives, primarily in the townships, leaving the villages, until the *saemaŭl* movement (the final element of the rural plan), without direct government mobilization centers. A titular misnomer, cooperatives were a series of government-sponsored organizations coordinated at the provincial level, the bottom of a highly centralized command structure at the bidding of the Seoul authorities. The cooperatives had a 97 percent monopoly on institutional rural credit (the other 3 percent came from the post office) and were the government agents for the purchase of rice and barley and for the distribution of fertilizer. Productive credit for seed, fertilizer, and mechanization were all subsidized in varying degrees, as were housing loans. The National Agricultural Cooperative Federation reinforced and implemented central government policies.

The third element in rural development and control was the "guidance" system. In 1961, on the recommendation of U.S. advisors, Park had merged the offices concerned with agricultural research and extension services into an Office of Rural Development. Thus, when in the early 1970s, as rural labor costs rose, technological improvements became available—namely, the high-yielding varieties of rice that were a cross between the traditional *japonica* and the southern *indica* varieties, adequate and appropriate fertilizer, and pesticides and herbicides—the delivery mechanism for these was in place at the local level. In contrast to extension systems in many countries, in Korea the bulk of the staff was in the field. The guidance system enveloped the nation in constant cries, exhortations, and warnings about when and what to plant, how to increase production, which insects were harmful, and what fertilizers, pesticides, and herbicides to use. It was so effective, and the results so good so quickly, that hardly a farm in the nation, even in the most remote areas, went unvisited by these guidance workers.

The final element of this integrated rural control system was the *saemaŭl undong*, or "new community movement." The government had early abandoned the uneconomic village-level cooperatives, consolidating them at the *myŏn,* so *saemaŭl* moved direct government intervention back into the villages. The program was placed under the control of the Ministry of Home Affairs and in the early 1980s was headed by President Chun's younger brother (who was in 1988 charged with corruption), although it was purported to be nongovernmental. By 1986, $9.3 billion had been spent on it since its inception; of this amount, $5.5 billion came from government, the remainder from the villagers. Acting as a type of local government at the village level, the *saemaŭl* movement appointed leaders, who were often young and vigorous and were not part of the traditional village elite pattern. It set goals for material accomplishments; attempted to stress moral regeneration, loyalty to the state, and obedience to authority; acted as a type of local tax agency; and allocated labor requirements by family. There was scarcely a village that lacked an action plan, in military, flip-chart form, indicating the annual objectives for village improvement.

Begun with the distribution of surplus cement on a village basis, the program expanded to include the elimination of grass roofs and the construction of bridges and culverts, village access roads, and latrines; it has also improved farm production and animal husbandry. It implemented what may be the most extensive and effective national reforestation program in the world, one that has transformed the ecological and aesthetic rural continuum. In its later stages, it sponsored the mass building (with subsidized loans totaling $747 million) of 306,000 improved units of new, Western-style housing of dubious aesthetic qualities. It was broadened to include a rural factory movement of more than seven hundred plants. For the most part, that factory program failed, but the *saemaŭl* movement in the early 1980s was expanded to include urban factories, schools, and workplaces.

There is no question about the accomplishments of the movement as measured by such physical changes as houses "modernized," kilometers of roads or culverts built, latrines dug, or any other material measure. Virtually every village has vehicular access, every farmhouse can be reached with a rototiller. By any standard, the program, which originally involved extensive government subsidization but has now shifted the burden to the villagers, is remarkable for the visual transformation it brought to the Korean countryside.

It was also designed to change traditional farmer concepts, to modernize the rural sector, and perhaps as a subsidiary benefit, to change the traditionally depreciatory attitude of the elite toward farmers. If many observers complain that the program is too centralized and authoritarian, others argue that, even if this is true, villagers have had more opportunity to control their destinies under the *saemaŭl* movement than at any point in Korean history. The *saemaŭl* movement, by providing status to young, nontraditional leadership, has been one of the most effective means of destroying the traditional *yangban*-oriented social system, one of the goals of the movement.

A separate element in the national mobilization process, one that is not confined to rural settings but operates in urban areas as well, was the *pansanghoe*. This block or village organization meets monthly, under the auspices of and with an agenda set by the Ministry of Home Affairs. Its purpose is local improvement, perhaps the planting of flowers or the cleaning of public areas, but attendance is mandatory for someone from each household and fines are levied for absence. The potential for mobilization is obvious. Few societies in ostensibly democratic states are so mobilized and controlled.

The pressures to raise production were supplemented by important economic incentives, without which farm income would not have risen so dramatically. Primary was the increase in the price of paddy to the farmer, a change in policy that the government felt was politically necessary or desirable and worth the economic costs. Rice prices rose from below world prices to more than double those on the world market, with prices subsidized for both the producer and the urban consumer. This brought about spectacular increases in rural income but at considerable cost. By 1984, the subsidy program (called the Grain Management Fund), which also included barley, had resulted in a cumulative deficit of $1.7 billion and could no longer be sustained or justified. Fertilizer production and sales also were subsidized, resulting in an additional deficit of $700 million by 1983. Subsidization also extended to the construction or improvement of roads and irrigation systems, as well as to the provision of electricity and the operation of uneconomic village-level bus routes. As structural adjustment policies were implemented in the early 1980s, subsidization dropped as inflation reduced the protection rate. With the presidential election of 1987, however, the government promised to increase producer subsidies for rice by 17 percent, undercutting opposition cries for improved rural living conditions.

Technological changes were both sophisticated and expensive, as well as simple and cheap. As urban labor costs rose, so did rural wages. Thus, it became necessary to cut labor intensity; the practice began of laying plastic between vegetable rows to cut moisture loss and to eliminate weeds; mechanization was introduced; herbicides were sold; and plastic greenhouses became ubiquitous as new, improved winter vegetables supplemented the Korean diet. It became uneconomic to grow barley, except for beer. Major rice fields were consolidated and leveled, increasing productive capacity by reducing boundaries and allowing greater mechanization. The rural transportation infrastructure, carefully constructed in the 1970s, turned Korea from a series of individual, isolated valley economies into one national market. There were only 503 miles (812 kilometers) of paved roads in the nation in 1958; in 1985 there were 12,445 miles (20,072 kilometers) (see Table 10.10). Electricity reached virtually every village. By 1984, more than 84 percent of all households had television, 68 percent had piped water, 38 percent had refrigerators, and by 1985, 48 percent had telephones. Although farm family lives are still hard, improvement has been remarkable, accomplished through a series of subsidized efforts, as pervasive as they have been effective.

EQUITY IN THE KOREAN DEVELOPMENT PROCESS

No subject concerned with economic development is probably more politically explosive, more difficult to measure, or causes more trauma among donors than the issue of equity. However defined, there are few, if any, complex social systems in which it is not regarded by some as a problem. Although there is a presumption among many economists that fast growth will increase the income disparities among elements of the population, the available statistics on Korea offer important qualifications to that hypothesis.

Korean income distribution, along with that of Taiwan, is among the least skewed in the developing, noncommunist world (see Table 10.11). The reasons may be found in several factors that strongly influenced not only income distribution but the development process as a whole. In comparative terms, the Korean experience is highly praiseworthy, but important questions should be asked about the accuracy of the data, likely changes, the prospects for the disadvantaged, and the extent to which such relatively favorable income distribution came about as an intended consequence of governmental policies or actions.

Ethnic homogeneity, so important in Korean history and in developmental mobilization, is also a positive element in income distribution. Lacking ethnically separate classes, or castes, whether elite or subordinate groups, Korea begins with an advantage that many other states lack. Early and, in general, equal access to and motivation for primary education allowed the society to become broadly literate (in comparative perspective), far in excess of what might be expected from its per capita income. By the 1980s, access to higher education had increased extensively.

Equally important was the land reform, embarked on by the U.S. military occupation in response to the Japanese alienation of much of the best arable land. In its second phase, it was designed to counter a previously instituted North Korean reform. Although the second reform

TABLE 10.10
Selected Statistics on Transportation, Tourism, and Private
Consumption, 1958-1986

	Registered Motor Vehicles	Paved Roads (km.)	Express Highways (km.)
1958	28,933	812	---
1966	48,838	1,934	---
1980	527,729	15,599	1,224
1985	1,113,430	20,072 [a]	1,415
1986	1,309,434		

a-In 1986, 77.1% of roads were paved.

	Foreign Visitors
1966	67,965
1980	976,415
1985	1,426,045
1986	1,659,972 [b]

b-791,011 were Japanese; 202,061 Koreans abroad

Private Consumption (percent of expenditures)	1965	1984
food	59.5	37.2
beverage	2.6	4.3
tobacco	2.5	3.4
clothing/personal effects	8.4	7.5
rent/water	5.7	5.5
fuel/light	4.5	4.4
furniture/household equipment	1.4	5.8
personal care/health	3.4	7.5
recreation	4.1	5.6
miscellaneous	2.7	7.8

Source: Economic Planning Board, various yearbooks.

TABLE 10.11
National Income Distribution, 1976, 1985

	Lowest 20%	Second Quintile	Third Quintile	Fourth Quintile	Highest 20%	Highest 10%
1976	5.7	11.2	15.4	22.4	45.3	27.5
1985	6.8	11.6	16.1	22.3	43.7	28.3

(In the United States in 1986: lowest 20% had 3.8% of total income;
highest 20% had 46.1%.)

Source: Economic Planning Board, various yearbooks

was carried out under the republic, its models were U.S. efforts in Japan and Taiwan and its motivation was political rather than equity oriented.

Korea traditionally had a more highly structured and rigid class system than China, but the elimination of the court obliterated the acme of income discrepancies. The *yangban* grew rapidly during the Yi Dynasty. Although belonging to that class had important residual social benefits, large elements of that group were no better off financially than the *sangmin*. The class structure had decayed and lost much of its economic meaning toward the close of the Yi Dynasty. After liberation, it never functioned with class solidarity or with defined class goals in the traditional Marxist sense. Today, some residual elements of *yangban* status remain in social relations. Although the educational system in the past served to revalidate social and economic status, at various levels mobility has become apparent, especially through the military and in the lower reaches of the business community. Class is no longer an important factor in equity and may be expected to decrease in influence.

Although Korean income-distribution figures have long been subject to question, there is little doubt about the existence of a major gap between urban and rural incomes. This inequity has pushed migration to urban areas, encouraging the young to leave the farm, and has resulted in the aging of farm families (who in part depend on their children's remittances to supplement farm income). By the late 1960s, rural income had fallen to about half that of urban, salaried wage workers (not the urban population as a whole, as higher-level civil servants, professional groups, businesspeople, and academicians were not included in the statistics, thus rendering the results inaccurate as a portrayal of the whole nation). With the increase in rice prices and other rural development efforts, parity was approximately achieved for a short period in 1975. Since then, with growing urban wages and falling subsidies for agricultural produce (until the 1987 election), major disparities have once again appeared.[2] Almost one-third of farm income today comes from nonfarm sources, such as urban remittances. There has been little opportunity to date for the off-farm employment that has been so important to rural incomes in both Japan and Taiwan.

Wages and real living standards of urban workers have risen, in spite of the setback in the inflationary and adjustment period of the early 1980s.[3] They have improved, however, not because of government policy, nor because Korean unions had been successful up until 1987 in negotiating such increases, but because, as industry and services expanded, labor shortages forced wages to higher levels. These wages sometimes paralleled and sometimes fell short of increases in productivity. Korea had refused to join the International Labor Organization, which stipulates minimum-wage legislation, which Korea avoided until 1987.

TABLE 10.12
Labor Force, 1960-1986
(percents)

	1960	1980	1986
Agriculture	66	34	23.6
Industry	9	29	25.9
Services	25	37	50.5

Labor Force Participation			
	1965	1975	1986
Male	76.6	74.5	69.6
Female	36.5	36.9	40.6

Source: Economic Planning Board, various yearbooks.

In addition, rigid Korean government control over unions had effectively eliminated them as bargaining agents. There is increasing concern that labor, which has on many occasions taken to the streets to express opposition to government policies, will become both radicalized and noncompetitive on the international export markets. Between fifteen hundred and five thousand students expelled from universities have surreptitiously joined the labor movement, in which they have tried to organize workers; firms would not have hired them had their backgrounds been known.

Women are important elements of both the modern and traditional work force, although only 40 percent participate (see Table 10.12). In the modern work force, they numbered about 32 percent in 1979, up from 25 percent two decades earlier. Both numbers mask the extent of their contribution. Women generally enter the work force before marriage and leave under social pressure either when they marry or on the birth of their first child. Almost 90 percent of the women in the modern sector are under thirty years old. Thus, there is a constant movement in and out of the work force, allowing employers to recruit entry-level female workers at the lowest wages and to avoid longer-term economic commitments to them. Women receive less than half the pay of men overall and about two-thirds of men's pay in selected positions. They work an average of 9.7 hours per day, compared to 9 hours for men; 85 percent of female urban workers earned less than the minimum family cost of living. There are few women in the higher levels of the bureaucracy, although women are well represented in higher education.[4] Women have constitutional equality with men, but in fact there is no gender equity in Korea for females.

All the various Korean governments have tried to provide reasonably equal access to education—first, to primary education, and more recently, to expanded higher education. The development of rural roads provided the means for farm children, previously limited to primary school, to receive middle-school or high school education, for buses and bicycles carry them farther afield. The government has subsidized bus routes in some remote areas. It also spent 20.1 percent of its budget on education in 1986. There is more equity in educational access than in many other sectors. Still, among the urban population, 9 percent have gone to college, whereas only 1 percent of those in rural areas have done so.

Better transportation has also meant better access to health facilities, although of all the social services, Korea has lagged farther behind in the provision of adequate, affordable health care for the poor than in any other social service. Government health expenditures average about 1 percent of its budget. Health care is still largely privately sponsored. At the township level, more than 82 percent of the people are not under medical protection, compared to 57 percent in urban areas. Cities have ten times more doctors than do rural areas, and far more nurses. Better transportation has meant better access to the cities, where health facilities exist.

Regional income disparities have also been important. In most developing nations, the growth of the primate city and its environs is common. Thus, the largest increases in industry and income have been in Seoul[5] and in the surrounding Kyonggi Province. The Kyongsang provinces in the southeast, however, and the city of Pusan in that region have grown far out of proportion in industry, income, and investment, as well as infrastructure, and have had fewer business failures than the Cholla provinces in the southwest. This has been a long-standing issue. There have been charges that Syngman Rhee tried to ignore the development of the Chollas, because his opposition was centered there. Park was from North Kyongsang Province, as was Chun. Kim Dae Jung, their archrival, was from South Cholla. Strong regional economic disparities have contributed to the regionalism that found its fatal culmination in the Kwangju massacre.

Developmental equity also demands equal access to the market in economies that are supposed to be dominated by the private sector. Such equality of access to credit has been lacking in Korea. The leading *chaebŏl* have monopolized institutional credit. In 1983, the thirty largest conglomerates had 48 percent of total bank credit, the top five holding 24.2 percent. Such credit has been limited, thus forcing the small businessperson or entrepreneur to the curb market, where interest charges are much higher. This discrimination against small business has had a marked effect on equity for the growing middle, business class and thus has limited mobility except for those within the employment of the

TABLE 10.13
Social Statistics, Selected Years, 1960-1982

	1960	1982
Life expectancy at birth		
Male	52	64
Female	56	71
Infant mortality (per 000 live births)	78	32
Population per physician	3,540	1,440 [a]
Population per nurse	3,240	350
Students in primary school	(percent of age group)	
Male	99	108
Female	83	91
Total	94	107
Students in Secondary school	27	85
Students in Higher education	5	18

a. 1,166 in 1986.

Government expenditures (percent of budget)	1972	1981
Education	15.9	17.9
Health	1.2	1.3

National savings rate (percent of GDP)

1967	11.4	1975	16.8	1980	20.8	1986	32.8

Source: Derived from Economic Planning Board, yearbooks and statistics.

chaebŏl, which still remain family-controlled firms and thus are closed to mobility at the top, although not at mid-levels.

Income distribution is comparatively, but not absolutely, good. The lowest 20 percent of the population in 1985 received 6.8 percent of income (slightly up from 1975) (see Table 10.11). The top 10 percent received 28.3 percent (also slightly up). For technical and political reasons, income distribution figures are often skewed, but it is evident that Korean income distribution is perhaps twice as good as that of the Philippines and perhaps equal to that of the United States and Japan.

Equity has been mercurial. Yet, overall, there is no question that substantial progress has occurred. In the 1960s, approximately 40 percent of the total population lived below the poverty line; in the 1980s, that figure is 10 percent. A surrogate indicator for improved income is lower infant mortality figures, as the poorest elements of the population are usually those most affected by infant death (see Table 10.13). Growth in equity has been remarkable, but inequities still exist and may be expected to increase, as is noted in Chapter 12.

*   *   *

Korean economic development was in part a product of political will, sound economic policies, effective implementation, mass mobilization, a skilled but often exploited labor force, a vigorous private sector under the guidance and control of an interventionist centralizing government, a strong subsidization program to induce exports and rural growth and to open new sectors for expansion, and an international scene conducive to Korean exports. (In 1986, Korean exports were 42.6 percent of GNP; they had risen from 13.6 percent in 1967, to 28.2 percent in 1975, to 34.4 percent in 1980.) Autocratic government alone (under Rhee) was not sufficient. Throughout the world, at various times, highly centralized states have failed, private and public sectors have performed poorly, sound policies have been poorly implemented, and subsidies have not produced expected results. The unique mix at the right international moment was Korea's special genius.

Increasing political dissatisfaction together with the rise of Korean nationalism has heightened interest, especially among Korean youth, in alternative explanations for Korea's remarkable economic growth and its international relations. These students have turned to dependency theory for such an explanation. Born out of analysis of the economic stagnation of much of Latin America, dependency theory defined growth in terms of center and periphery and relegated much of the Third World and the newly industrializing nations to the periphery, which was seen as subjugated and exploited by the industrialized center.

Although highly popular among Korean students, dependency theory, however accurate for Latin America, is severely wanting for much of East Asia. Foreign investment and multinational corporations have had marginal impact on Korea, and Korea has confounded dependency theorists by its stellar economic performance and its unprecedented economic competition with the industrialized center. Korea, it may be argued, was a client state of the United States, and a general characteristic of such states is that they tend to make their governments more isolated from and less responsive to their social and economic groups. This may have been true during the Rhee period, but by the Park era Korea was pursuing an independent foreign policy in the Middle East and developing an increasingly competitive rather than a client relationship with the United States in the economic sphere.

Espousal of dependency theory is less a reflection of economic accuracy than it is of political frustration. Korea, however, is dependent, not in economic terms but in matters of international security. And if South Korea may be considered dependent in security matters, North Korea is in the same position. Security issues hinge on North Korean–South Korean relations and the relations between South Korea and the United States. To this subject we now turn.

11

Korea and Its External Relations

Do not be deceived by the Soviets
Don't count on the Americans
The Japanese will soon rise again
So Koreans, be careful!

—Popular Korean saying after liberation

Korean foreign relations, formal and informal, have historically been responses to regional Eastern or Western power and political influences. Until the end of the nineteenth century, those forces emanating from the mainland predominated. For the longest periods, and with the strongest cultural impact, China was Korea's diplomatic mentor. Korea was part of the Sino-centric world order from the second century before Christ, when China established a military administration in Korea. Korean emissaries brought tribute to the Chinese (or Mongol or Manchu) court (linguistically and ideologically the center of the world), a requirement that was inherent in the Chinese conceptualization of the world order (and which was to cause problems for Europeans later). Presents were given in exchange, and the Chinese ratified the claims of new monarchs as to the propriety of their accession to the Korean throne. Thus, the tribute system was often disguised trade of considerable magnitude, and the Chinese conferring of titles gave Korean monarchs political legitimacy in the eyes of the *yangban*. Koreans also brought back new technology and philosophical ideas, such as neo-Confucianism and, indeed, Christianity. The system was holistic in that it satisfied most of Korean external needs.

There were aberrations, of course, over this long period. Korea (Koguryŏ, the kingdom in the northern portion of the peninsula) fought and defeated the Sui and T'ang Dynasties. As "barbarians"—such as the Mongols and the Manchus—moved on China, Korea was incorporated into their imperial systems. Korea engaged in small, regulated trade with Japan through Pusan.

With the opening of Korea in 1876, the pattern began to change, with Japan assuming the predominant role, one that it did not relinquish until 1945 and one that has partly been reasserted in the economic sphere since 1965. In one sense, since 1945 the United States has been thrust into the traditional position in relation to South Korea that China had occupied earlier, while China and the Soviet Union play balancing acts with the North. Responsible for defense, the major trading partner, sometimes mentor, and a contributor to political legitimacy, the United States is less assured of its role and less consistent in it, playing its part with the South with considerably less aplomb than did the Chinese in imperial times.

Since 1945 and the unhappy division of Korea along the 38th parallel, North Korea has probably been the major determinant of South Korean external relations and internal policies. Diplomatic competition with the North defined until 1973 the nations with which South Korea had relations; under the "Hallstein Doctrine" (based on a German model), if a third nation recognized the North, the South demurred to recognize that other nation. The U.S. defense treaty and military assistance are designed to frustrate the obviously hostile intentions the North has exhibited toward the South on numerous occasions. Economic development in the South is in part a response to the North or is at least given an urgency that would not exist without the threat from the North. Rigid political and social controls—indeed coups, martial law decrees, and repression—over the South Korean population are continuously justified by various governments as needed because of the threats from the North.

In this chapter we will concentrate on relations with North Korea and the United States. Those with Japan, the other major force affecting the South, have been treated in Chapters 5 and 10.

NORTH KOREA AND THE ISSUE OF REUNIFICATION

Cultural and linguistic homogeneity, historical unity continuously since 668, natural geographic boundaries, and uri-ism ("we-ness") in the face of stronger neighbors have given the Korean division a sense of poignancy that is difficult for others emotionally to comprehend. No other national people in modern times has undergone such a traumatic split. Reunification is as vibrant an issue as is the retention of the Korean culture in a hostile environment.

The need for unity is reinforced by a variety of forces. More than 2 million refugees, or about 10 percent of the republic's population, fled to the South between liberation and the end of the Korean War, so family separation is a constant theme now affecting perhaps 10 million people. The division was not a Korean product; it was imposed from the outside on the Korean people (even though it may also have been perpetuated by internal forces), who were pawns in a global geopolitical game. Time has intensified this concern—much as it has petrified that border—rather than ameliorating the emotions involved. The ideological differences that separate North and South are less important to southern youth than to their parents, as the young did not experience the horrors of the Korean War and the North's brief but memorable occupation. As South Korea has developed economically, many Koreans now believe that neither Japan nor the United States wants to see a unified—even nonaligned—Korea, which would pose an economic threat to both nations given the size of the Korean economies, their vigor, and their general complementarity. This perception, true or false, contributes to anti-U.S. sentiment.

Each South Korean government has viewed the issue of reunification with suspicion, and it has moved to coopt the field in the South by establishing a ministerial-level department to deal with it. Positive statements about its importance from nongovernmental sectors are often regarded as subversive unless emanating from approved sources. Those making statements placing reunification above anticommunism (such as statements made by the 1987 opposition leadership) could have been subject to prosecution. Even advocating a neutralized Korea (singular or plural) has been an indictable offense at various times. Writings about North Korea are carefully reviewed; visits to North Korea by South Korean citizens without government approval are considered acts of treason.

The South views the North with justified suspicion. North Korea has defense treaties with both China and the USSR, both dating from 1961. The continuity of North Korean leadership under Kim Il Sung (and the expected rule of his son, Kim Jong Il) gives the South little hope for early change. The Korean War; constant infiltration and espionage (it is not known how much goes north); the attempted assassination of President Park Chung Hee in 1968 and again in 1974, when his wife was killed; the Rangoon bombings of 1983; tunnels under the DMZ; constant vying for the loyalties of the Korean population in Japan and overseas in general; and the antigovernment students who have used North Korean slogans in their demonstrations—all constantly remind many in the South of dangers from the North. With a quarter of the population of the country in Seoul, only 30 miles (48 kilometers) from the border, not much prompting is required.

It is equally true that each South Korean government has used these justifiable fears for its own political ends. Restrictions on individual, institutional, and press freedoms have been profound but have been constantly excused or justified because of the perceived threat of a country with which the South is still (technically) at war. The viability of an open democracy is often questioned, and not only by those in government, because it might lead to dissent and disunity in the face of the monolithic North. Although an outsider might argue persuasively that repression in the name of national unity, even in the face of foreign threats, may lead to greater future instability, the government has demonstrated that the most serious offenses, real or imagined, are those involving a purported relationship with, support of, or even lukewarm attitudes toward North Korea. A foreign focus of concern is a traditional pattern used by many regimes to deflect criticism of their shortcomings as well as to maintain power; South Korean governments have used this threat for both purposes.

The United States has been caught in a dilemma. Its objectives in Korea have included the maintenance of the close security relationship with the South together with a desire for political liberalization and democratization. As it has in many other countries, in such circumstances the United States has reluctantly regarded security as of priority. In a real sense the United States has been a captive of its ally, the South. Washington has refused to negotiate separately with North Korea on any issue on the grounds that this would undercut the republic, and that the North and South should negotiate directly with each other. The United States has been sensitive to any accommodation that would undermine the republic's position on the peninsula or elsewhere in the world, or diminish the capacity of the South to respond militarily to the North, which has improved its relations with the Soviet Union. Soviet military assistance has increased, and North Korea's volume of trade with the USSR has almost doubled since 1980, reaching 43 percent of the North's total trade in 1985. The United States has constantly sought to maintain the political status quo and military balance in the area.

Washington has negotiated quietly behind the scenes to ameliorate the gross excesses of the republic's regimes. The U.S. government can be informally credited with saving the life of Kim Dae Jung, for example, as well as privately warning the Korean government against various actual, proposed, or rumored repressive measures and against retaliatory strikes against the North. Its influence, however, has been limited, for fear of the North means that security remains the cardinal focus in the region.

With the fall of Syngman Rhee in 1960, the North proposed a confederated state with separate political systems, but the South rejected the proposal. In 1971, the North advocated the withdrawal of U.S. troops, the reduction of the military on both borders, democratic elections and political parties with the release of all political prisoners, a joint economic committee if not confederation, and consultative meetings by various political private groups.

Previously, in 1970, President Park had proposed talks with North Korea, and over the next four years discussions took place. Many of them were carried out under the auspices of the Red Cross, but the results were disappointing. Their pinnacle came early in a joint July 4, 1972, communiqué in which both sides pledged that efforts would be made toward peaceful reunification without external (that is, U.S., Soviet, or Chinese) help, and that "a great national unity, transcending differences in ideas, ideologies, and systems shall be sought first."

The meaning of this agreement was almost immediately disputed. (Did it, for example, first require the withdrawal of U.S. troops? The North said yes, the South no.) Six full sessions under Red Cross auspices were held over twelve months, but without effect. In August 1973, North Korea broke off the full discussions following Park's June 23, 1973, offer to withdraw objection to UN membership for both Koreas. In fact, this concession was the South's recognition that North Korea had already been quite successful in its UN campaign, having been admitted to the World Health Organization that year. High-ranking representatives paid visits to each country, the head of the South Korean CIA visiting Pyongyang, for example. Most of the discussions concerned issues involving the reunification of families, exchanges of visits or mail, and other humanitarian questions. Included in these discussions, and the sporadic meetings that were held at Panmunjom after the talks broke down in 1973, was a great deal of posturing on both sides.

In 1980, North Korea in a communication with the South formally used the South's official name for the first time, and in October 1980 (following President Park's assassination) Kim Il Sung at the Sixth Korea Workers party meeting proposed a "Democratic Confederal Republic of Koryŏ" that would be neutral, democratic, and increasingly collaborative in a variety of fields. President Chun in January 1982 proposed a Consultative Conference for National Reunification to draft a constitution, but this was rejected by the North. The Republic of Korea also rejected a 1984 proposal from the North that would have for the first time given the South equal status in North Korean–U.S. discussions: North Korea and the United States to sign a peace treaty (South Korea never did sign the armistice), and North and South to sign a nonaggression pact. The South rejected this approach, for it wanted the USSR and China to make equal presentations to the South if the United States were, in effect, to recognize the North.

Some positive steps, however, have occurred. North Korea delivered cement and other commodities to Seoul in a gesture of flood relief for South Korean victims in 1984. In 1988 discussions were under way on how to deal with the thorny issue of the summer Olympics, which Seoul officially hosted and in which Pyongyang wished to share.

The competition between Pyongyang and Seoul is diplomatic and economic as well as military. The South's spectacular economic successes have clearly overshadowed progress in the North. Although statistics are not readily available, Seoul's GNP is some 5.5 times that of Pyongyang and 2.6 times as large on a per capita basis (as the North's population is about half that of the South). The South's trade is about twenty-two times that of the North. Yet, the growing disparities between the two should not mask Pyongyang's early accomplishments (during the First Republic, growth in the North exceeded that in the South). However, in the 1970s North Korea was in economic trouble; it defaulted on some foreign loans in 1974. North Korea, in comparative world developmental terms, has done quite well. Its economic accomplishments considerably dwarf those of most of Africa and Latin America. To attribute this solely—positively or negatively—to a socialist economy is misleading. One need only note the poor economic performances of Burma and Tanzania, both avowedly socialist regimes.

If the economic race has been to the South, the diplomatic competition has been a stalemate. Although each Korea has its coterie of states that recognize it alone, the bulk of each group is obviously influenced by great-power bloc considerations rather than the merits of either regime. By October 1985, 67 nations recognized both governments. South Korea had relations with 118 additional nations, North Korea with 101, although the North is still ahead among the nonaligned group. By 1986, South Korea belonged to fourteen of the fifteen UN specialized agencies, North Korea to ten. If both Koreas continue to remain apart, as is more than likely, then over time joint recognition will grow.

The United States softened its approaches to the North in 1987, allowing U.S. diplomats to talk informally with North Koreans, something that had been prohibited, but both Washington and Seoul remain adamant in maintaining the troops on the peninsula, a factor continuously decried by the North. That very modest opening was stopped, however, a few months later, after a Korean Airlines flight was destroyed by North Korean sabotage over Burma.

Meanwhile, squabbling between the United States and the North continues; acrimonious, essentially meaningless, negative platitudes are exchanged in periodic armistice meetings at Panmunjom. As North Korea incites unrest in the South, the South's fear of the North remains unabated. The South also fears that the North's construction of the major Kumgangsan Dam just north of the DMZ would pose a flood threat to Seoul, and the South has built the first stage of its own dam to counter the one in the North.

The opening of North-South communications, even for a limited period such as during the Olympics, might help alleviate some of the more immediate tensions but is unlikely to resolve the fundamental issues, which revolve around the distribution of power on the peninsula. A wide variety of suggestions has been made, formally and informally, on reunification; possibilities range from a unitary structure to a federal one that would retain separate economic and political regimes in each area but with various joint activities. The North has continuously called for U.S. troop withdrawals from the South (the Chinese left North Korea in 1958), but clearly growing informal acceptance of the economic importance of South Korea by the North's two powerful neighbors, South Korean political liberalization, Soviet and Chinese plans to participate in the Olympics, as well as the North's desire to participate also, have seemed to make the North more conciliatory, at least verbally.

None of the adversaries on the peninsula officially recognizes each other; China, the Soviet Union, and North Korea do not officially have diplomatic relations with South Korea, nor is the reverse the case. Yet, South Korea, through intermediaries, does over $2 billion in annual trade with China and $500 million with the Soviet Union; by March 1988, South Korea and Hungary had opened trade offices in one another's countries, presaging an increase in Eastern European–South Korean commerce. North Korea's trade with Japan is about $400–500 million annually. South Korean academics attend meetings in the Soviet Union and China. China sent a large delegation to the Asian Games in Seoul in 1986, and South Korean athletes have been to China. But the North-South problem remains the sticking point.

KOREAN-U.S. RELATIONS

In 1982, with considerable acclaim and ceremony, Korea and the United States celebrated a centennial of diplomatic relations. Speeches were made, symposia held, commissions formed and grants given in a self-congratulatory spurt of goodwill. The events were both public and private; not only were the lives of many in both nations intertwined through choice or happenstance, but each government used the occasion for its own purposes. The Chun administration sought through these diverse celebrations to wrap itself in the mantle of political legitimacy;

the Reagan administration wished to reinforce the improvement in relations with Korea that had taken place since the Carter years.

In retrospect, however, this century has been one of turbulence in relations, more so for the Koreans but with crises for the United States as well. The U.S.-Korean relationship included the U.S. betrayal of Korea to the Japanese in 1904–1905; a major U.S. missionary commitment to Korea's modernization; the liberation of the country from colonial rule; the division of Korea; a three-year military government; a war to preserve Korean independence; the provision of over $13 billion in economic and military aid; the training of tens of thousands of Koreans in the United States; scandals that for a period cast discredit on the Korean government and on highly placed elected officials in the United States; a generation during which the United States acted as mentor to Korea; and, as the centenary ended, growing joint concern over increasing trade frictions.

It may be said that to the U.S. public, the relationship has been divided into three periods of decreasing length: ignorance until the Korean War, dismay until about 1980, and increasingly positive attitudes since then. In the early 1980s, surveys indicated that more than half the U.S. population admitted to knowing almost nothing about Korea, in spite of the presence of almost a million Koreans in the United States and of perhaps a million U.S. soldiers who had served in Korea during and after the war. Those who had heard of Korea often knew of it because of the television program "M*A*S*H," the dark comedy look at war and its degradations. The Korean War created images that persisted in American minds for many years after the event: cold, mud, poverty, filth, and squalor. These visions were perpetuated, much to the chagrin of the Korean government, not only because of "M*A*S*H," but because private American philanthropic organizations felt they needed such images to raise money for their welfare activities.

Some Americans, a relatively small, urbane group who live in cities, may have ventured into the "Koreatowns" of New York or Los Angeles or noted the increasing numbers of small, Korean-owned and family-run businesses in many major cities. A smaller number may have tried p'ulgogi (barbecued beef), kalbi (shortribs), or kimch'i in one of the increasingly common Korean restaurants. Few Americans, however, will think of Korea by evoking images of individual Koreans or the nation as a whole from literary sources. No matter how spurious the stereotypes, how quaint, curious, exotic, and erroneous the impressions, U.S. views of the Chinese are probably more favorable because of Charlie Chan, not to mention Judge Dee and Kai Lung, and U.S. views of the Japanese owe much to Mr. Moto. Until Richard Kim's 1965 best-selling novel, The Martyred, there were no popular portraits in English that humanized Koreans. There was not even a Mikado, let alone a Madama Butterfly.

A new era in U.S. perceptions about Korea has recently emerged, and these perceptions are diversely stamped on the American consciousness. They are variegated, but positive overall. They are composed of impressions of Korean scholarship and academic achievement in competitive U.S. fora, of hardworking Korean businessmen and families who have taken over small retail trade in many areas, and of the increasing size of the Korean presence in the United States. Korean immigration has not only increased, its class composition has changed. From World War II until changes in the U.S. immigration laws in the 1960s, immigrants were often of *yangban* and wealthy origins; today, they are increasingly blue-collar.

With demographic change has come product change. Residual consciousness of Korea is reinforced by ubiquitous color television sets, microwave ovens, shoes and footwear, textiles, and toys. No member of an American family can escape the Korean label or, more recently, the Korean brands made in the United States. In itself, the Korean brand is a significant sign of economic status and respectability. In the late 1980s, Korean products have increased in sophistication: Computers and microchips are common. More important for perceptions of Korea is the automobile. As the United States is a car-oriented society, the importation of Korean cars will have a singular effect on U.S. impressions of Korea, more than any other single product or combination of products.

Korean views of the United States have been, by contrast, both more naive and more sophisticated, more sustained, more permeating, and yet more unrealistic. As U.S. troops liberated Korea from the Japanese, and as food and aid followed in their wake, the United States was seen to be the savior of the society, the idol of a type of sophisticated cargo cult. This image was reinforced during the Korean War and the rehabilitation that followed under the U.S. military protective shield. Westernized culture (and counterculture) swept in as well, with fashions, products, literature, films, and even heroes making their Korean mark.

Korean naiveté surfaced not so much in the wholesale adoption of things American but rather in the motives that the Koreans attributed to their American friends. U.S. support was regarded as altruistic, borne and sustained by selfless humanitarian concerns. Pro-U.S. feelings were (and are) genuine, but they have been reinforced by all Korean governments, as well as by many of the opposition parties and factions, each of which sought to use the American label for its own (sometimes quite appropriate) purposes. Governments have also restricted criticism of the United States in the controlled press except when such criticism seemed to serve their own needs.

As the U.S.-Korean relationship shifted from donor/recipient and teacher/student to one approaching peer status, in spite of the economic disparities between the two nations, the mutuality of security needs and economic ties has become increasingly clear. So, too, the individual national interests of each nation as articulated by its government illustrate when such interests diverge, or even conflict. Such conflicts are often rooted in the internal political vulnerabilities of each regime, which defines the steps that each feels it must take to satisfy local, often highly explosive, but parochial views.

The growing Korean public realization that the United States is not an altruistic cargo cult deity, together with recognition of the real mistakes in U.S. foreign policy and U.S. self-interest (especially in trade issues), increases the level, depth, and articulation of anti-U.S. sentiment. Within the international comparative context, this feeling is still remarkably limited; its growth from a very low base has increased its internal visibility, however, and it therefore has attracted more attention in U.S. circles. Attitudes toward the United States are still grounded in a remarkably solid and widespread general aura of goodwill. Anti-U.S. feeling as practiced in Korea also contains elements of rising Korean self-confidence and nationalism, of ambivalence about the protective screen provided by the U.S. security program and Korean dependency and about U.S. trade pressures and Korean reliance on U.S. markets for exports, and, at the same time, of the need to seek autonomy of action.

Anti-U.S. actions are sometimes seen as dramatic means to illustrate concern and attract attention. The burning of the U.S. cultural center in Pusan in 1982, the bombing of the Taegu center in 1983, and the student occupation of the U.S. center in Seoul in 1985 (on the fifth anniversary of Kwangju) were symbolic acts of identity and defiance. As important as they are, they are not representative of general sentiment. Dissatisfaction about the United States may be grouped around three central themes: general policy issues, political problems, and economic relations. Dissatisfaction based on these issues may be expected to intensify.

Koreans correctly blame the United States for the division of their people (although there were few, if any, feasible alternatives). They perceive that the United States seems to place more importance on Japan than on Korea and that Washington regards the bilateral defense treaty with Japan as its most critical relationship in the region—many would say, in the world. Koreans sometimes feel that their role is once again that of the proverbial shrimp among whales. Some of the younger Koreans, those most vociferous in their criticism, note their government's implacable opposition to North Korea and claim that Washington encourages it because the United States does not want to see a unified Korean nation.

Political issues have centered around U.S. support for any regime, including those formed by coups. Extremists have even theorized that Washington has been responsible for the two military coups, but this is a type of conspiratorial historical revisionism without foundation. More prevalent are beliefs that the United States, at virtually almost any internal Korean political cost, is prepared to sacrifice the interests of the Korean people and democratic government for stability and security concerns. The assumption in this argument is that Washington has "leverage" with any Korean regime and can force or influence decisions should it wish to do so.

The U.S. position is that its leverage is quite limited. It can be exerted at a price on individual matters of a technical or transitory nature, and not at all frequently, but rarely when key issues concerning the internal distribution of power in Korean society are involved. Such leverage may be marginal, but it can also be critical. It is also evident that the past role and mere presence of the United States incites expectations of positive intervention (for example, on behalf of the government in international affairs; for the opposition in the Kwangju negotiations) that the United States has often tried to avoid. The U.S. position is that it is concerned with the process of democratization, not with the choice of individual parties or candidates. In fact, Korea is important to Washington because of the multitude of U.S. interests in the future of that society. Thus, there rarely is unanimity within the U.S. government (and between that government and its people) that the importance of any particular issue, except overarching security matters, warrants use of this potential, limited leverage. The Korean government is well aware of this situation and has been able to counter cries for internal political liberalization with dire warnings of the threats to security from the North. There are usually elements of truth in such alarms, and often the warnings are effective, if overplayed. As a general rule, the more intense are U.S. interests in a nation, the more diverse such interests are likely to be, and thus less leverage is likely to be available for internal changes that affect the internal distribution of power.

Criticisms of U.S. economic policies have shifted over time. In the liberalization following the overthrow of Syngman Rhee, Korean academics were able to write about the shortcomings of the U.S. economic assistance program, which included justified charges that the United States did not engage in any major productive (as opposed to consumption-oriented) economic assistance and that much of the funds were not effectively used.

The charges in the 1980s are different. They include complaints that Washington is treating Korea like another Japan and, thus, has restricted through informal mechanisms the importation of Korean goods or, more recently and more formally, is considering tariffs against Korean products. At the same time, Koreans charge that the United States is attempting to force the Korean government to accede to the liberalization of imports into the Korean market or to enable U.S. firms to compete in the service field against Korean companies. These economic issues come not only from the students, the bastion of Korean nationalism, but increasingly from the *chaebŏl* and smaller manufacturers or service industries that see themselves threatened. The opening of less than 1 percent of the Korean tobacco market to the United States (under strong, public U.S. pressure) in 1986 created a nationalistic furor far out of proportion to its economic effect, accompanied by some feeling that at least some of the complaints were government-inspired. No government in Korea (or no opposition party) wants to be perceived as having to acquiesce to U.S. economic pressure.

In fact, it is possible that as a more participatory politics develops in Korea, student and other discontent, which had been concentrated on the Korean government, may be redirected toward the United States. It would be ironic if the very factor (liberalization) that the United States had hoped would succeed in Korea intensified attitudes critical of the United States. But the 1 million Koreans in the United States and their families in Korea, the strong economic bonds between the two nations, the security relationship, and the evidence (in the light of events in the Philippines and the overthrow of the Marcos government) that the United States now looks more carefully at internal political events in Korea, and is prepared to speak out more openly about them—all these indicate that although anti-U.S. sentiment may be expected to grow as a result of the maturity of the Korean national ego, Korean ties with the United States may also be expected to remain strong.

KOREAN RELATIONS WITH OTHER NATIONS

Growing Korean economic confidence has shaped Korean relations with the rest of the world and encouraged Korea to enlarge its contacts, engage in autonomous foreign policy ventures, and seek a unique role for itself.

Korea has always regarded itself as having a special relationship with the United Nations. It was, after all, the UN that supervised the elections that founded the Republic of Korea; it was under UN auspices that the republic was saved from the North Korean invasion; and it has been under the UN flag that Korean forces still operate. Korea has been an observer at the UN (as has North Korea), and UN economic assistance was the only significant official and continuous support to Korea beyond that of the United States until the early 1960s. Korea has supported the activities of UN agencies, such as UNESCO, and has been an active participant in other UN programs.

South Korean relations with Eastern bloc nations have traditionally been cool. For many years no South Korean was allowed to visit such countries, and even the playing of Soviet music composed since the revolution (such as works by Shostakovich) was banned. That era is over. Koreans participate in academic meetings in Moscow and in Eastern Europe, and Soviets and others have been to Korea. Trade between the two sides, however, is minuscule.

By contrast, trade is the key element in Korean relations with the People's Republic of China. Through intermediaries, Korea exports over $2 billion to China annually (and buys Chinese coal and corn), and it is likely that this trade will grow, as China needs the technological products at competitive prices that Korea has to offer. Korea has also negotiated directly with the Chinese, in an incident in 1983 concerning a defecting Chinese pilot. The Chinese participated in the Asian Games of 1986. China might like closer ties with South Korea, partly to ensure that the Soviet Union does not establish these first and perhaps because the South might give technological assistance, but China is not likely to jeopardize its ties with the North to achieve that end, no matter how important trade becomes.

Although Seoul has been cultivating Beijing, it has continued to maintain close relations with Taiwan. Taiwan is an economic competitor, but the strong anticommunist stance of both governments (General MacArthur wanted to use Taiwanese troops in Korea against the Chinese communists during the Korean War) together with the autocratic nature, but now liberalization, of both regimes have given them a natural affinity that is reflected in trade and in frequent exchanges of cultural, political, and economic delegations.

In general, however, Korean diplomatic initiatives toward the rest of the world have been determined by its trading patterns. During the late 1970s and early 1980s, half a million Koreans were employed in the Middle East. Many of those Koreans were working in the construction industry, contracting more than $13 billion in one year in foreign exchange from projects in that region. Korea pursued a foreign policy independent from that of the United States to ensure that its supply of oil was continuous—for example, engaging in major construction contracts in Libya at a time when U.S. relations with that country were strained or broken. Korea's trade with Asia (including Japan) and the Middle East are fast-expanding elements in the success of Korean exports. Korean exports to Asia rose from $105 million in 1966 to $10.2 billion in 1985, of which less than half went to Japan. Korea's two-way trade with

ASEAN (Association of Southeast Asian Nations) countries rose from $175 million in 1971 to $2.6 billion in 1980. Korea established an Overseas Economic Development Fund in 1987 as a type of foreign economic assistance. Managed by the Ministry of Foreign Affairs, it will begin with $90 million in expenditures during its first year, rising to $350 million in five years. It is expected to improve both economic and diplomatic relations with a number of nations.

Japan looms largest in any discussion of Korean foreign relations. This has historically, but tragically, been the case. Today, Japan is most important to Korea for economic reasons—in terms of trade, investment ($1.3 billion until 1985, or half of all foreign investment in Korea), and the import of technology. Japan's success has proven to be an unadmitted and inchoate model for many of Korea's policies and programs. Japanese tourism is also important to Korea (one-half of the 1.4 million foreigners who visited Korea in 1985 were Japanese [see Table 10.10]), and the more than six hundred thousand Koreans resident in Japan (split between adherents of North and South) are important social and economic links, as well as a source of tensions, between the two countries. Korea provides security, through its massive army, for Japanese prosperity just as Japan has been a spur for Korea's economic growth. Yet, Japan still treats Korea (as well as other Asian nations) with insensitivity, such as in its proposed revision of Japanese textbooks that play down Japan's repressive role in the colonial period. The Koreans, however, have reason to feel these slights more acutely.

Korea is at the threshold of a new order in international relations, of which the 1988 Olympics may be the beginning. It has demonstrated its economic capacity through its growth and the reputation of its products. In 1987, it had begun to erase its image as a country of political repression. Its diplomatic competence and sensitivity have expanded. If Korea continues along these paths with the vigor it has demonstrated in the past, then its international position will be further strengthened.

12

The Future of Korea

We the people of Korea, proud of a resplendent history and traditions dating from time immemorial, upholding the cause of the Provisional Republic of Korea Government born of the March First Independence Movement of 1919 and the democratic ideals of the April Nineteenth Uprising of 1960 against injustice, having assumed the mission of democratic reform and peaceful unification of our homeland and having determined to consolidate national unity with justice, humanitarianism and brotherly love, and
   To destroy all social vices and injustice, and
   To afford equal opportunities to every person and to provide for the fullest development of individual capabilities in all fields, including political, economic, civic and cultural life by further strengthening the basic free and democratic order conducive to private initiative and public harmony. . . .
      —The Constitution of the Republic of Korea
      (as amended, 1987)

Few Koreans or knowledgeable observers in the dark aftermath of the Korean War could have imagined the profound changes that have taken place in Korea since that war. In only three decades a society intentionally transformed itself, metamorphosed into a burgeoning industrial state, urban rather than rural, international rather than insular. Korea has assumed an importance worldwide few would have imagined.

How hazardous, then, to prognosticate on Korea, for although its history, judiciously explored, should give us clues to its future, the record of success is not an enviable one. Korea has confounded the experts, internal and external, and can do so again. Although our knowledge of Korea has grown, Korea's international importance has outstripped our understanding of its dynamics. Yet, there are lessons from Korea's past and broad, discernable trends that may provide insights into the future, however tenuous our forecasts must remain.

The traditional characteristics of Korean political and economic culture are often cited to include such factors as a strong sense of hierarchy, centralization, paternalism, aspirations for social mobility, a

172

willingness to take risks, familism, factionalism, all within recognition of residual Confucian virtues that also include concepts of a meritocracy, a government monopoly on political morality, and a sense of state legitimacy that has precluded a strong concept of a "loyal opposition." Although such a disparate catalogue may be marginally helpful, it is also selective and misleading, ignoring change, defying analysis of the relative weights of each, and oblivious of new, perhaps equally or more important international trends that mix and contradict the traditional social order.

Our record for social prognosis is not inspiring. As late as three decades ago, the pervasive academic analysis was that Confucianism was an anachronism, a developmental fetter holding the society to premodern, and thus economically inappropriate, views that would continuously retard economic progress. Economic issues were downplayed in the traditional Confucian state, and the status of production and commerce socially vilified. Leading scholars argued—referring to the century-old debate in East Asia that focused on retaining traditional values but using modern, Western technology for practical affairs—that the degradation of China was in part caused by such dichotomous attitudes; a state should be thoroughly modern if it is to progress.

Now, however, Singapore and Taiwan, as well as Korea, all stellar economic performers over time, have consciously introduced Confucian virtues into their educational systems. Japan has successfully blended much that is contemporary with traditional Confucian views in management and industrial relations. We now recognize that traditional values can play modernizing roles under certain circumstances. Our former conclusions were faulty, as our analysis was incomplete and superficial, and, indeed, the accurate, quantifiable role of Confucianism in development may still defy analysis. Having learned, however, something from our past spurious analyses, perhaps we are in a better position to avoid those mistakes as we look to the Korean future.

The movement of social, political, and economic forces and influences has rapidly accelerated. Some of these new or strengthened elements will profoundly affect Korea's future and, indeed, the reinterpretation by Koreans of their own society. Although Koreans may be culturally and linguistically homogeneous, attitudinal variety exists, and, as the history of Korean factionalism and political parties demonstrates, it can be exceedingly acerbic. There is likely to be intense debate over many of these points.

URBANIZATION AND PLURALISM

The single most profound, influential trend in Korea—which now affects the whole society but which will affect the future even more strongly—has been the urbanization of the nation. Korea is an urban society, with more than 65 percent of the total population living in urban areas of over 50,000 people, and one-quarter living in the capital alone (on liberation, Seoul had 5 percent of the population). The ramifications of this continuous process of migration and change, which forcibly influences the rural sector as well and, in essense, is an internal "brain drain" of rural talent to Seoul and other cities, may not be undone. Over time, this process of urbanization will profoundly compromise traditional values and affect political and economic institutions and the culture itself. Its influence is immediate in politics, but its impact far transcends imminent issues.

With urbanization, both as cause and effect, have come vast changes that cannot always be either channeled into discrete, preordained directions or dammed. These include such factors as the growth of a wage economy, the rise in the status of women and their mass entry (at least for a period in their lives) into the modern labor force, the predominance of the nuclear family, the increased internationalization of the society, and the broadening and strengthening of the middle class. These trends are coupled with the expansion of higher education, the great enlargement and growth of prestige of the business sector, and the economic integration of the nation into a single economy. Because of these forces, we are witnessing the budding, perhaps the flowering, of a type and degree of Korean pluralism unique in Korean history.

The centralized court suppressed the development of alternative centers of power and influence in the traditional period. Then, during the Japanese colonial era, any such nascent tendencies were rigorously eliminated under alien rule. Since independence, the more modern and sophisticated approach to ensuring centralized power has not only involved reversion to the more traditional, blatant means of suppression, which have been extensive, but also cooptation: The state and its organs have enveloped organizations or movements that seemed to have the potential for growth and influence, either positive or negative. Few institutions between the family or clan and the state were free from domination by the center.

The relatively small size of the Korean elite community effectively eliminated the possibility of differentiation among social, political, or economic centers of alternative power and their isolation. The Korean government, for example, has continuously had the capacity and power to prevent private employers in any field from hiring individuals whom it wished to see isolated. Given the concept of monopolistic political morality, all had to be controlled. The limited geographic area of Korea and the absence of distinct ethnic or linguistic entities prevented isolated pockets of dissent from flourishing undisturbed.

As long as Korea was internationally isolated (as it was during the monarchy and colonial periods and, to a lesser but significant degree, by the censorship of the governments under the republic) and insofar as internally Korea was essentially a series of relatively isolated economies, cooptation and control were easier. But as an urban nation, even with the inchoate retention of traditional attitudes of a single, centralized political ethic, such methods are infinitely more difficult to implement and less acceptable to an increasingly better educated populace; thus, their effectiveness is more unlikely. Coupled with the increasing extent and influence of international exposure at all levels of the society, with openings that are no longer limited to the elite as they were just three decades ago, any future government will find the old coercive methods of sociopolitical control less effective—indeed, less possible—if it wishes to employ them. The massive urban demonstrations of June 1987, ending in the government's volte-face on democratization on June 29, are evidence that even many of those in authority recognize these changes. If you cannot suppress them, join them.

Persuasive evidence also exists from the elective process over three decades. Until 1987, opposition to any strong regime has been concentrated and demonstrated in antigovernment majorities in urban areas (but not in rural districts), where the government is less capable of wielding its extensive instruments of power and hortatory influence. At any given moment, of course, and on whatever pretext, the vast coercive forces at the disposal of the state can physically prevent pluralism from continuing, but these explosions of governmental wrath, however violent and intimidating, must be ephemeral and will in the future arouse extensive popular unrest and perhaps even resistance from elements within government. Any use of the military will be justified by real or perceived national security interests; such justification, overused in the past, will be far less tolerated in the future unless the dangers are clearly present and objectively real. The trend toward pluralism will increase.

Centers of pluralism already exist and cannot continuously be held in check or their influence limited. Although student demonstrations had for years been forcibly confined to the campuses, their influence, if not their physical presence, extended beyond those enclaves. Similarly, more diffuse groups have expanded their reach beyond their organizations and, increasingly, beyond the physical power of the state to suppress. As these groups demonstrate capacity in articulating their grievances, their preemptive effect on state policy may be as pronounced and as real as if their impact were more strident and physical.

THE ROLE OF BUSINESS

Foremost in terms of direct and immediate influence on the state is the business community, especially the *chaebŏl*. Long a captive of the administration because of state control of financial institutions, major corporations now realize that effective relationships between the state and business are mutually reinforcing, not one-sidedly dependent. The need of these corporations for simple, direct reliance on the government—without pursuit of their own, perhaps now more varied, interests—is waning. Their internal requirement for more autonomy is increasingly recognized as the economy has grown in size and complexity. Big business acknowledges that *dirigiste* interventions have been sometimes ill-conceived. At some future time, business could determine that state policies were subverting the economic well-being of the nation. Although these interests may not directly compete for political power for some time, they could influence those institutions and individuals who might do so.

The government for its part has attempted to intimidate big business, allowing a major conglomerate to fail as an object lesson on the need for effective business management and restructuring whole sectors to improve Korean international competitiveness. Although the business sector has not yet attempted to vie for political power, either directly or through admission of its members into the National Assembly (one member was elected in 1988 as an independent), it is becoming more vocal in opposing government politics, such as import liberalization, that it regards as inimical to its interests. As the business sector's role has expanded, so has its status and prestige in the society. It has broken the monopoly of the bureaucracy and the literati on the middle class. More and more, the business and administrative links that once were so profoundly intertwined will loosen. Business will become one or perhaps many alternative sources of political pluralism.

SOCIAL ISSUES

Another major shift has been the growth of all forms of Christianity. The Christian churches have spread their influence faster and more profoundly in Korea than in any other nation in Asia in the modern period. Their expansion parallels Korea's economic growth, although no causal relationship is implied. Although the reasons for their influence may be in dispute, the churches are the most important uncontrolled social link beyond family and clan for many in the society. This is also true for Buddhist institutions, which have also seen a renaissance but to a lesser degree. Indigenous sects and new religions have also spread.

Some of the churches have taken strong stands on social issues, such as on the importance of equity in the role of labor and on the right of political dissent. Although the Christian churches have in general been socially and politically conservative, some elements have become radicalized, as in the modern tradition of the Latin American clergy. A *minjung* (mass or people's) theology has evolved on the Latin American model. Although individual church leaders may work with government, and some have been most circumspect about protest, a significant church involvement in social issues, including social equity as well as political protest, is likely to continue.

The government has been in a dilemma over suppression of some church activities (such as the threatened storming of Seoul's Catholic cathedral, in which protesting students had taken refuge in the spring of 1987), as this could result in profoundly repugnant publicity about Korea in the West, thus vitiating some important external links in the South's continuous propaganda campaign against North Korea and jeopardize explicit U.S. approval of the regime. Such approval still carries weight even with increasing Korean nationalist sentiment and anti-U.S. feeling. It is likely that the influence of the churches will spread and that the government will have to treat them gingerly.

Urbanization has led to intense speculation in urban real estate, which the government has from time to time attempted to suppress through taxation and preventive business regulations. Extremely high land values have meant growing housing shortages (especially for the young), smaller housing units in the form of apartments (a rarity even in 1960), and thus the rise of the nuclear family. The young of both sexes are pulled to urban areas, not only because of the prospects of jobs, but also because of the attractions of urban living, however full of hardship such a life may appear to outsiders. The escape from the drudgery of farm life and the still prevalent restrictions of village Confucianism have become important motivations to youth. The anonymity of urban living lifts social restrictions on personal, political, or protest activities, eviscerating much of dictatorial governmental authority and creating both broad political cynicism concerning any government and political expectations.

With urbanization has come enhanced roles and status for women, who, in spite of constitutional provisions, are still a subjugated group. Although Korean women are in general socially conservative, especially on issues such as marriage, they have been increasingly active and obvious in protest. Because of the nature of much of Korean industry, in fields such as textiles and, more recently, microchips, women are an important part of the labor force and have been prominent in union activities. They also have been leaders in the church movements. An increased activist role for women is likely and perhaps the formation of new women's groups influencing social and political activities. In 1986, the progressive Federation of Women's Associations, composed of twenty-one organizations, was formed, supplementing the more middle-class National Council of Women's Organizations, made up of twenty-five groups. Both groups may be expected to influence public concern for the extension of expanded social legislation.

The rise of the middle class, by its members' own perception encompassing in 1988 over 55 percent of the population, is also a product of economic growth and the urbanizing experience. The middle class is articulate, informed, and mobile and will make increasing demands on the society and government. Compared to middle-class attitudes in many other societies, the political conservatism of the Korean middle class is of a different stripe in that it is tolerant of strong leadership and governmental direction, but not of excessive authoritarianism, and it is skeptical of government. The population as a whole is literate, but the middle class, because of its education and its expectations, will force any government to listen closely to its social and political demands.

Social mobility is also likely to continue; class distinctions are changing and new hierarchies being formed. It is unlikely that Korea, either North or South, will become a classless society. Although the rapid economic expansion has generally fostered far greater upward mobility than decline, this mobility will be less automatic. Higher education, once the premier avenue to changing status, will no longer have the automatic function of status imprimatur; it may be a necessary but not sufficient means for social change. Unemployment among college graduates in 1985 was officially 9.8 percent for females and 5.8 percent for males, but these figures are likely undercalculations. Other figures indicate that 43 percent of graduates were unemployed for at least a significant period following graduation. The unemployment rate for those with higher education is likely to increase. Emigration, permanent or temporary, has been a means to limit economic frustration, which is likely to increase within this group.

The labor organizations, so long under surveillance and control by the government, have at each point in the liberalization process after the Rhee and Park regimes, and again in 1987, attempted to press their demands for more equitable treatment. Management is unlikely to accede to labor's ultimate wage and benefit goals, but labor is also likely to continue to demand better conditions for workers, although it is the larger corporations that can and do provide such amelioration of conditions and better pay. Workers in small firms and unorganized day workers are the worst off. Labor will likely play a more significant role in the search for equity, but Korean governments, to remain competitive in international markets as the economy moves into higher technology, will demand greater productivity in return for increases in wages.

Korea is also a youthful nation, and as youth has increasingly fled the countryside, the farming population has aged and the cities have become young. Sixty percent of the population in 1987 was under twenty-nine years old, and 58 percent of the total electorate was under thirty. Youth are more adaptable to new trends and needs; they are also the most vociferous in articulating their rights, in their cynicism toward all government, and in their liberal views. In the cities, they are more free from governmental manipulation in the electoral process. All those under forty years old, some three-quarters of the population, have no personal memory of the Korean War and the North Korean occupation. Nor do they remember American largesse. Youth is the most antiforeign group, both toward Japan and the United States.

POLITICAL PLURALISM

Political pluralism does not emerge exclusively from forces external to the government or from the opposition. It may become more difficult for future administrations to control dissent within their own political ranks and party than it has been for past governments to control the opposition through coercion, the buying of votes, or other inducements. One of the salient reasons for Korean economic success in both policy formation and implementation has been the insulation of economic technocrats from the vagaries of public opinion and internal bureaucratic infighting. Sanctioned and protected by the Blue House, they could perform subject only to the personal intervention of the leader (as in the case of the *saemaŭl* movement and the heavy and defense industries policies).

Although political parties in Korea have in the past been the mere expression of their leader's will, that situation will change with a peaceful transfer of authority, even within the same political party. New leadership will have to establish its authority not through the coup process, nor simply by having the past leader hand the mantle down to his chosen successor; rather, successors will have to build political constituencies among the people and within their own parties. It is likely that any party, even if it is capable of manipulating some of the electoral results, will be more responsive to public concerns and will express those concerns to the executive branch. Pluralism may well express itself even within the state-controlled political system, between the government-controlled party and the executive branch. The process has already begun. If the executive and legislative branches are controlled by different parties, as in 1988, then the debate will be more obvious and probably more confrontational. Any of these situations may well lead to a less economically efficient Korean state in the sense that policy formation will be far less insulated, and less determined by abstracted economic criteria. But such a state will also be more concerned with dealing with the needs of its population.

The most obvious form of dissent is, of course, the opposition political parties. These have been extremely numerous; their name changes mask the continuities of personalities and orientation. Their record since independence has been less than inspiring. Grouped around often brave and strongly principled individuals, the opposition parties have more often reflected simple opposition as a sometimes vocal counterpoise to state views than a means to develop cohesive, alternative policies. All legal political parties of any magnitude in Korea have lacked a comprehensive, discernible political or economic policy. Policy formulation has been captive to the views of the leader, but once those views have been articulated, then the party and/or the bureaucracy implement them with alacrity. Insofar as government has allowed them to exist, the opposition parties have continuously upheld aspects of government policy to scrutiny and have expressed their views within the National Assembly.

The National Assembly has been a sounding board, subject to occasional physical intimidation and intrusion by the state, and only able to influence perhaps 20 percent of the national budget. The assembly may not yet have grown in power commensurate with the economy, but the political process by which its members are elected certainly has been transformed in importance and prestige, and its role has increased in influence. The anomalies that had marked all elections in Korea since independence—with the single exception of an election during the Second Republic—have been far reduced, the degree of public interest expanded, and the opportunities greatly heightened for a real change of power based solely on the voting (and not on proportional appointments or other nonelective means to maintain power). If the opposition did not legally win in 1985, the government clearly lost, although it was able to maintain control through nonelective, appointive mechanisms. The 1988 assembly elections, in which the government clearly was defeated, offers a profound challenge to the Korean political process. Over time, an opposition candidate, party, or coalition may be able to defeat a government at the polls, but the military will carefully scrutinize the political process and could step in to halt pluralism, but not for very long.

There will also likely be a reconfiguration of the political process, a substantive change from parties clustered on the Right to a system having the more usual spectrum of groups from Right to Left. Although such parties will probably reflect the ideological predilections of their leaderships, the increased access to information and impatience with traditional Korean political practices will likely engender in both Left and Right more concern about policies and lead them to formulate more policy platforms. Individual leadership will probably continue to be an exceptionally strong factor in Korean politics.

Although the Korean army has never been monolithic, it is probably more cohesive than any other major institution in Korean society. The pervasive influence of the military, in uniform or in mufti, is so great and the forces at its disposal so vast that it could for a period prevent an opposition political party from achieving power or a government leader (even a military one) from remaining in office. An intense crisis or social ferment, such as nationwide demonstrations, a major defeat of the government at the polls, or a discrediting of the state in the public eye might prompt some elements of the military to try to replace the ruling regime with one or some of its own members, with the ostensible purpose of protecting the state in the face of perceived foreign threats. Yet, even under such dire circumstances, the influence of the pluralistic forces in the society would eventually come to the fore. Such a military eventuality is increasingly unlikely primarily because of internal social changes (the military may not want to sully itself unnecessarily with politics), but also because the United States will be likely to deplore such actions publicly.

INTERNATIONAL TRENDS

The gnawing—and to Koreans, unnatural—fact of partition of an ethnically homogeneous people will continue to influence popular emotions. Although talks between the two Koreas may continue, and under the most optimistic of scenarios some exchanges and trade may take place, barring a massive realignment in the Northeast Asian power configuration, it is unrealistic in the forseeable future to expect a political or major change that would amalgamate both regimes under a united or federal structure. A unified Korea as part of an Eastern bloc power system would, of course, be anathema to both the United States and Japan. A neutral Korea or one aligned with the West and part of the world trading system—consisting of the economic raw materials and production of the North joined with the industrial sophistication of the South—would likely be viewed with dismay by China and the USSR and would be a competitor that many nations might fear.

It could be argued that greater economic development by both South and North could harden the regimes, virtually setting up more concrete barriers to reunification. Much also depends on the personalities of the leaders of both countries. Although pressures from youth in the

South for reunification will probably grow, and are articulated in the 1987 amended constitution that serves as epigraph for this chapter, vested interests on both sides of the DMZ will likely resist them. Reunification is unlikely to happen in the forseeable future. The most that can realistically be expected is that the increased confidence of the South Korean government will allow the United States to negotiate directly with the North, enhancing the prospects of eventual cross-recognition of both South and North by one another and by the United States, Japan, China, and the Soviet Union. There are many small steps that might be taken to reduce tension, but even these appear to require greater trust on all sides than seems currently possibly.

Although politicians have been jailed in Korea for calling for neutralization, and complete neutralization is unlikely, movement toward a more open political and economic stance toward the rest of the world, and thus away from the United States, is probable. Anti-U.S. feeling in Korea has grown continuously, partly because uncritical faith in U.S. altruism toward Korea was unfounded, unwise, and proved to be wrong, but also because the United States, as global security interests were paramount in its approach to regionally specific issues, ignored, at least publicly, the excesses of various governments and the grievances of the people. Korean foreign trade policies will most likely continue to reflect pragmatism more than ideology.

But access to more information, worldwide leftist or liberal trends among youth, and other factors have fired a new form of anti-U.S. sentiment beyond the past patterns associated with U.S. sins of commission or omission. These earlier patterns have persisted, but a deeper, more ideologically based opposition has emerged among a narrower, more radical, youth group. Given the inherent disputes over economic and security issues, which are unlikely to disappear, anti-U.S. sentiments will continue but will probably not reflect majority opinion, even among youth. Paradoxically, Christianity, which had been a force both for democracy and pro-U.S. sentiment, has become an element in anti-Americanism, as some church groups have been most strident in criticizing U.S. policies supportive of governments in power. In fact, the less obvious the reason for protest against the government, the more general frustration may be directed toward the United States.

Trade will continue to be a major point of tension between the two nations. As U.S. trade policies toward Korea place a higher priority on internal U.S. political issues than on foreign policy problems, protectionism in its various guises will likely grow. Whatever legal barriers are placed or retaliation taken by the United States in regard to imports from Korea—and they will likely be considerable—Korea will also, because of its own growth of political pluralism, find it difficult to satisfy the U.S. government that it has liberalized its imports and service industries to the extent that Korean governmental rhetoric seemed to have indicated. As pluralism grows, it will be more difficult for any Korean government to satisfy the United States on economic liberalization issues, even as the Koreans achieve more in the democratization process, also an important aspect of U.S. policy.

Economically, the new emphasis on pluralism is already reflected to some degree in the Sixth Five-Year Plan (1987–1991). The plan calls for reduced emphasis on export expansion (a recognition of increased protectionism) and more expenditures on social services. There will likely be less restrictive labor laws, perhaps fueling inflation to some degree; stress on small and medium-sized industries; and increased use of economic policies for political ends and short-term interests. An open political process will probably result in increasing expenditures for overtly political influence or political ends. The draft plan calls for external debt to decrease to $29.5 billion by 1991 and for exports to rise by 9 percent per year to $59 billion (representing about 2 percent of world trade). There will probably be increasing liberalization, especially in the financial sector, and accelerated import substitution in machinery and components. More women are likely to be employed.

The United States, economically disabled by its trade imbalance, may be expected to continue its pressures on Korea for a more open economy, but with only marginal effects. Although some have called for a U.S.-Korea free-trade zone (on the U.S.-Israeli model or that proposed between the United States and Canada), there is far less internal U.S. political and economic interest in such a relationship. A free-trade relationship would, in addition, essentially destroy traditional Korean rice agriculture, as well as the dairy and beef industries there. This would be politically disastrous for any government in power, especially a democratic one more responsive to internal pluralistic forces. As the military contains many officers from poorer rural backgrounds, it would probably be unsympathetic to any such move.

A new factor in Korean-U.S relations, but one with a broad impact, is the growing population of Koreans outside Korea, and especially in the United States. The Koreans have not yet become a major political force, even in areas of the United States where they are concentrated, but they are likely to become so as Koreans take advantage of U.S. educational opportunities and continue the work ethic that has made them one of the most successful of minority groups in the United States. Just as developments in Korea have an impact on the Korean community in the United States, so will Koreans in the United States, through frequent travel and family ties, play an important role in the internationalization of the Korean nation. Their influence, perhaps even their

The Olympic stadium, dedicated Sept. 29, 1984

funds, may help shape the future Korean political system and the U.S. response to it.

There were few contrasts between the early Korean immigration patterns to Japan and to the United States. Japan was able to recruit and draft unskilled Korean labor for its war industries partly because poverty in Korea spurred migration. Korean workers came to the United States (essentially to Hawaii) for the same reason. The patterns of immigration to the United States changed markedly after liberation, however. The first Koreans to go to the United States thereafter went mostly for education and came from the upper class. They had the educational prerequisites, and their families could afford the costs. With the change in U.S. immigration laws in the 1960s, a wide variety of blue-collar workers found their way to the United States, so that the present mix of Koreans is far more representative of the society as a whole than the previous pattern had been. This new pattern also means that the influence of Korean immigrants is spread more widely within Korea than it once was. Scarcely a family in Korea does not have a relative who lives or has lived in the United States or Japan, or who has worked abroad in some capacity, or who fought in Vietnam.

Some have called the Koreans xenophobic, but the necessity for cultural preservation through uri-ism ("we-ness") was an acquired and necessary trait that does not necessarily equate with hatred or fear of foreigners in general. On the contrary, there are few societies that have adjusted as quickly and as easily to foreign influences as have the

Koreans. Because of such foreign experience, together with the influx of foreign goods, media, and culture, Korea could now be called the gregarious, rather than a hermit, nation. No future Korean government will be able to insulate Koreans from international trends. In retrospect, the pursuit of an export-led policy suited the Korean personality, which has become more international in a shorter period of time than any other in the region. There will be no turning back, although there will be many who decry the loss of traditional values and customs. Change, and adaptation to change, has become part of the Korean social pattern.

How has the 1988 Olympics affected Korea? Many Koreans regard the Olympics as a national *rite de passage*, the international coming of age of the nation. Pride and the prospect of enhanced international recognition are in the minds of many. Whatever the economic costs and returns, a spectacular Olympics successfully organized and managed were a significant national return on the massive investments estimated in the billions of dollars and have had an even greater impact on the national psyche. The Korean government sees its legitimacy strengthened internally and internationally and its trading prospects improved, and the successful Olympics wiped out the previous image of poverty and deprivation. For the people, such an Olympics ended the long sentence of national humiliation under the Japanese, the mendicant mentality of the Korean War, and the abuses that followed.

The Olympics have had other effects as well. With the events surrounding the overthrow of Marcos in the Philippines still fresh in the minds of the international public, both the government and opposition in Korea understood that the Olympics focused attention on Korea and that continuing political upheavals and demonstrations undercut Korean prestige. Thus, the government probably realized that it could no longer continue to suppress the growing demonstrations for political liberalization, and the opposition probably also concluded that it must seek to ameliorate its political stridency. The Olympics may have affected President Chun's decision to step down and the army's decision not to step in.

What, then, remains after the Olympics? Korea may not again return to normalcy, for what was once normal during the five republics preceding the Olympics may never be possible again. Yet, basic tendencies that have characterized the Korean social system will be difficult to change. Hierarchy, stress, mercurial politics, and the tendencies toward orthodoxy and away from compromise and conciliation are unlikely to be easily overcome. In the background, a proud, patriotic, and concerned Korean military will watch these developments as the U.S. military (with lower troop levels) and State Department play diminished roles with less immediate influence and urgency.

The Korean people and their increasingly eclectic culture will remain vibrant whether or not these predictions about Korean society and development are accurate. Whatever political or economic vicissitudes the society may undergo, it will retain much of what is old but adopt and adapt much that is new in a vital and expressive manner that will be quintessentially Korean.

Koreans can look back with pride, not unmixed with regret and many tears, over their history; but they can also look back over their more contemporary accomplishments with considerable satisfaction, for they have done what a hundred other nations have hoped and tried to do, but they have done it better and more quickly.

There are causes for concern, and many have suffered, some unnecessarily, for what has been accomplished, but the Koreans have entered in a spectacular manner an economic era that none would have imagined years ago. Although politics and rights have not kept pace with increased prosperity, and I do not contend that the economic ends have justified the political means, I am confident that pluralism, so evidently growing in Korean society, will correct some of these imbalances and that emulation of Korea as an economic model will be only part of the Korean success story.

13

Epilogue: Development Lessons from the Korean Experience

In the golden age of Asia
Korea was one of its lamp bearers
And that lamp is waiting to be lighted once again
For the Illumination in the East

— Rabindranath Tagore (1861–1941)

The reality of the spectacular Korean development process is father to speculation about the origins and reasons for such progress, producing both myths and analyses. If many of the results are clear, understanding why and how Korea was able to achieve what it has accomplished is exceedingly difficult. We are bound by our disciplinary predilections, our desire for easily articulated conclusions, and our traditional neglect for things Korean. Developmental economists search for hard data, yet clues from some of the soft social sciences may be equally or more germane.

Experience in Korea and elsewhere indicates that single-factor explanations are wanting. If sound economic policies were the only solution to national stasis or decay, more nations would have been successful. If a cultural (Confucian) heritage were the key, then how does one explain centuries of economic stagnation? If autocratic leadership were the answer, then what happened under Syngman Rhee? The interplay between the hard social science—economics—and its softer historical, cultural, social, and political relatives may provide hypotheses, if not complete answers.

To seek developmental lessons from the Korean experience is important, but to mistake those elements, treat them as universally applicable, or skew them to fit our own theories of what ought to be;

187

to assign credit for efforts that were peripheral to the results; and to generalize loosely from the Korean experience all subvert the process of understanding and improving economic well-being in other nations.

There are lessons to be drawn from Korean growth, but they must be considered contextually and temporally in the dynamic of the internal Korean political and social situation, and its external relations and world conditions, as well as adapted to the singular needs of any other developing nation. Pat answers and universally applicable formulae are thus unlikely to be relevant and indeed could be harmful. Perhaps the first, generic lesson to be drawn from Korea is that such analyses must be done with cultural deftness. The second is that universally applicable rules of development are unlikely to be universally sound.

We must begin with a set of general conditions that are inherent in the Korean scene. Some are unique, and some are contributory factors in Korea's economic success. Primary is the cultural, ethnic, and linguistic homogeneity of the Korean people. This homogeneity gave Korea a developmental edge. It provided an easier milieu in which a powerful regime could mobilize for developmental (or political) purposes. It encouraged cultural and nationalistic identity that enabled a government to seek mass dedication toward specific goals. It meant there were no dominant or inferior distinct social or ethnic groups that either controlled economic or political power or had to be assisted in raising their economic standards. Korea lacked the Chinese of Southeast Asia, the Indians of Burma or East Africa, the Lebanese in West Africa, or caste or pariah groups. Compared to the tribally differentiated nations of Africa, the Latin American split between indigenous Indian and foreign elements, and the multiethnic dimension of most Asian nations, Korea had a powerful and distinct advantage. North Korea shared this asset.

The colonial period, however traumatic politically and culturally, and whatever the economic and social costs were to the Koreans who were deprived of their most elemental rights, created the preconditions for economic growth. These preconditions were not, of course, created with the benefit of Koreans in mind, nor were they a necessity for growth; they did give Korea a comparative colonial advantage, however, which it again shared with North Korea, whose industrial base was much greater. Whether the creation of the regionally unified economic system consisting of Japan, Korea, and Taiwan—and devoted to the expansion of Japan's economic and military power—was a unique and necessary element in future progress in all three states requires further study, but it produced a base that few colonial nations had. This should not imply that later economic growth in any manner justified the Japanese occupation, but the contribution of that occupation, although inadvertent, was considerable. On independence, Korea had a modern, albeit small, industrial sector, a modern agricultural system, some trained entrepreneurs and managers, and effective internal communications. It had as well a reinforced heritage of a centralized command structure.

The Confucian tradition, when transformed into a modern setting and with other elements in place, provided in some manner as yet unclear an impetus to economic achievement. Whether this impetus consisted of a sense of personal efficacy that was instilled through an essentially authoritarian and hierarchical educational and social system; whether it was a respect for and love of literacy and learning; a pragmatic approach to problem solving at least in economics; or whether some other factors, such as social and/or clan unity, were important, the accomplishments of all the Confucian—or as some say the "post-Confucian"—societies of East Asia are more than mere happenstance. The growth of this group of nations from Japan to Singapore, together with the achievements of the Chinese in Southeast Asia and of East Asians in general in the United States and elsewhere—each different yet all bound by a Confucian link—cannot summarily be dismissed as accident. (Vietnam, which has a Confucian heritage, demonstrates that this background is not a sufficient explanation for progress. Ideology has subverted the efficacy of the Confucian ethic there.) If the Confucian tradition was an important element, it clearly cannot be considered either necessary or sufficient in any worldwide generalized theory. It was important in the East Asia context, in combination with other factors.

Land reform was important to Korea in equity terms in both South and North. It may have only marginally improved production and did not in any major sense redistribute income in the society as a whole, but more important, in the short term it produced a state of shared rural poverty that, with other factors, defused political activism in the countryside; in the longer perspective, land reform prevented some of the inequities of maldistribution of income in the early years of independence. Whether the reform was accompanied most effectively is a separate issue, but all the Confucian states have implemented major land reforms (China, Japan, Korea, Taiwan, Vietnam) or, like Singapore and Hong Kong, have no rural base. If other nations wish to achieve some degree of equity along with growth, land or agrarian reform (including dealing with the issue of the rural landless) seems essential.

The pragmatic nature of Confucian societies, including Korea, where religion may be important but not dominant, has meant that there were no conservative religious elites with either ideological or economic interests that could attempt to stem the process of economic development and social change. In the East Asian context, this of course does not appear as a major factor of comparative advantage, but in comparison with the Middle East or other areas, it has meant that there were few social forces in the society that could deter a determined government from implementing a policy of economic development once that decision had been made.

When Korea entered into its export drive, the new military government was not beholden to any of the traditional elite groups in the country, including the bureaucrats, the literati, or those with vested interests in import-substitution industries. Thus, the government had virtually absolute discretion in pursuing internal policies, subject only to broad stabilization efforts that were affected by U.S. assistance. In much the same way that land reform was accomplished in Taiwan because there were no Taiwanese landlords in the Kuomintang (and, indeed, no Ministry of Agriculture at that time), so in Korea economic change could come through a military that did not have to accommodate to vested interests in any industrial policy or program. In other societies, entrenched clienteles can inhibit development reforms.

Korea had another distinct advantage as it entered its period of intense export-led growth: It had virtually no external debt. The foreign assistance it received from the United States until the Park government was essentially all grant funds, and the only other, relatively modest, assistance—from UN agencies and private and voluntary groups—was also of this nature. Other nations today that try to emulate Korea will be unable to match the Korean advantage (and interest rates are now substantially higher). This is especially true for most developing countries on the lower end of the economic spectrum, the ones that need development most and that generally export primary products. With the fall of world market prices for most of their export commodities, combined with the continuing escalation of international prices for industrial, intermediate, and consumer imports, the developing countries are caught with increasing external debt burdens and greater local demands. Thus, however sound their economic policies may be, and however effective the implementation of these, such countries are disadvantaged compared to Korea in the early 1960s.

The external dimensions of development are now different as well. Not only did world prices escalate following the two oil shocks of the 1970s, after Korea had already formulated and implemented its export drive, but the growth of exports from countries like Japan and Korea have also created some production economies that few countries will be able to match in the shorter term, even with lower labor costs. Perhaps more important, a growing worldwide trend toward protectionism will undercut the ability of many of these nations to achieve substantial increases in economic development and income though an export-led strategy. Thus, Korea's success undercuts the possibility of other Korea-like successes.

There is also a myth concerning the efficacy of a Korean single-focused export development strategy. Korea was able to combine overall export promotion with import substitution, first in rice and later in heavy and defense industries. The Korean case demonstrates the value of a sense of pragmatism in economic strategy—a sense that is sometimes lacking in development theory. This pragmatism is important. Bound in no economic ideological net, Korea has evolved strategies to suit both its needs and international conditions. It has been less subject to a historic or political tradition that demanded a specific economic orientation (socialist or capitalist) for acceptance and legitimacy.

A view prevalent in conservative economic circles, especially in the United States, is that the efficacy of the private sector and the marketplace was generally responsible for worldwide economic growth and was the major factor in Korean development. The Korean case demonstrates, however, that the private sector was under the clear command of government and was used by government to achieve national economic development targets. There is no doubt that private industry was effective overall, but without government assistance, incentives, and, in many cases, subsidies, punishments, and general supervision, the state probably would not have been able to achieve many of its economic targets within the determined periods.

The market played little internal role in the early spurt of Korean growth, although it obviously was critical in Korea's international competitive pricing policies. Government intervention not only provided incentives; it eliminated the worst speculative, manipulative, and rent-seeking aspects of the Rhee economy, thus forcing entrepreneurs into productive modes. The government, through subsidization of interest rates and allocation of resources, was able to intervene in the market process and influence, even control, development of both the sectors and the pace of internal industrial and rural development. A vast and complex system of subsidies was instituted for sectors that the government deemed economically or politically vital. Internal market forces had little to do with the salient field of Korean economic growth. If there was an invisible hand, it was in the government's iron glove.

This is not to imply that nonmarket interventions were or are necessarily effective, nor that other governments should adopt the Korean system. It seems obvious that a good dose of private-sector initiative is a critical factor in growth, as many nations today are belatedly learning, but Korea is not the example that should be followed if that is a primary lesson.

Here a difference with North Korea may be noted. Both regimes have been *dirigiste*, but the micromanagement of the North Korean economy and centralized planning to a degree unknown even in the

South, together with the North's ideological fixations, have probably influenced the relatively slow economic performance of the North since the early 1960s. Such management-intensive policies may also have influenced the more rapid growth of the North in the years immediately following the Korean War, as communist regimes seem to have been adept at rebuilding shattered economies but not at maintaining their well-being. North Korean military spending approaches that of the South, but with a GNP of far smaller size these expenditures probably contribute to the lack of stellar North Korean economic performance.

The South Korean case also demonstrates that public enterprises can be run efficiently and that "privatization," a hallmark of contemporary U.S. economic dogma, should be considered selectively. In those nations with bloated and protected public sectors run by inefficient management, privatization may be justified, but Korea's extensive public sector has been run prudently, and its management was responsive to central directives calling for efficiency and innovation.

Two controversial lessons emerge from the Korean experience, both focused on the issue of the responsiveness of government to its people and internal political and social pressures. The first is that political will at the apex of the administration is an effective and necessary element of economic growth. Whether such leadership need be dictatorial is moot, but at a minimum it must be able to carry with it or reflect an overall societal consensus. Korea has been a hard state, where economic decisions were made that involved sacrifices by portions of the population to longer-range national goals, and these groups had no part in the process of determining either the level of their contribution or the appropriateness of these goals.

Certainly, the insulation of economic policymakers from the overt political process and from the checks and balances of representative institutions allowed the formation of policy in Korea to be remarkably efficient internally and quickly responsive to changing worldwide conditions. Korean economists were thus able to gear their policies to new national needs without concern over vested economic or social interests. What Korea gained in economic efficiency it lost in internal social and economic responsiveness, however. The degree of insulation from or responsiveness to societal demands that is needed for effective economic development is likely to continue to be disputed. There is no formula, for extremes of hermetic isolation from pluralistic or democratically articulated needs and subservience to diverse special interests are both likely to be ineffective. Political and economic tolerance levels are culturally defined, and the globe is studded with states with powerful, but extremely inefficient, leaders.

Korea's growth is also attributable to a most effective implementation system, and the lesson from its experience is that concentration on economic policies to the neglect of their implementation is likely to produce little. The particular nature of the Korean system of governance probably has little relevance to other nations, so efforts of the government to instruct foreigners in, for example, the *saemaŭl* movement methods of implementation would probably be ineffective. This top-down system of control may also produce problems as well as successes, as Korea's hasty expansion of the *t'ongil* rice varieties or the development of defense industries demonstrate.

Perhaps a lesson yet to be learned from Korea, for it is in the process of ferment, is that as growth proceeds, as economic and other centers of influence and power appear, there will be more pluralism in the society and more diffusion and stress in the process of economic decision making. Thus, it may well be ironic that as a society like Korea is able to grow at remarkable rates in part—and only in part—because it was insulated from diffuse influences that might have diverted attention and resources from growth, the very success of its efforts created the seeds of a more economically inefficient but more responsive system, which will better reflect internal needs as expressed by its people. The seeds of success thus germinate into the growth of increasing inefficiency in economic policy formulation.

The Korean case also demonstrates that external tensions can galvanize a regime to perform if other factors are in place. The threat from North Korea and the constant competition with that state have enabled the South Korean government to marshal its resources, and evoke from significant elements of its population support for its economic policies. As Dr. Johnson said, "Believe me, sir. When a man is about to be hanged it concentrates the mind wonderfully."

The relationship of Korea to its external donors also demonstrates that policy dialogue that recommends that a regime diminish its centralized political power is unlikely to be heeded. Decentralization or devolution of authority, privatization, and other pluralistic measures have only been pursued when governments have regarded them as in their own political interests. On the other hand, technical assistance that reinforces the attainment of national goals may be readily adopted.

The development of Korea also clearly puts into question the simple dependency theory of development, which was in any case based on a Latin American model. The Korean experience indicates that the periphery can industrialize and that multinational corporations need not exert undue influence, although dependency does create specialized problems, ones that are not covered by the neo-Marxist theoretical analysis. Korean growth points to the possible marginal role of foreign investment in economic growth. Although technological transfer may be critical to economic development, it can be accomplished through a variety of means, of which investment is only one.

Finally, the Korean experience demonstrates that no single, simple solution or abstracted principle is likely to lead to success in any particular nation at any point in time in the international economic scene. To force the Korean mold on another, different society, at a different time, would be inappropriate and ineffective. Donor nations and institutions must carefully tailor their developmental programs to the particular needs of the recipients. Thus, U.S. policy supports an "agriculture first" development plan, but Korea proceeded with industrialization first, putting its surpluses back into agriculture rather than the reverse. Korea's success may also require the restructuring of administrative assistance systems and a review of the personnel policies of multilateral and bilateral donors to ensure understanding of the individual dynamics of developing nations.

If there is a Korean formula for economic success, how "Korean" has it been? If it is Korean, then the North Korean experience must be explained and discrepancies and similarities noted. If it is simply a matter of the "right" economic policies, then South Korea is merely illustrative. Is the Korean development experience sui generis or generic?

There are commonalities in both North and South masked by opposing regimes: external enemies, ethnic and linguistic homogeneity, strong leadership, a pervasive work ethic, and a totally literate population. Both states also share a strong sense of hierarchy, an effective command system, and a penchant for centralized state intervention in the economy.

North Korea, in a sense, chose politics over economics. It pushed a *chuch'e* ideology of autonomy effectively, isolating itself from much of the world while copying Eastern bloc models, such as China's Great Leap Forward. South Korea followed a policy of external orientation, letting economics remain separate from politics. It is paradoxical that South Korea's international dependency on exports has proven more effective than North Korea's self-sufficiency. In the South, export-led growth has resulted in political liberalization and the destruction of the autocratic regimes that gave birth to rapid development, but in the North *chuch'e* has neither produced political liberalization nor economic innovation.

Although the evidence is unclear, problems of the North Korean economy after its initial spurt may result from the policies of its economic mentors: a lower level of transferred technology, limited export opportunities within the bloc, ideological rigidity, and micromanagement. Thus, as South Korea's success may in part be attributed to the "Korean-ness" of its regime, the lack of similar progress in the North may be a product of its regional alliances.

The Republic of Korea then emerges as a society so complex that its economic successes can best be understood only in relation to its own internal dynamic. Korea's lessons for other nations and for developmental theory in general must be extrapolated with care and finesse. The Korean people throughout history have endured much to preserve their culture and today persevere in spite of a variety of economic and political hardships. Their successes and their needs combine to produce a dynamism—often progressive, sometimes destructive—that increasingly will count on the world economic scene. In two generations, Korea has transformed itself and its place and image in the world. This is a remarkable achievement, and Korea's continuing development thus becomes increasingly a matter of international interest and possible, if careful, international emulation.

Notes

Chapter 1

1. Vassily Aksyonov, *The Island of Crimea* (New York: Random House, 1983).

Chapter 2

1. Cornelius Osgood, *The Koreans and Their Culture* (New York: Ronald Press, 1951).

Chapter 4

1. Peter H. Lee, *Anthology of Korean Poetry* (New York: John Day, 1964).

Chapter 5

1. Peter H. Lee, *Anthology of Korean Poetry* (New York: John Day, 1964).

Chapter 6

1. Yi I (Yulgok), *Sung-hak Jip-yo*, Book 7, Part 4, Chapter 4. Quoted by Lee Hahn Been, in the keynote address at the UCLA Conference on the Korean Bureaucracy and Development, August 1987.
2. Young Whan Kihl, *Politics and Policies in Divided Korea: Regimes in Contest* (Boulder, Colo.: Westview Press, 1984).

Chapter 7

1. Lee O-young, *In This Earth and in That Wind: This Is Korea*, translated by David I. Steinberg (Seoul: Royal Asiatic Society, Korea Branch, 1968, 1983).
2. Ibid.
3. Peter H. Lee, *Anthology of Korean Poetry* (New York: John Day, 1964).
4. Ibid. The poem "Celadon" is by Pak Chong-hwa (b. 1901).

Chapter 8

1. Peter H. Lee, *Anthology of Korean Poetry* (New York: John Day, 1964).

Chapter 9

1. "The Profession of Arms," in Dewey C. Johnson, ed., *Concepts of Air Force Leadership* (Colorado Springs: Air University, 1970).

Chapter 10

1. Japanese direct investment in the Pacific during 1980–1985 totaled $25.1 billion; $13.2 billion was invested in the United States. Investment in Korea was relatively small. In the same period, the United States invested $16.9 billion in the Pacific nations, of which 38 percent was in Japan.

2. Rural indebtedness as a percentage of rural assets (including land) was 106 percent in 1965, 20 percent in 1976, and 82 percent in 1982. By 1981, 46 percent of farmers were full or partial tenants, and 22 percent of land was tenanted.

3. World Bank figures on comparative hourly wages in the textile industry in 1980 were as follows: West Germany, $10.65; United States, $6.37; Japan, $4.35; South Korea, $.78; India, $.60; Thailand, $.33. The Korea Development Institute calculated hourly compensation in manufacturing as a whole in 1987 as follows: United States, $13.09; West Germany, $16; United Kingdom, $8.19; Japan, $10.94; South Korea, $1.68; Taiwan, $2.08; Singapore, $2.51; and Hong Kong, $1.87.

4. In 1985, of the 5.8 million female workers in the labor force, 1.2 million were in production, 1.6 million in mining and fisheries, 1 million were in services, .6 million in clerical work, and only .3 million in the professional, technical, or administrative fields.

5. In 1981, Seoul had 40 percent of all registered cars; 43 percent of all firms employing more than five persons; 62 percent of all bank loans; 53 percent of all domestic tax collections; 36 percent of all telephones; 37 percent of all college and university enrollment; 44 percent of all medical doctors—but only 22.3 percent of the population.

In 1967, Seoul per capita income was 7.2 times that of the Cholla or Kyongsang provinces. In 1982, per capita incomes for the Seoul and Kyongsang areas were the same but were 1.8 times that of the Chollas, graphically indicating the decline of the Cholla provinces in relation to the Kyongsang provinces.

Glossary and Acronyms

GLOSSARY

ajŏn	traditional social class of petty clerks
amhaengŏsa	secret royal inspector
bansanghoe	village or block citizens' organization supervised by the Ministry of Home Affairs
Blue House	Korean White House
chaebŏl	conglomerate, or large multifunction business concern, similar to the Japanese *zaibatsu*
ch'ima param	"The wind of skirts," popular expression of women's influence
Chiphyonjŏn	Royal Academy in the Yi Dynasty
Ch'ŏndogyo	"Religion of the Heavenly Way," also known as *Tonghak*
chuch'e	autonomy, or self-reliance, the slogan of Kim Il Sung in North Korea
Chungch'uwŏn	Royal Secretariat in the Koryŏ Dynasty
chung'in	social class of technicians below the gentry
do	province
hancha	Chinese characters
han'gul	Korean alphabet, invented in 1444
hwarang	Silla Dynasty elite youth group, reconstituted under Park Chung Hee
hyangban	local *yangban* or gentry, usually of modest means
hyangch'al	early Korean script, the link between Chinese and Korean
kalbi	shortribs, a Korean beef dish
kamikaze	"divine wind" of Japan, which saved Japan from Mongol invasions
kayagŭm	zitherlike stringed instrument from the Kaya state
kimch'i	Korean pickled vegetables, a staple of the diet, hotter or more sour by region and class
kisaeng	female entertainer, similar to the Japanese *geisha*
kun	county, unit of government under a province
kunsu	county chief, centrally appointed head of a county
minjung	mass or people's, referring to theology and similar to liberation theology

mudang	shaman sorceress
myŏn	township, unit of government under a county
ondŏl	traditional Korean floor radiant heating
p'an'gwan	to be henpecked (slang)
p'ansori	traditional form of vocal music and oral narrative, usually of stories, sung by *kisaeng* in traditional times
p'ulgogi	broiled beef
pulsun punja	"impure elements"
sadae juŭi	"serving the great"; toadyism, in present usage. Originally not perjorative but used so today; traditionally referred to China
saemaŭl undong	"new community movement," a rural development and mobilization effort begun by Park Chung Hee in 1971
sahoe ch'ŏnghwa	"social purification"
sakura	"cherry blossom," in Japanese. Used in Korea to denote government-paid opposition candidates used to split opposition votes
Samil	"3-1," March 1, 1919, the date of the Korean Independence Movement
Samsŏng	Three Chancelleries, in the Koryŏ period
sangmin	commoners, as distinct from *yangban*
sangnom	common person, used today in perjorative sense
sasang oyŏm	"ideological pollution"
sijo	classical poetry of forty-seven syllables, originally meant to be chanted or sung
Sirhak	"Practical Learning" school of Neo-Confucianism in the Yi Dynasty
Sinminhoe	"New People's Organization," a Korean anti-Japanese nationalist group
sŏngbun	inherent nature, used to determine class affiliation of North Korea
sŏwŏn	traditional school to teach Confucian classics, usually sponsored by a family or clan
Tohwasŏ	Academy of Art in the Yi Dynasty
Tonghak	"Eastern Learning," a nineteenth-century religion, later known as *Ch'ŏndogyo* ("Religion of the Heavenly Way")
t'ongil	"unification," a name given to a high-yielding variety of rice
uri-ism	"we-ism," Korean solidarity in relation to foreign influence or pressure
wakō	Japanese pirates
yangban	literally, the "two classes," civilian and military. Used for the gentry
zaibatsu	Japanese business conglomerates

ACRONYMS

ASEAN	Association of Southeast Asian Nations
DJP	Democratic Justice party (government party of the 5th and 6th Republics)

DMZ	Demilitarized Zone (between North and South Korea)
DPRK	Democratic People's Republic of Korea (North Korea)
DRP	Democratic Republican party
GNP	gross national product
KATUSA	Korean Augmentation to the U.S. Army
KCIA	Korean Central Intelligence Agency (renamed the Agency for National Security Planning in the Fifth Republic)
KMA	Korean Military Academy
NATO	North Atlantic Treaty Organization
ROK	Republic of Korea
UNESCO	United Nations Educational, Scientific, and Cultural Organisation

Dramatis Personae

Korean names are complex for three reasons. There are very few surnames, and half a dozen predominate (Kim, Lee, Park, Choi, etc.). There is also no standard .romanization system for personal names, as each Korean uses that romanization most suitable to his or her interests. Thus, the same Chinese character may be romanized as Lee, Li, Yi, Yee, Rhee, Leigh, etc. Last, the order of names, although clear in Korean, becomes confusing when put in English, as there is no standard order. Most Korean surnames are listed first and are single syllables (Park Chung Hee); the few that are double—such as SaKong, HwangBo—are normally printed without hyphens. Personal names, which follow family names, may be one syllable or two, but if two they may or may not be hyphenated, printed as one word, or left separate; but in modern practice, names are no longer hyphenated. For foreign consumption, some Koreans reverse the Korean order and place their surname last (Syngman Rhee). This practice normally presents no problem with common surnames, but it can cause confusion with some homonyms that could be either first or last names. Only major modern figures are included in this section; others are listed in the index.

Chang Myŏn   (John M. Chang) 1896–1966. Democratic party leader from North Korea. Vice president under Syngman Rhee; prime minister, 1960–1961; overthrown by Park Chung Hee coup of 1961.

Chang To Yŏng   Born 1923. Chief of staff, Korean Army, 1961; titular coup leader 1961; and chairman of the Supreme Council for National Reconstruction.

Choi Kyu-ha   Born 1919. Educated at Tokyo College of Education. Professor, Seoul National University, 1945; Foreign Ministry, 1951–1959; vice minister, 1959–1960; ambassador, Malaysia, 1964; acting prime minister, 1975; prime minister, 1976–1979; acting president October-December 1979.

Chun Doo Hwan   Born 1931 in a farming village in South Kyongsang Province;

grew up in Taegu. Graduated from the Korean Military Academy, Eleventh Class (1955). Various military posts (including short-term training in the United States): deputy commander, First Paratrooper Special Forces, 1966; battalion commander, Metropolitan Defense Division, 1967; commander, 29th Regiment, 9th Division, Vietnam; commander, 1st Division, 1978; commander, Defense Security Command, 1979; president, 1980–1988.

Chung Il Kwŏn Born 1917. First Class, Korean Military Academy. Chief of staff, army, 1954–1956; chairman, Joint Chiefs of Staff, 1956; general, 1957; ambassador to Turkey, 1957, to France, 1959, to the United States, 1960–1963; minister of foreign affairs, 1963; prime minister, 1964–1970; acting chairman, DRP, 1972–1973; National Assembly speaker, 1973–1979.

Hŏ Chŏng Born 1896 in Pusan. Educated at Posong College, in law. Exiled following *Samil* movement. Secretary, Korean Peoples' party, 1945; elected to the National Assembly, 1948; minister of transport, social affairs; deputy prime minister, 1951; Seoul mayor, 1957; minister of foreign affairs, 1960; prime minister, 1961.

Kim Il Sung Born 1912 in Pyongju as Kim Song Ju. Formed Young Communist League, 1927; imprisoned 1929–1930; founded Korean Revolutionary Army, 1930; joined Korean Communist party, 1931; anti-Japanese activities, 1932–1945; founded Workers Party of Korea, chairman, 1945; premier, 1948–1971. President 1972–.

Kim Dae Jung Born 1925. Graduate, Konkuk University, 1953; Graduate School of Business Administration, Korea University, 1964; Kyunghee University Graduate School, 1969. President, the newspaper *Mokpo Ilbo*. National Assembly, 1960–1971 (spokesman, Democratic party, Minjung party spokesman 1965); presidential candidate, 1971; kidnapped in Tokyo, 1973; jailed at various times since then; lived in the United States, 1982–1985; presidential candidate, 1987.

Kim Jae Kyu First Class, Korean Military Academy. Head, KCIA. Assassinated President Park Chung Hee, October 26, 1979. Executed in 1980.

Kim Jong Il Born 1941 in the USSR, first son of Kim Il Sung and his first wife. Attended Mangyongdae Revolutionary School; graduated, Namsan Middle–High School, Pyongyang, 1958; attended Air Academy, East Germany, 1960; graduated, Kim Il Sung University, 1963. Held various party-government posts. Designated as political heir to Kim Il Sung.

Kim Jong Pil	Born 1926. Educated Seoul National University and Korean Military Academy. Chief, KCIA, 1961; retired (1963) brigadier general; chairman, DRP, 1967–1968; vice president, DRP, 1971–1973; prime minister, 1971–1975.
Kim Ku	1876–1949. Rival of Syngman Rhee. Independence leader; ran Korean government in exile, Shanghai, 1919. Assassinated, 1949.
Kim Sŏng Ju	Original name of Kim Il Sung.
Kim Yong Sam	Born 1927. Seoul National University, 1951. Secretary to premier, 1951; National Assembly, 1954–1973 (Democratic party, Civil Rule party, New Democratic party); president, New Democratic party, 1974, 1979.
Park Chung Hee	1917–1979. Born North Kyongsang Province. Taegu Normal School; Japanese Military Academy. Teacher, 1937–1940; Japanese army, 1940–1945; Korean army, 1945–1963; deputy commander, 2nd Army; deputy chairman, Supreme Council for National Reconstruction, 1961, chairman, 1961–1963; acting president, 1962–1963; president, 1963–1979. Assassinated.
Rhee Syngman	1875–1965. Born Kaesong. Helped form Independence Club, 1896; imprisoned, 1897–1904; went to United States, received Ph.D. from Princeton University, 1910. Returned to Korea, 1910; exiled, 1919; president, exiled Korean Provisional Government; returned to Korea, 1948; president, 1948–1960; obliged to resign, lived in exile in the United States.
Roh Tae Woo	Born 1932. Educated Korean Military Academy, 1955. Commander, Airborne Special Warfare Brigade, 1974; commander, Capitol Garrison Command, 1979; commander, Defense Security Command, 1980; chairman, Olympic Committee, 1983–1985; chairman, DJP, 1985–1986, presidential candidate, DJP, 1987; president, 1988.
Yun Po Sŏn	Born 1897. Educated Edinburgh, Scotland. Mayor, Seoul, 1948–1949; minister of trade and industry, 1949–1950; president, 1960–1962; member, Sixth National Assembly, 1963–1966; presidential candidate, 1963, 1967 under New Democratic party.

Suggested Readings

These references are chosen from the wealth of material available in English on aspects of Korea. By far, the greatest number in any single discipline relate to economic development, reflecting the importance of the subject and the focus of this book. The titles of many salient articles are not included here but are nevertheless important and may be found in the reference lists of works cited. Works dealing exclusively or mainly with North Korea are excluded. The categories are arbitrary, for none of these fields is self-contained. I am indebted to the authors and translators of these works for their inadvertent contributions to this book.

General History

Bunge, Frederica M., et al. *Area Handbook for South Korea*. Washington, D.C.: The American University, 1981. One of a series of volumes that set forth in summary form a great many factual aspects of the society in question. A worthwhile reference, although without sources cited.

Han, Woo-keun. *The History of Korea*. Translated by Lee Kyung-shik, edited by Grafton K. Mintz. Seoul: Eul-yoo Publishing Company, 1970. One of the several standard histories, stopping at the student revolution.

Henthorn, William E. *A History of Korea*. New York: Free Press, 1971. A history covering the time up to the end of the Yi Dynasty that stresses topical, rather than chronological, events.

Hulbert, Homer B. *History of Korea*. Edited by Clarence N. Weems. London: Routledge & Kegan Paul, 1962. A classic, two-volume work first published in 1905.

Lee, Ki-baik. *A New History of Korea*. Translated by Edward W. Wagner with Edward J. Shultz. Cambridge: Harvard University Press, 1984. This is probably the premier general history of Korea. It unfolds the story through the student revolution of 1961.

Rutt, Richard. *James Scarth Gale and His History of the Korean People*. Seoul: Royal Asiatic Society, Korea Branch, 1972. A biography of this missionary to Korea together with his history, which was originally published in 1925.

Sohn Pow-key, Kim Chol-choon, and Hong Yi-sup. *The History of Korea.* Seoul: Korean National Commission for UNESCO, 1970. A standard history through independence, with some notes through the Korean War.

Geography

Bartz, Patricia M. *South Korea.* Oxford: Clarendon Press, 1970. The most comprehensive physical geography.

McCune, Shannon. *Korea's Heritage: A Regional and Social Geography.* Rutland, Vt.: Charles E. Tuttle, 1956. Stresses the social and cultural factors in geography.

Sociology and Anthropology

Brandt, Vincent S. R. *A Korean Village Between Farm and Sea.* Cambridge: Harvard University Press, 1971. The best of the village studies.

Mattielli, Sandra, ed. *Virtues in Conflict: Tradition and the Korean Woman Today.* Seoul: Royal Asiatic Society, Korea Branch, 1977. The best single volume (a series of essays) on Korean women.

Osgood, Cornelius. *The Koreans and Their Culture.* Tokyo: Charles E. Tuttle, 1951. The only early and useful study of a Korean community (Kanghwa Island) on the verge of modernization.

Political Science

Cumings, Bruce. *The Origins of the Korean War.* Princeton, N.J.: Princeton University Press, 1981. The first of two volumes that promises to be the definitive study of the period beginning with liberation.

Hahm, Pyong Choon. *Korean Jurisprudence, Politics and Culture.* Seoul: Yonsei University Press, 1986. The collected writings of a most articulate Korean professor and diplomat on law, politics, culture, and society.

Han, Sung Joo. *The Failure of Democracy in South Korea.* Berkeley: University of California Press, 1974.

Henderson, Gregory. *Korea: The Politics of the Vortex.* Cambridge: Harvard University Press, 1968. This highly controversial book is the first in English to theorize about the nature of Korean society and politics. Required reading for the serious student of Korea.

Jacobs, Norman. *The Korean Road to Modernization and Development.* Urbana: University of Illinois Press, 1985. Korea dissected through a Weberian patrimonial analysis. An important, often overlooked, work.

Kihl, Young Won. *Politics and Policies in Divided Korea: Regimes in Contest.* Boulder, Colo.: Westview Press, 1984. A good survey of North and South Korea.

Kim, Quee-Young. *The Fall of Syngman Rhee.* Berkeley: Institute of East Asian Studies, Korea Research Monograph 7, 1983. A detailed study of the last period of Rhee.

Kim, Se-Jin. *The Politics of Military Revolution in Korea.* Chapel Hill: University of North Carolina Press, 1971. Important study of the military coup, its background and consequences.

Lee, Chong-sik. *The Politics of Korean Nationalism.* Berkeley: University of California Press, 1965. The classic study of the rise of the nationalist movement from the end of the nineteenth century.

————. *Japan and Korea: The Political Dimension.* Stanford, Calif.: Hoover Institution Press, 1985. A new and useful summary of this critical relationship.

Lee, Hahn-Been. *Korea: Time, Change, and Administration.* Honolulu: East-West Center Press, 1968. The best available study of public administration theory applied in Korea.

Macdonald, Donald. *The Koreans: Contemporary Politics and Society.* Boulder, Colo.: Westview Press, 1988. The newest comprehensive text on both South and North Korea.

Oh, John Kie-Chiang. *Korea: Democracy on Trail.* Ithaca, N.Y.: Cornell University Press, 1968. A political analysis through the beginnings of the Third Republic.

Palais, James B. *Politics and Polity in Traditional Korea.* Cambridge: Harvard University Press, 1975. The best study of the political economy at the close of the Yi Dynasty.

Reeve, W. D. *The Republic of Korea: A Political and Economic Study.* London: Oxford University Press, 1963. A good study, through the military coup period.

Suh, Dae-sook, and Chae-jin Lee, eds. *Political Leadership in Korea.* Seattle: University of Washington Press, 1976. An important set of essays.

Wright, Edward R., ed. *Korean Politics in Transition.* Seattle: University of Washington Press, 1975. A collection of eleven important essays by well-known scholars on aspects of Korean politics.

Economics

There is a burgeoning literature on the economic development of Korea as well as a wealth of dissertations on aspects of the process. What follows is a sample of the better-known and more-available works. Also notable are a variety of specialized studies by the World Bank.

Burmeister, Larry L. *Research, Realpolitik, and Development in Korea: The State and the Green Revolution.* Boulder, Colo., and London: Westview Press, 1987. An important study of a neglected topic.

Cole, David C., and Princeton N. Lyman. *Korean Development: The Interplay of Politics and Economics.* Cambridge: Harvard University Press, 1971. The best single study of the development process in that period.

Kim, Joungwon Alexander. *Divided Korea: The Politics of Development, 1945–72.* Cambridge: East Asia Research Center, Harvard University, 1975. The political economy of both South and North Korea.

Kuznets, Paul W. *Economic Growth and Structure in the Republic of Korea.* New Haven: Yale University Press, 1977. The best single-volume study of the topic.

Moskowitz, Karl, ed. *From Patron to Partner: The Development of U.S.-Korean Business and Trade Relations.* Lexington, Mass.: D.C. Heath, 1974. A collection of essays on an increasingly important economic relationship.

Parvez, Hasan. *Korea: Problems and Issues in a Rapidly Growing Economy.* Baltimore: Johns Hopkins University Press, 1976 (published for the World Bank). A detailed and useful study.

Studies in the Modernization of the Republic of Korea 1945–1975. Cambridge: Harvard University Press for the Harvard Institute for International Development and the Korea Development Institute. Probably the most comprehensive study of development in any one country. These volumes are recommended; the first is the summary volume:

Mason, Edward S., et al. *The Economic and Social Modernization of the Republic of Korea.* 1980.

Bahl, Roy, et al. *Public Finances During the Korean Modernization Process.* 1986.

Ban, Sung Hwan, et al. *Rural Development.* 1980.

Cole, David C., and Yung Chul Park. *Financial Development in Korea, 1945–1978.* 1983.

Jones, Leroy P., and SaKong Il. *Government, Business, and Entrepreneurship in Economic Development: The Korean Case.* 1980.

Kim, Kwang Suk. *Growth and Structural Transformation.* 1979.

Krueger, Anne O. *The Developmental Role of the Foreign Sector and Aid.* 1979.

McGinn, Noel P., et al. *Education and Development in Korea.* 1980.

Mills, Edwin S., and Byung-Nak Song. *Urbanization and Urban Problems.* 1979.

Repetto, Robert, et al. *Economic Development, Population Policy, and Demographic Transition in the Republic of Korea.* 1981.

Wade, L. L., and B. S. Kim. *Economic Development of South Korea: The Political Economy of Success.* New York: Praeger Publishers, 1978. A helpful study of this issue.

World Bank. *Development in a Global Context.* Washington, D.C.: 1986.

———. *Managing the Industrial Transition,* 2 vols. Washington, D.C.: 1987. Vol. 2 deals with textiles, shipping, and electronics. Detailed studies of the Korean economy.

Literature

There is a growing body of material on Korean culture, including a wide variety of works published in English in Korea. Some of these materials are good, many are popularized. The best overall source is the monthly *Korea Journal,* published in Seoul (but widely distributed) by the Korea National Commission for UNESCO. The Korea Branch of the Royal Asiatic Society has also published a variety of works, some of which are cited here; its *Transactions,* published since 1900 (with exceptions), are important sources. Many translations of Korean poetry and short stories are now available in Korea. Peter Lee is generally regarded as the most eminent translator of Korean literature.

Lee, O-young. *In This Earth and in That Wind: This Is Korea.* Translated by David I. Steinberg. Seoul: Royal Asiatic Society, Korea Branch, 1968, 1983. Delightful essays on aspects of Korean life.

Lee, Peter H. *Anthology of Korean Poetry: From the Earliest Era to the Present.* New York: John Day Company, for UNESCO, 1964.

————. *Korean Literature: Topics and Themes.* Tuscon: University of Arizona Press, for the Association for Asian Studies, 1965.

————, ed. *Flowers of Fire: Twentieth-Century Korean Stories.* Honolulu: University of Hawaii Press, 1974.

————, ed. *The Silence of Love: Twentieth-Century Korean Poetry.* Honolulu: University of Hawaii Press, 1980.

Rutt, Richard, trans. *The Bamboo Grove: An Introduction to Sijo.* Berkeley: University of California Press, 1971. One of the most delightful commentators on Korea, Rutt, who is an Anglican priest, ably translates Korean poetry.

Rutt, Richard, and Kim Chong-un, trans. *Virtuous Women: Three Masterpieces of Traditional Korean Fiction.* Seoul: Korean National Commission for UNESCO, 1974. Translations of "A Nine Cloud Dream," "The True History of Queen Inhyon," and "The Song of the Faithful Wife, Ch'un-Hyang."

Religion

Clark, Charles Allen. *Religions of Old Korea.* Korea, 1961. Lectures delivered in 1921 at Princeton Theological Seminary on Buddhism, Confucianism, Ch'ŏndogyo, and Shamanism.

de Bary, Wm. Theodore, and JaHyun Kim Haboush. *The Rise of Neo-Confucianism in Korea.* New York: Columbia University Press, 1985. The most thorough and important collection of essays on the major philosophical school of the Yi Dynasty.

Janelli, Roger, and Dawnhee Yim. *Ancestor Worship and Korean Society.* Stanford: Stanford University Press, 1982. A detailed and standard work on the subject.

Kendall, Laurel. *Shamens, Housewives, and Other Restless Spirits. Women in Korean Ritual Life.* Honolulu: Hawaii University Press, 1985. An important study of women and the indigenous religion of Korea.

International Relations

Baldwin, Frank, ed. *Without Parallel: The American-Korean Relationship Since 1945.* New York: Pantheon Books, 1973. A hard look at Korea's most important contemporary foreign relationship.

Clough, Ralph. *Embattled Korea.* Boulder, Colo.: Westview Press, 1987. A comprehensive and detailed study covering both North and South Korea.

Koh, Byongchul. *The Foreign Policy Systems of North and South Korea.* Berkeley: University of California Press, 1984. Helpful study of both North and South Korea.

The Korean War

Goulden, Joseph C. *Korea: The Untold Story of the War.* New York: 1982. New information on the war.

Kaufman, Burton I. *The Korean War: Challenges in Crisis, Credibility, and Command.* New York: Alfred Knopf, 1986. Useful study that cites recently declassified material.

Knox, Donald. *The Korean War: An Oral History.* New York: Harcourt Brace Jovanovich, 1985. A readable series of personal accounts of the war.

Rees, David. *Korea: The Limited War.* New York: St. Martin's Press, 1964; Penguin Books, 1970. The best work on this subject.

Stone, I. F. *The Hidden History of the Korean War.* New York: Monthly Review Press, 1952. Iconoclastic, and leftist, view of the war.

Korean Arts

Gompertz, G. St. G. M. *Korean Celadon.* London: Faber and Faber, 1963. The standard English work on this subject.

————. *Korean Pottery and Porcelain of the Yi Period.* New York: Frederick A. Praeger, 1968. The companion piece to *Korean Celadon;* another recommended study by an eminent authority.

Honey, W. B. *Corean Pottery.* London: Faber and Faber, 1953. The first major work on Korean pottery in English.

Kim, Chewon, and Lena Kim Lee. *Arts of Korea.* Tokyo: Kodansha, 1974. A most beautiful and authoritative work.

Kim, Chewon, and Won-Yong Kim. *Treasures of Korean Art: 2,000 Years of Ceramics, Sculpture, and Jeweled Arts.* New York: Harry N. Abrams, 1966. An important work by two authorities.

Wright, Edward Reynolds. *Korean Furniture: Elegance and Tradition.* Tokyo: Kodansha, 1984. The best treatment of this delightful subject.

Personal Memoirs

Kang, Younghill. *The Grass Roof.* New York: Charles Scribners, 1931. The earliest, and a charming, account of growing up in Korea.

Kim, Richard E. *Lost Names.* New York: Praeger Publishers, 1970. Memoir of Korea under the Japanese by a well-known novelist.

Pahk, Induk. *September Monkey.* London: Victor Gallancz, 1953. A Christian remembrance.

Li Mirok. *The Yalu Flows.* London: Harvill Press, 1954; East Lansing: Michigan State University Press, 1956. Evocative memoir first published in German.

Early Views

Bishop, Isabella Bird. *Korea and Her Neighbors,* 2 vols. London: John Murray, 1905. A fascinating study by one of Asia's intrepid travelers.

Hamilton, Angus. *Korea.* London: Heinemann, 1904.

Hulbert, Homer B. *The Passing of Korea.* 1906, reprinted Seoul: Yonsei University Press, 1969.

Ledyard, Gari. *The Dutch Come to Korea.* Seoul: Royal Asiatic Society, Korea Branch, 1971. The narrative of Hamell's shipwreck and travels in Korea in 1653, together with a commentary.

Guidebooks

Korea. Hong Kong: APA Productions, Insight Guides, 1983. A beautiful, thoughtful guide to Korea. Recommended.

Koreans Abroad

Choy, Bong-Youn. *Koreans in America.* Chicago: Nelson-Hall, 1979. The first third of the volume is on Korean-U.S. relations; the rest is on immigration and Koreans in the United States.

Lee, Chai-jin. *China's Korean Minority.* Boulder, Colo.: Westview Press, 1986. An important study of education in the Yanbien Korean Autonomous Region in Manchuria.

Mitchell, Richard H. *The Korean Minority in Japan.* Berkeley: University of California Press, 1967. Important study of a major problem in Korean-Japanese relations.

Patterson, Wayne. *The Korean Frontier in America. Immigration to Hawaii, 1896–1910.* A study of the earliest immigration of Koreans to the United States.

Bibliography

Kim, Han-kyo. *Studies on Korea: A Scholar's Guide.* Honolulu: University of Hawaii Press, 1967. Important guide to bibliographies and services.

Index

Acheson, Dean, 51
Activism. *See* Government opposition; Student demonstrations
Agriculture, 46, 52, 54, 128, 147
Ajŏn, 31
Alphabet, Korean, 32, 78–79, 85
Ancestor reverence, 99
Anticommunism, 103, 160
Anti-Japanese sentiment, 38, 39, 47
Anti-U.S. sentiment, 58, 60–61, 116, 118, 143, 160, 167, 177, 182
Army. *See* Military
Arts, Korean, 6, 19, 22, 83–85, 87. *See also* Calligraphy; Painting; Pottery
ASEAN. *See* Association of Southeast Asian Nations
Association of Southeast Asian Nations (ASEAN), 171
Automobiles, 69, 143, 166
Autonomy, 5. *See also* Self-sufficiency

Banking system, 41, 141, 143
Barley, 146, 150
Blue House, 97, 179
"Bone rank," 25, 72, 93
Buddhism, 5, 9, 22, 25–26, 28, 32, 34, 72, 89
Bureaucracy, 12, 34, 73–74, 91, 92–93, 95
Business community, 176. *See also* Commerce

Cairo Declaration (December 1, 1943), 48
Calligraphy, 85
Carter, Jimmy, 60, 119
Catholicism, 34, 89. *See also* Christianity
Celadons, 83–84

Censorship, 82. *See also* News reportage
Centralization, 96–97, 98, 102, 172
Ceramics. *See* Pottery
Chaebŏl, 60, 114, 135, 140, 143, 155–156, 169, 176
Chan, Charlie, 169
Chang Myon, 54, 55, 82, 125, 202
Chang To Yŏng, 202
Cheju Island, 10, 13, 30
Choi Kyu Ha, 59, 202
Christianity, 34, 72, 89, 158, 176, 182
Chuch'e concept. *See* Autonomy; Self-sufficiency
Chun Doo Hwan, 59, 60, 62, 81, 97, 106, 120, 125, 155, 162, 164, 202–203
    coup against, 63, 64, 65, 116
    and economic growth, 138
Chung Il Kwan, 108, 112–113, 203
Chung'in, 31, 73
Ch'unhyang Chŏn, 87
Clan system, 20, 30, 71, 89, 99. *See also* Family relations
Coinage. *See* Currency
Cold war, 49, 51
Colonial era, 39, 44–47, 174, 188. *See also* Anti-Japanese sentiment
Combined Command, 115–116, 117–118
Commerce, 34, 96. *See also* Business community; Chaebŏl
Commoners. *See* Sangmin
Computers, 69, 143, 166, 177
Confucianism, 5, 34, 87, 103, 173, 177
    and class structure, 74
    and economic growth, 173, 187, 189
    and family relations, 25, 71–72, 99
    as ideology of the court, 7, 25, 26, 30
    and morality, 7

213

.